D1386322

BUSINESS GUIDE TO THE UNITED KINGDOM 2017

BREXIT, INVESTMENT AND TRADE

Edited by
Jonathan Reuvid

Legend Business Ltd,
107-111 Fleet Street, London, EC4A 2AB
info@legend-paperbooks.co.uk | www.legendpress.co.uk

Contents © Legend Business, Jonathan Reuvid and Individual Contributors 2017
The right of the above authors to be identified as the authors of this work has been asserted in accordance with the
Copyright, Designs and Patents Act 1988. British Library Cataloguing in Publication Data available.

Print ISBN 978-1-7850791-3-9
Ebook ISBN 978-17-850791-2-2
Set in Times. Printed by Opolgraf SA.
Cover design by Simon Levy www.simonlevyassociates.co.uk

Publishers Note
Every possible effort has been made to ensure that the information contained in this book is accurate at the time
of going to press, and the publishers and authors cannot accept responsibility for any errors or omissions, however
caused. No responsibility for loss or damage occasioned to any person acting, or refraining from action, as a result
of the material in this publication can be accepted by the editor, the publisher or any of the authors.

All rights reserved. No part of this publication may be reproduced, stored in or introduced into a retrieval system,
or transmitted, in any form, or by any means electronic, mechanical, photocopying, recording or otherwise, without
the prior permission of the publisher. Any person who commits any unauthorised act in relation to this publication
may be liable to criminal prosecution and civil claims for damages.

CONTENTS

Contents

FOREWORD TO UK BUSINESS GUIDE

At the time of writing, Brexit negotiations have just begun. The exact nature of the UK's future trading relationship with the other 27 countries in the European Union is therefore uncertain, and many business organisations, including COBCOE, are working hard to help ensure a stable outcome.

What is clear, however, is that Britain will not leave Europe geographically, and international business between the UK and the EU27 will find a way to continue. I also believe that business will continue to be a unifying force across Europe and beyond.

The UK has, in recent years, been a leading destination globally for foreign direct investment (FDI), attracting more investment than any other country in Europe. Speculation about this continuing post-Brexit is only natural, although any changes to Britain's trading relationships will undoubtedly bring new opportunities as well as challenges.

For businesses investing in the UK from overseas, there is a wealth of useful information in this guide. All the key considerations are clearly laid out, from the economic outlook to employment and intellectual property law and from the immigration regime to grants and incentives.

When it comes to finding practical support in the UK, the Department for International Trade and grass roots business organisations have much to offer.

As Executive Chairman of COBCOE, an organisation representing chambers of commerce, it is worth recognising the contribution that chambers of commerce make in supporting and helping to coordinate inward investment.

Across the country, these independent business organisations, funded by their memberships, partnerships and the services they provide, work closely with 'tried and tested' professional service firms and members of the wider business community in their local areas with whom they have close and long-standing relationships.

Cities and regions around the UK are promoted as business locations by chambers of commerce. These chambers have strong links with the Department for International Trade as well as international chambers of commerce networks, such as our own. I am proud to say that one such chamber, Thames Valley Chamber of Commerce Group, recently became the first UK-based member of COBCOE earlier this year, following a change to our articles of association.

Additionally, if you are looking to export from the UK, chambers of commerce can also provide information and practical support services, such as document processing services.

My organisation, COBCOE, was established in 1973, when the UK entered what was then the European Economic Community, to represent British chambers of commerce located in Europe. Since that time, we have grown our network and have a British chamber member in nearly all European countries, representing a total of around 12,000 businesses. We have also developed a network of affiliated chambers of commerce around the world.

We are working with our members, corporate partners and affiliated organisations to create a hub for international trade and investment support, commercial services and best practice in business. Our networks and our new digital platform, COBCOE Connects, featured in this guide, provide access to local market expertise and assist in building the local relationships that help businesses to succeed. (Please visit www.cobcoe.eu for more information.)

We wish you well in your international business venture and hope that you will find the information you need through this guide.

David Thomas MBE
Executive Chairman, COBCOE
Council of British Chambers of Commerce in Europe
July 2017

LIST OF CONTRIBUTORS

MAZARS LLP

Mazars is an international, integrated and independent organisation, specialising In audit, accountancy, tax and advisory services. Mazars can rely on the skills of 18,000 professionals in 79 countries across Europe, Africa, the Middle East, Asia Pacific, North America, Latin America and the Caribbean. The organisation also has correspondents and joint ventures in 15 additional countries.

Financial Report & Accounting

Stephen Brown is a Partner at Mazars LLP specialising in Audit and Assurance services. His client base ranges from owner-managed businesses, charities and not for profit organisations to international groups, either based in the UK or reporting to overseas parent companies.

Business Tax and Business Tax Planning

Andrew Ross is a Tax Director at Mazars LLP with extensive experience of both UK and non-UK/cross-border tax issues, including tax efficient corporate restructuring and transaction planning (for both acquisitions and disposals/exists). He advises a range of clients, ranging from multi-national corporate groups to owner-managed businesses.

Company Formation

Helen Harvey is a Senior Manager at Mazars and has over 20 years' experience in providing company secretarial services to a wide variety of UK and foreign-owned companies. She also provides transactional support to businesses including share capital reductions, share buy backs, restructuring and reorganisations.

Helen provides clients with company law and compliance advice in respect of running a business, together with advice in setting up a UK entity. She joined Mazars in February 2014 and is a Fellow of the Institute of Chartered Secretaries and Administrators. Before joining Mazars, Helen was the manager of the Company Secretarial Department of a law firm for 18 years.

UK Taxation for Foreign Nationals

Paul Barham is a Private Client Director at Mazars LLP specialising in all aspects of individual international tax planning, including tax residency issues and offshore trust tax planning. He is the firm's national expert on the rules surrounding non-domiciled individuals and regularly advises clients on a range of remittance planning from small remittances to transfers in excess of £1 million.

Immigration and Money Laundering

Alison Hutton is a Director at Mazars LLP leading their International Immigration Services practice. She advises a wide range of clients, from private individuals and small start-ups to large multinationals, on a broad spectrum of UK and global immigration matters. Amongst other things, this includes providing assistance to businesses in obtaining a sponsor licence for the UK, advisory work relating to preventing illegal employment and the right to work in the UK and many other types of visa application under the UK Immigration Rules. Alison is an OISC registered immigration adviser.

Jac Berry is an audit partner and a member of the UK Executive Board of Mazars LLP, with responsibility for quality and risk. As Head of Quality within Mazars since January 2016, she is responsible for leading the firm's legal, compliance and risk management teams across all service lines and UK entities. From an international perspective, Jac is a member of the Global Mazars Quality and Risk Management Board and is a member of the international quality control review team, with responsibility for reviews and developing teams in a number of the firm's more challenging regions. She is the Money Laundering Reporting Officer for Mazars LLP.

Regulation of Financial Services

Sarah Ourbya is a Partner at Mazars LLP specialising in the regulation of the financial services industry. Sarah has over 20 years' experience working in the financial services sector and has worked with firms covering a wide range of regulatory matters including regulatory applications and authorisations, specialist reviews for the regulators and advice and assistance regarding compliance/implementation of regulation.

Swagat Bannick is a Manager at Mazars LLP providing advice to clients in the financial services sector on governance and conduct related matters. Swagat has worked extensively with the financial consulting team across the US and Japan on critical assignments involving compliance and governance functions. His experience in financial services has included regulatory compliance mainly around prudential risks, risk management and governance reviews for both domestic and international firms across the retail, corporate and Asian banking sectors. Swagat specialises in assisting the UK subsidiaries of overseas financial institutions with regulatory compliance in the UK.

James Smalley is a Partner at Mazars LLP specialising in Accounting and Outsourcing Solutions. He has a broad client base and works with a large number of international businesses setting up in the UK and supporting them in their growth as they expand internationally.

Olga Diamond is a Manager within the Corporate Finance and Deal Advisory services team at Mazars LLP and her experience includes working on disposals, acquisitions and finance raising transactions. She has acted for a number of overseas companies searching for acquisition targets in the UK. Mazars offers a proactive acquisition search service that identifies targets that are not formally up for sale. Olga was shortlisted for Young Dealmaker of the Year in the 2016 and 2017 South East Dealmakers Awards.

Richard Metcalfe is a Partner at Mazars Financial Services & Capital Markets and leads the firm's Financial Services & Capital Markets Assurance practice covering Insurance, Banking, Asset Management and Capital Markets reporting services. He has over 20 years' experience and has acted as lead engagement partner for numerous listed and international audit clients and as reporting accountant on IPOs, secondary debt and equity offerings and M&A transactions.

Ben Winder is a Senior Manager within the Mazars Transaction Services team in London. He is responsible for the day-to-day delivery of capital market transactions, with extensive experience of reporting accountant assignments to both the main Market and AIM in the UK. He also manages financial due diligence assignments - both buy-side and vendor - and other assurance reporting assignments to corporates, private equity sponsors and banks. Ben has substantial experience of supporting clients investing in the UK. He previously worked within Mazars Industry & Commerce audit team where he was responsible for the delivery of audits to a wide ranging portfolio of clients.

Pensions

Howard Finch is a Director at Mazars Employee Benefits. He is authorised and regulated by the Financial Conduct Authority (FCA). Howard advises clients on developing and managing their employee benefits in a modern and effective way. This involves reviewing existing arrangements through to designing and implementing new schemes to enhance clients' benefits package.

WATSON FARLEY AND WILLIAMS LLP

Competition

Jeremy Robinson is a Competition Partner at Watson Farley & Williams LLP. He counsels clients on asserting their EU and competition law rights, whether in competition investigations before EU and UK competition authorities, litigation, and commercial transactions. His work covers: international merger control, restrictive agreements, abuse of dominance, competition compliance, State aid, public procurement, economic regulation in the transport and energy sectors and the legal implications of "Brexit."

Employment

Asha Kumar is a Partner of Watson Farley and Williams LLP specialising in employment law and regularly assists inward investors on a range of employment law matters affecting start-up operations. She also advises companies on how to safeguard their growing business interests.

Property

Gary Ritter is a Partner of Watson Farley & Williams LLP. Gary specialises in advising on a broad range of residential and commercial property matters, including development, investment and landlord and tenant. He acts for substantial companies as well as for individual investors.

Charlotte Williams is a senior associate at Watson, Farley & Williams LLP. Charlotte advises on a wide range of commercial property matters, including sales and purchases, commercial lettings, development work (including in the energy sector) and secured lending, acting for individual investors, companies, funds and financial institutions.

OTHER CONTRIBUTORS

Marcus Dolman is Vice President, ECA & Sales Finance, Rolls-Royce plc. He was appointed Co-Chairman of the British Exporters Association (BExA) in 2016 with specific responsibility for the Large Exporter members. He has been the Rolls-Royce representative at BExA since 2013 and was previously Chairman of the Industry Committee. Marcus is the focal point for all of the Rolls-Royce Group's ECA activity including maintaining its relationship with various government ECA departments, specifically UKEF, US ExIm and GIEK in Norway. He is also responsible for all Customer Financing activity in the Americas and Europe for Rolls-Royce's aerospace customers and globally for any land based power projects. He obtained an MBA from the Open University in 2004 as part of the Rolls-Royce Management Development Curriculum.

Nick Hood is a Partner within Carter Jonas, a Director of St. John's Innovation Centre Ltd, The City of Cambridge Education Foundation, and is a Chartered Surveyor. Nick leads the Carter Jonas Technology Team which specializes in the development and marketing of Science Parks and Innovation Centres. Carter Jonas is one of the leading property consultants in the Science Park sector. The Technology Team offers a broad spectrum of services to both public and private sector clients including feasibility studies, demands and needs studies, development agreements, marketing strategy reports, lettings and acquisitions of incubators, laboratory and/or R&D buildings.

Jonathan Reuvid is an editor and author of business books and a partner in Legend Business. He has edited all eight editions of 'The Investors' Guide to the United Kingdom' and has more than 80 editions of over 30 titles to his name as editor and part-author including 'The Handbook of International Trade', 'The Handbook of World Trade', 'Managing Cybersecurity Risk' and business guides to China, the 10 countries that joined the EU in 2004, South Africa and Morocco. Before taking up a second career in business publishing Jonathan was Director of European Operations of the manufacturing subsidiaries of a Fortune 500 multinational. From 1984 to 2005 he engaged in joint venture development and start-ups in China. He is also a founder director of IPR Events, the quality exhibition organizer and President-elect of the charity, Community First Oxfordshire.

Guy Robinson is a Deputy Director in the Innovation Directorate at the Intellectual Property Office. Guy heads up policy teams that help people to make informed choices about IP, to derive value from the IP that they own and to mitigate risks around IP ownership. He has 17 years of IP experience both in policy and operations, he begin his career at in the IPO as a patent examiner in 1999. The Intellectual Property Office (IPO) is the official UK government body responsible for intellectual property (IP) rights including patents, designs, trade marks and copyright. The IPO is an executive agency of the Department for Business, Energy & Industrial Strategy.

Susan Ross is an Account Director at Aon Credit International. She is an export credit insurance broker at Aon, placing risk in the London Market, whole turnover market and with UK Export Finance (UKEF). Susan chaired BExA from 2009-2012, during which time she successfully campaigned for the re-launch of the UKEF Bond Support scheme. In addition, she introduced and edited several of the well regarded series of BExA Guides, which provide exporters with practical and concise instructions on various export related subjects. Susan continues to be an active member of BExA in her current role of Vice President, and was awarded an MBE in the Queen's Birthday Honours 2017 for voluntary services to UK exports.

Olaf Swanzy is the PNO Group UK sector specialist for innovation with close working relationships with all principal funding bodies in this sector. He joined the PNO Group in 2004 to help establish the UK operation with an initial focus on technology development within the Environmental Sector. Over the past 9 years Olaf has worked with an extensive range of SMEs and large companies across all industry sectors and academia to advance research and innovation activities through the procure ment of government funding from national and EU sources. Since 2008, he has been involved in the delivery of training to SMEs in the areas of government funding for innovation investment activities. In 2009 alone he secured in excess of £15 million of grant support for clients.

David Thomas MBE is Executive Chairman of COBCOE and a non-executive director of several public companies. He owns and runs Net Investing sp z o o, the leading P2P business financing portal in Poland, and is founder of the leading Polish fintech financing platform. He has held senior roles with HSBC, ING, Schroders and Coopers & Lybrand. David is a co-founder of the Hope Foundation, a Polish charity, and the Association for Geographic Information. He has a BA from the School of Oriental and African Studies and an MSc DIC from Imperial College, London.

Glynis Whiting is Managing Partner at TIAO and a founding partner in two startups providing digital transformation for membership organisations and companies. She has 30 years leadership experience in EU and UK public policy, business development, innovation and high impact projects to address global challenges. A resident of Brussels, Glynis set up West Midlands In Europe in 2000 with over 90 stakeholder partners. She is a founder member of the European Regions Research and Innovation Network.

BUSINESS GUIDE TO THE UNITED KINGDOM

INTRODUCTION

Unlike the previous Legend Business investors' guide, focused on inward investment, the scope of Business Guide to the United Kingdom has been expanded to include overviews of the post-Brexit international trade outlook for companies locating in the UK as an export hub.

As before, the first four parts of the book provide authoritative information on the regulatory environment and legal framework, audit, accountancy and the taxation regimes for UK registered companies. Also covered are the immigration and visa regime for foreign nationals working in the UK, employment laws and pension practice. These are all issues for serious study by prospective investors before commitment and are presented and discussed by our content partners, the international accountancy firm Mazars and law firm Watson, Farley and Williams.

Additional background information is provided in Part One on the UK's economic environment, grants and incentives available to UK registered companies, the prime sectors of infrastructure investment and science parks and business incubators. Part Four focuses on financial regulation, mergers and acquisitions processes, the Aim market of the London Stock Exchange and investment in commercial property.

Part Five is the additional foreign trade content of the book with chapters on the WTO, on the UK's position after leaving the EU and on the trade outlook after disengagement, supplemented by chapters from the Council of British Chambers of Commerce in Europe (COBCOE) and the British Export Association. Appendix I, to be read in conjunction with Chapter 5.2, will be of interest to all UK exporters seeking new markets beyond the EU. It provides profiles of each of nine target countries in the form of digests of the leading international data sources most used by desk researchers and economists. These profiles supplement the headline information available on the Department for International Trade's websites.

As editor, I express my grateful thanks to the more than 20 authors who have written and without whose contributions this book could not be published. Their further advice is available to all readers through the Contributors' Contacts listed in Appendix II. My appreciation also to David Thomas, Chairman of COBCOE, for his Foreword.

Jonathan Reuvid, Editor

Part One

Investment in the United Kingdom: The Current Outlook

1.1 THE UK ECONOMY AND INWARD INVESTMENT

Jonathan Reuvid, Legend Business

The outcome of the June 2016 Referendum on UK membership of the EU had little visible effect on the UK economy up to March 2017 when the Prime Minister invoked Section 50 of the Treaty of Rome confirming termination from March 2019. Following the intervention of the UK General Parliamentary Election called in April, negotiations on the terms of departure were delayed until 19th June when formal negotiations in Brussels opened. Understandably, uncertainties which surround the likely outcomes and which will persist until there is an outline agreement on the future relationship between the EU and the UK are now having a dampening effect on the economy.

However, the economy remains robust and there are encouraging signs of possible bilateral trade deals with some leading global economies beyond the EU when Brexit finally takes place. (Profiles of these economies and their foreign trade are included in Appendix I of this book.) The UK Department for International Trade is leading these initiatives.

MACRO-ECONOMIC INDICATORS

Forecasts for 2017/18
Composite forecasts for the basics of the UK economy published by HM Treasury are highlighted in Table 1.1.1.

Table 1.1.1 Macro-economic indicators June 2017

	2017			2018		
	Lowest	Highest	Average	Lowest	Highest	Average
GDP growth (%)	1.1	2.1	1.6	0.4	2.6	1.4
Inflation Q4 (%)						
- CPI	2.1	3.6	3	1.7	3	2.5
- RPI	3.2	4.9	3.9	2.6	4	3.3
Unemployment (Q4%)	4.4	5.5	4.8	4.1	6.4	5.1
Current Account (£bn)	-89.5	-17	-60.4	-82.7	-19.8	-49.5
PSNB (2017-18, 2018-19: £bn)	42.8	79.8	58	23.9	70.2	46.8

Source: Macroeconomic Co-ordination & Strategy Team, HM Treasury No. 361, June 2017

The highest and lowest forecasts are extracted and the averages calculated from the forecasts made by 20 City banks and accredited advisers and by 19 international institutes and professionals during the previous three months excluding May. The non-City institutions include the European Commission, OECD, IMF, the Economist Intelligence Unit (EIU), the Confederation of British Industry (CBI) and the British Chamber of Commerce (BCC).

Growth prospects for the UK are compared with those of other major advanced economies and the emerging and developing economies in Table 1.1.2 by reference to the most recent OECD forecasts of real GDP.

Table 1.1.2 Forecast GDP growth for 2017 and 2018 vs 2016

	2016 %	2017 %	2018 %
Advanced economies			
UK	1.8	1.6	1.0
US	1.6	2.1	2.4
Australia	2.4	2.5	2.9
Canada	1.4	2.8	2.3
France	1.1	1.3	1.5
Germany	1.8	2.0	2.0
Italy	1.0	1.0	0.8
Japan	1.0	1.4	1.0
Spain	3.2	2.8	2.4
Euro Area	1.7	1.8	1.8
Emerging and developing Asian economies			
China	6.7	6.6	6.4
India	7.1	7.3	7.7
Korea	2.8	2.6	2.8
Total OECD	1.8	2.1	2.1

Source: OECD statistical Table 1, June 2017

The lower rate of growth projections by the OECD for the UK in 2018 compared to HM Treasury's current forecasts reflects a more pessimistic view of the progress of Brexit negotiations . Nevertheless, it is clear that the short-term outlook for the UK economy is significantly weaker than for North America and for the larger EU countries other than Italy. All of these are overshadowed by the continuing high growth rates of Asia's two biggest economies.

The UK Population

At mid-year 2016 the population total stood at 65.6 million having increased by 538,100 over the previous year. Of this increase net immigration accounted for 336,000, representing 62.4%.(Source: Office of National Statistics, June 2017).

As of May 2017, 32.1 million were in work, 324,000 more than a year earlier. As of July the jobless rate stands at 4.5% (www.tradingconomics.com). Applying the international measurement standard, the UK's unemployment rate compares favourably with the EU average of 9.3% (source: Eurostat, 2017) although higher than the US (4.4%) and Germany (3.9%).

The last UK census of population was taken in 2011, when 83.9% of the population were resident in England, 8.4% in Scotland, 4.9% in Wales and 2.8% in Northern Ireland. Of those living in the UK at that time 8.4 million (13%) were born abroad.

UK INWARD INVESTMENT

The UK enjoyed a successful year in 2016-17 with the number of projects rising by 2% compared with the previous year to 2,265, creating 75,226 new jobs and protecting a further 32,672 jobs. However, the total of jobs related to inward investment projects declined from 115,974 in 2015-16 to 107,986. Of the new projects registered 1,053 were funded by investors new to the UK and 1,212 by existing investors extending their UK engagements. Over the past five years, the number of new FDI projects in the UK has increased steadily each year as illustrated in Table 1.1.3.

Table 1.1.3 FDI performance over five years

	2012-13	2013-14	2014-15	2015-16	2016-17
New projects	1,559	1,773	1,368	2,213	2,265
New jobs created	89,153	66,390	84,693	82,650	75,326
New investments	777	820	1,058	1,130	1,237
Expansions	577	677	740	821	782
Mergers & acquisitions	205	276	190	262	246

Source: Department for International Trade

Inward investment flows to the UK over the past four years have been impressive by comparison with EU fellow members and the EU in total according to UNCTAD statistics (World Investment Report 2017).

Table 1.1.4 Value of FDI inflows

US$ milion

	2013	2014	2015	2016
UK	51,676	44,821	33,003	253,826
France	34,270	2,689	46,991	28,352
Germany	15,573	3,954	33,312	9,526
Total EU	336,811	256,613	483,839	566,234
UK share (%)	15.3	17.4	6.82	44.8

Source: United Nations Conference on Trade and Development

In terms of accumulated investment UK inward FDI in 2016 reached USD$1.2 trillion, representing 15.6% of the EU total and compared to US$771 billion for Germany and US$698 billion for France. UK outward FDI stocks, net of disposals, stood at US$1.4 trillion.

Sources of FDI

The top sources of UK FDI in 2016-17 in descending order are listed in Table 1.1.5 together with the new jobs created and safeguarded jobs.

Table 1.1.5 The UK'S major investment sources

Country	FDI projects	New jobs	Safeguarded jobs
United States	557	24,607	7,197
China and Hong Kong	160	3,326	1,444
France	131	5,831	2,182
India	127	3,999	7,645
Australia and New Zealand	127	2,197	1,803
Japan	116	3,511	6,095
Germany	100	5,802	426
Italy	99	1,482	167
Canada	72	1,788	122
Spain	70	1,789	1,152
Ireland	56	2,914	752
Netherlands	53	2,292	546
Switzerland	49	1,428	643
Other Europe, Middle East, Africa	261	6,867	923
Other American countries	59	1,080	206
Other Asian Pacific countries	82	1,896	394

Source: Department for International Trade

Regional dispersion

FDI in 2016-17 was spread widely among the regions with the Greater London Area taking the lion's share as Table 1.1.6 demonstrates:

Table 1.1.6 Regional dispersion of 2016-17 FDI

	No. of projects	*New jobs created*
London	891	20,753
South East	217	5,432
North West	147	6,501
West Midlands	151	6,570
Yorkshire and the Humber	132	3,872
East of England	125	3,634
South West	101	3,402
East Midlands	74	1,796
North East	69	4,609
England	1,907	56.569
Scotland	183	5,547
Wales	85	2,581
Northern Ireland	34	1,652

Source: Department for International Trade

Sectoral focus of 2016-17 FDI

As the report issued by the Department for International Trade for 2016-17shows, the tech sector attracted the greatest number of new projects with the second highest number of new jobs after the business and consumer services sector. Many of these are located in the Greater London area and at the beginning of July London & Partners reported a record level of investments in UK tech companies in the first six months of 2017 accounting for £1.3 billion. The UK remains the leading destination for venture capital investments, attracting more than twice as much invested than in Berlin.

The sectoral dispersion of investment and job creation is illustrated in Table 1.1.7.

Table 1.1.7 Sector results 2016-17

	FDI projects	New jobs	Safeguarded jobs	Total jobs
Advanced engineering and supply chain	146	3,716	7,913	11,629
Aerospace	47	1,818	1,275	3,093
Automotive	127	5,711	8,803	14,514
Biotechnology and pharmaceuticals	90	2,329	896	3,225
Business and consumer services	211	13,603	1,353	14,956
Chemicals and agriculture	50	787	1,044	1,831
Creative and media	151	3,654	89	3,743
Electronics and communications	115	3,170	902	4,072
Environment, infrastructure and transportation	184	6,302	1,301	7,604
Extraction industries	49	642	758	1,400
Financial services	217	8,847	2,661	11,508
Food and drink	144	4,620	2,417	7,037
Life sciences	116	2,457	1,385	3,822
Renewable energy	87	2,749	344	3,093
Software and computer services	418	10,971	1,476	12,447
Wholesale	113	3,850	74	3,924

Source: Department for International Trade

Among the other sectors receiving the most new projects creating high numbers of jobs and protecting existing jobs are advanced engineering and software. Together with the automotive, financial and business services sectors they are all driven by digitisation as they seek to generate innovation and new products.

Funding for tech investment after Brexit

The funding sources available to all companies located in the UK are identified and explored extensively in Chapter 1.2. However, inward investors may have concerns about the continued availability of EU funding for UK enterprises after March 19, particularly in the tech sector, from the European Investment Fund (EIF). At this early stage all outcomes of Brexit negotiations are unknown, but it seems unlikely that the UK can retain its role in the Fund. The EIF's parent body is the European Investment Bank which is wholly controlled by EU member states and under the oversight of the European Court of Justice. In the event of withdrawal from the EIF, the UK government is expected to provide alternative sources to maintain support funding, possibly through UK Innovation which is increasingly proactive or through a major expansion of the British Business Bank. Repatriation of the Barclays Bank and Scottish Enterprise stakes in the EIB would provide seed funding for establishing an alternative mechanism.

THE UK AS A BASE FOR INTERNATIONAL TRADE

A major factor in encouraging new and repeat investment in the UK has been tariff free access to the rest of the EU for foreign investors establishing manufacturing operations and service centres in the UK. Some of the consequences should the UK fail to maintain open access to EU markets are explored in Part 5 of this book. While it is plain that the tariff effect of transferring to independent WTO membership will have to be addressed on an industry by industry basis, the administrative burden of leaving the EU customs union, which would fall on all, will be mitigated to some degree by new opportunities to build exports and establish bilateral free trade agreements elsewhere worldwide.

The patterns of UK exports in merchandise and services in 2015 are summarised in the current WTO data of Table 1.1.8.

Table 1.1.8   UK export shares by destination

	Merchandise	Services
	%	%
European Union	43.8	37.2
United States	14.9	23.3
Switzerland	7.3	5.8
China	5.9	-
Japan	-	2.6
Other	28.1	31.1

Source: WTO country profiles

Note: Merchandise exports to Japan and services exports to China are included under the 'Other' categories

The sub-sector of other commercial services and goods-related services accounts for 74% of total services. of which financial services in turn accounted for one third in 2015.

The top 10 product groups in UK exports and imports represent the following shares of the merchandise totals:

Table 1.1.9 Top export and import product goups

	Exports			Imports	
	US$ Bn	*%*		*US$Bn*	*%*
Gold	41.6	9.8	Cars	49.9	8.2
Cars	40.8	9.6	Packaged medicaments	21.0	3.5
Packaged medicaments	19.9	4.7	Refined petroleum	20.2	3.3
Gas turbines	14.7	3.5	Crude petroleum	17.3	2.9
Refined petroleum	13.2	3.1	Vehicle parts	15.0	2.5
Crude petroleum	12.9	3.0	Gold	11.8	1.9
Aerospace parts	10.8	2.5	Petroleum gas	10.8	1.8
Hard liquor	7.8	1.8	Broadcasting equipment	10.0	1.6
Vehicle parts	5.8	1.4	Planes, helicopters etc,	9.9	1.6
Nucleic acids	4.7	1.1	Delivery trucks	9.0	1.5

Source: https://atlas.media.edu/en/profile/country

For readers researching the foreign trade opportunities for the UK beyond the EU, nine priority markets including the US, China, Japan and Switzerland are identified in Chapter 5.2 and profiled in Appendix I.

SUMMARY

Overall, with its world beating combination of permissive regulations and transparency, innovative businesses, access to talent and interconnected sectors, the UK remains a highly attractive location for FDI and as a hub for international trade.

Note: Much of the statistical content for this chapter relating to inward investment is derived from the Department for International Trade's 2016-17 report.

1.2 GRANTS AND INCENTIVES WITHIN THE UK

Olaf Swanzy, PNO Consultants Ltd

INTRODUCTION

Despite current political uncertainty surrounding the UK, there are numerous grant funding measures available to strengthen UK industry by stimulating growth, employment and the development of state-of-the-art technology which allows the UK to compete effectively in the global market. In particular, the UK grant landscape is extremely buoyant, with a regular supply of varied funding programmes which are beneficial over loan or equity investment as they are non-repayable and do not require the dilution of shareholdings.

Thousands of different grant schemes, worth well in excess of £5 billion each year, are available for UK companies in an attempt to encourage, amongst other things, innovation and economic development.

In general there are four types of public funding incentives available in the UK:

- **Grants** – where funding is secured ahead of the launch of a project;
- **Soft loans** – where loans are secured for projects that fall outside the parameters of normal business banking;
- **Tax incentives** – recognising advanced financial incentives for those with leading edge Research and Development (R&D) or capital programmes that are aligned with government strategy;
- **Awards** – that retrospectively recognise industry excellence in many functional areas of business – usually a financial prize, which has the advantage of significant PR.

Outside of the obvious fiscal benefits, for successful applicants the receipt of public funding can be also be used to achieve the following:

- Increased project leverage and project development;
- Improved company image (being awarded a grant is the equivalent of being awarded a quality stamp from a grantor body);
- A competitive advantage over others in your sector;
- Help raising additional 'harder finance' – comparable investment criteria;
- Establishment of collaborative relationships. Not all grants require a collaboration, but those that do provide an ideal opportunity to work with academia, or indeed other industrial organisations, including potential customers.

In all cases, funding is used by a Governmental Body or Policy Maker to address key policy issues and to stimulate first movers by reducing financial risk in that area. Such incentives are therefore always in line with Government policies and key drivers. It is important that this is kept clearly in mind for any potential applicant when positioning their applications.

Although other forms of public funding are available, this article will focus predominantly on grants which represent the larger sums of money available for UK business.

MAIN GRANTS AND INCENTIVES IN THE UK

One of the key funding bodies to support UK businesses is Innovate UK (formerly the Technology Strategy Board), a fully public funded executive body established in July 2007. Innovate UK is our national innovation agency, dedicated to driving innovation for wealth creation in the UK, so that technology-enabled businesses sustain or attain global significance. It provides particular support for Research and Development (R&D) to build partnerships between business, research and the Government to address major societal challenges and to run a wide range of knowledge exchange programmes to help innovation flourish. Funding is available for business and in some cases the academic base. The vision for Innovate UK is to make the UK a global leader in innovation and a magnet for innovative businesses, where technology is applied rapidly, effectively and sustainably to create wealth and enhance quality of life. Further information can be found at https://www.gov.uk/government/organisations/innovate-uk.

Other sources of guidance and support for UK investment include: www.ukti.gov.uk, www.scottish-enterprise.com, www.wales.gov.uk and www.investni.com.

In general, the range of funding programmes available for UK businesses can be broken down into the following three principal areas:

1. Research and Development;
2. Training and Education;
3. Capital Investment.

1. RESEARCH & DEVELOPMENT

Innovation remains the key focus area for the majority of UK funding bodies. A range of schemes are available for businesses irrespective of sector, company size and Technology Readiness Level (TRL). The core national funding programmes, designed to support businesses in their R&D activities, offer up to 70% grant funding for projects up to £1million in cost. They have been summarised below.

For technical feasibility studies and industrial research, funding rates are:
- 70% for small businesses
- 60% for medium-sized businesses
- 50% for large businesses

For experimental development projects, the funding rates are:
- 45% for small businesses
- 35% for medium-sized businesses
- 25% for large businesses

The Open Programme (Innovate UK)
Available for UK-based enterprises to support projects that aim to develop or demonstrate highly innovative processes, products or services that have the potential to deliver significant business growth. The competition, which is typically run across two calls per year, is open to all sectors and will support projects at different levels of maturity from initial ideas through to advanced prototype development. To be in scope, a proposal must show:

- cutting-edge, disruptive or game-changing innovation leading to novel, new products, processes or services; and
- a clear and anticipated growth impact leading to a significant return on investment.

Manufacturing and Materials (Innovate UK)
This competition, which is also deployed typically across two calls per year, aims to stimulate and broaden innovation in manufacturing and materials, to increase productivity, competitiveness and growth for UK businesses, especially SMEs. To be in scope, a project must cover at least one of two areas:

- innovation in a manufacturing system, technology, process or business model; e.g. more flexible or efficient processes and those that allow greater customisation of products;
- innovation in materials development, properties, integration or reuse; e.g. materials for ease of manufacture or for targeted performance;

- Each project must focus on the manufacturing or materials innovation, rather than a product innovation – the challenge should be in the manufacturing process or materials development.

All projects must enable a step change in productivity and competitiveness for at least one UK SME. Applications are particularly welcome where the innovation can impact on more than one sector.

Emerging & Enabling Technologies (Innovate UK)

This scheme aims to identify and invest in new technologies coming from the research base that allow things to be done that were not previously possible (emerging) and the underpinning capabilities that improve existing industries (enabling). Proposals must show innovation in one of the key priority areas (see below), have outputs applicable to more than one market or sector, and improved business growth, productivity or export opportunities. Key priority areas include:

- Emerging technologies, including biofilms, energy harvesting, graphene or novel single-layer (2D) materials, cutting-edge imaging technologies, and unconventional new computational paradigms such as biological computing;
- Digital, where there is significant development in one or more of: machine learning and artificial intelligence (AI), cyber security, data analytics or 'big data', distributed ledger technology (such as blockchain), Internet of Things (IoT), immersive technology (such as virtual or augmented reality) and innovative services or applications employing new forms of connectivity, including 5G;
- Enabling capabilities, such as electronics, sensors and photonics (ESP), robotics and autonomous systems and creative industry technologies;
- Space applications with innovation in at least one of satellite communications, satellite navigation, or earth observation and environmental monitoring services.

Health and Life Sciences (Innovate UK)

This scheme aims to stimulate innovation in health and life sciences that significantly increases competitiveness and productivity with a particular focus on SMEs. Key priority areas include:

- Agricultural productivity: advanced and precision engineering, fighting agro-chemical and antimicrobial resistance, biotic and abiotic stress resilience, individualized livestock/aquaculture nutrition and healthcare, and novel genetics and breeding;
- Food quality and sustainability: authenticity and traceability, nutritional value, food safety, modern food manufacturing methods, new and smarter ingredients, protein development, and smarter packaging;

- Precision medicine: the development of tests and/or diagnostic tools to select the best treatment, care pathways and disease management regimes for patients, paediatrics and child health, stratification in primary care and the community, companion diagnostics, antimicrobial resistance and developing capabilities to enable precision medicine (e.g. informatics, imaging techniques and biosciences);
- Advanced therapies: increasing commercial capacity/productivity to manufacture viral vectors for use in the development of clinical cell and gene therapies for the treatment of human disease and disorders;
- Preclinical technologies: innovative platforms for analysing, screening and optimising potential new medicines and novel in vitro and in vivo models that determine mechanism of action, efficacy or safety of potential new medicines;
- Biosciences: synthetic biology, computational systems biology, biological sample preparation technologies, cells, tissues and communities as bio-manufacturing platforms.

Infrastructure Systems (Innovate UK)

A scheme that aims to stimulate innovation in infrastructure systems that provide critical services to our economy, environment and society, across a range of sectors, including energy, transport and city/urban systems. Solutions can include technologies such as communications, digital, electronics, novel materials and sensors. Projects must meet one of the specific competition themes:

- 'Smart' infrastructure: smart, resilient and sustainable integrated infrastructure that adds intelligence to:
    * improve functionality, capacity, productivity, security or whole-life performance;
    * improve resilience and sustainability;
    * reduce the risk of failure;
    * reduce whole-life costs or environmental impact
- Energy systems: innovations in the ability to match energy supply and demand, which are smart systems solutions that integrate energy generation and demand at local, regional or national scales, and create significant improvements in value proposition, energy affordability, security and reduced carbon emissions;
- Nuclear fission: innovations that lead to major cost reductions, improved asset integrity and supply chain development for the UK and global civil nuclear markets, including decommissioning;
- Offshore wind: innovations that result in substantial reductions in the cost of energy from offshore wind;

- Connected transport: innovations that:
  * improve network capacity, efficiency and reduced operational cost, whilst (i) balancing transportation infrastructure peak demands, (ii) connecting different transport modes to provide better services, greater flexibility and reliability, and (iii) reducing logistics problems
  * offer greater system intelligence in existing transport networks
  * future-proof transport infrastructure for advanced vehicle technologies;

- Urban living: innovations that address citizens' challenges in cities and urban areas and offer citizen-centric solutions such as better health and wellbeing, increased productivity and higher resilience to change, by integrating different types of urban infrastructure systems.

The Catalyst Programmes (Innovate UK)

Catalysts are run jointly by Innovate UK and the Research Councils. A Catalyst is a form of research and development funding which focuses on a specific priority area and aims to help take projects from research to as close to commercial viability as possible.

The Catalyst model supports projects in priority areas where the UK research base has a leading position and where there is clear commercial potential. Three levels of funding are usually available, varying according to how close a project is to commercialisation, with applicants able to join at any phase. Current Catalyst programmes include:

1. The Biomedical Catalyst is open to both SMEs and academics looking to develop innovative solutions to healthcare challenges, either individually or in collaboration. Support will be available for projects arising from any sector or discipline that is aimed at addressing healthcare challenges. Two categories of grant are available, depending on the maturity of the research, including Early Stage and Late Stage Awards (both maximum grant £2.4 million, up to 50% support). Applications are accepted on a rolling basis with batch assessment dates typically every four to six months;
2. The Agri-Tech Catalyst supports businesses and academia in developing innovative solutions to challenges in the agri-tech sector. The Agri-Tech Catalyst will fund proposals relating to: primary crop and livestock production, including aquaculture, non-food uses of arable crops (for example, for biomass), food security and nutrition challenges in international development or challenges in downstream food processing, provided the solution lies in primary production;
3. The Energy Catalyst supports businesses and research organisations, including academia, to respond to challenges across the energy sector. It will fund projects delivering innovative solutions that address all elements of the energy trilemma.

The Energy Catalyst can fund projects from early concept stage through to pre-commercial technology validation.

Small Business Research Initiative (SBRI) (Innovate UK)

The SBRI supports the engagement of the public sector with industry during the early stages of development, supporting projects across a range of industry sectors through the stages of feasibility and prototyping. The initiative is particularly suitable for SMEs and early stage businesses, as it provides them with vital funding for the critical stages of product development, and gives them a fast track and simplified process for working with the public sector. Typically, funding available is £100,000 for a feasibility stage project and £1 million for a development stage project.

Full information regarding all Innovate UK managed funding programmes can be found at https://www.gov.uk/apply-funding-innovation

EUREKA Eurostars (joint programme between more than 30 EUREKA member countries and the European Union)

This programme supports research-performing SMEs to develop market orientated innovative products, processes and services in a transnational context i.e. involving at least one other partner from another Eurostars country. Any topic will be considered (with the exception of military applications). The main programme criteria are:

- Consortium leader is an R&D performing SME from a Eurostars country which includes the UK;
- Eurostars R&D performing SMEs contribution is 50% or more of the total project cost;
- The consortium is well balanced (no single participant or country is responsible for more than 75%);
- The project duration is up to three years;
- Market introduction is within two years of the project's completion;
- Any topic can be considered (with the exception of military projects).

In the UK, only research-performing SMEs are eligible for funding under Eurostars. UK Academics/universities and large companies are welcome to participate in a Eurostars project, but must fund their own participation or use funds from other sources. The same rules do not apply for other member states so for any potential collaboration please check the terms specific to that country. Up to 60% of eligible costs will be supported to a maximum grant level of €360,000 per UK partner in a Eurostars project. Further information can be found at https://www.eurostars-eureka.eu/.

Horizon 2020 (H2020) – European Funding

At a European Level, H2020 is the largest European funding programme for research and innovation, with nearly €80 billion of funding available over seven years (2014 to 2020). Horizon 2020 is the financial instrument implementing the Innovation Union and a Europe 2020 flagship initiative aimed at securing Europe's global competitiveness. With the emphasis on excellent science, industrial leadership and tackling societal challenges, Horizon 2020's goal is to ensure Europe produces world-class science, removes barriers to innovation and makes it easier for the public and private sectors to work together in delivering innovation. Horizon 2020 is open to everyone and has a simpler structure than previous programmes – reducing red tape and time so that participants can focus on what is really important. This approach helps new projects to get off the ground quickly – and achieve results faster. Full details can be found at http://ec.europa.eu/programmes/horizon2020/.

Please note that UK organisations can still participate in all H2020 programmes until the point that the UK leaves the EU. The potential to access support after this point will depend on the negotiation process.

2. TRAINING

Training or retraining of employees is of eminent importance to keep the workforce up to speed in rapidly changing environments. In some areas within the UK, these types of training courses may be eligible for public funding. The focus is on training for personnel below NVQ level 2 or minority groups such as asylum seekers.

3. CAPITAL INVESTMENT

Few CAPEX support programmes remain in the UK, with a greater number of smaller schemes available at a regional/local level, depending on location. For larger scale investments, the main national funding programme is the Regional Growth Fund (RGF). RGF is a £3.2 billion fund, helping companies throughout England to create jobs between now and the mid-2020s. The payment of RGF money is spread between 2011 and 2017. RGF supports projects and programmes that are using private sector investment to create economic growth and sustainable employment. The bid threshold (a minimum amount of funding that can be applied for) is £1 million. Any support will be phased in line with expenditure and/or job creation/safeguarding. If you are considering an investment that will lead to job creation, it is worth speaking initially to your Local Enterprise Partnership about the availability of funding: https://www.gov.uk/government/policies/local-enterprise-partnerships-leps-and-enterprise-zones.

THE GRANT APPLICATION PROCESS

Thorough preparation is the key to success in applying for grants. Having a credible business plan, a clear commercial or marketing strategy as well as a quality management team, before an application is submitted is a very important part of the application process. Application processing times differ significantly from scheme to scheme, with timescales ranging from four weeks to nine months. For any potential applicants it is important that project costs are not incurred before the grant application process is completed and grant agreements signed with the appropriate funding body.

Careful preparation of applications will naturally increase the chances of success. However, there are no guarantees that an application will succeed, regardless of its merits, as the majority of UK grants are discretionary, meaning that they are awarded on a case-by-case basis and, more commonly, on a competitive basis. It is therefore of vital importance to ensure that the application is of the highest quality so that it stands out against the competition. It is also prudent to maximise the chances of success by developing a total grants strategy, rather than pinning everything on just one application.

SUPPORT IN THE GRANT ACQUISITION PROCESS

Finding the most appropriate grant and applying for funds can often be prohibitive. Successful grant procurement requires dedicated time and resources which companies often do not possess internally. As a result some businesses choose to maximise the funding opportunities available by appointing external expertise. Support advice and providers can be found through bodies such the UK Government Business Link network and the Enterprise Europe Network as well as specialist funding consultants. One such public funding advisory is the PNO Group – Europe's leading innovation funding advisors. Employing over 270 staff across the EU, PNO's core business is advising organisations across all industrial sectors, in the context of the UK and EU grant funding landscape, helping them to identify and secure funds through available schemes.

Their client base include an extensive range of SMEs, Universities and Multinationals which include companies such as HP, Microsoft, Philips, P&G and Solvay (www.pnoconsultants.com). You can contact PNO's UK office to discuss the eligibility of any project ideas for funding potential on 0161 488 3488.

CONCLUSION

Public funding can provide a valuable means of supporting companies to achieve their strategic goals. For R&D activities in particular there are a range of schemes available to support projects across all stages of development from initial conception through to large scale demonstration.

With many businesses struggling to raise private and bank finance to advance their activities, it has never been more important to review all forms of funding available, including public funds. If you are serious about being a market leader in your field, grant funding is the ideal mechanism to help you to achieve your goal.

1.3 UK INFRASTRUCTURE INVESTMENT OPPORTUNITIES

Jonathan Reuvid, Legend Business

In March 2016, the UK government published a new National Infrastructure Delivery Plan that brought together all its plans for the current Parliament up to 2021 to support major UK infrastructure projects together with investment in large-scale housing and regeneration, new local schools, hospitals and prisons.

The Plan is based on a government commitment to invest more than £100 billion in infrastructure by 2020-21 and calls for significant investment by the private sector. The latest version of the National Infrastructure Pipeline is incorporated within the Plan, highlighting economic infrastructure investment of more than £425 billion in more than 600 projects and programmes across the UK and an additional £58 billion of public investment in social infrastructure over that period and beyond.

Following the general election of June 2017 the life of the new parliament is extended to 2022 and the Treasury has reconfirmed its investment commitments on infrastructure accordingly.

SECTORAL INVESTMENT

The National Infrastructure and Construction Pipeline (Autumn 2016) identifies by sector and sub-sector timing and expenditure on 728 projects and programmes totalling £502,249 million up to and beyond 2020-21. Table 1.3.1 summarises the detail by sector.

Table 1.3.1 Projected timing and expenditure of Infrastructure Pipeline

Sector	No. projects & programmes	2016/21 £m	post-2020/21 £m	Total £m
Energy	114	78,623	127,640	206,264
Transport	251	91,929	46,402	138,331
Utilities	96	59,218	15,600	74,812
Communications	8	19	15.377	15,396
Education	20	22,488	0	22,488
Housing & Regeneration	18	12,916	0	12,916
Ministry of Defence	47	5,780	2,594	8,374
Science & Research	25	5,913	265	6,178
Flood Defence	29	2,720	1,418	4,138
Health	32	2,886	57	2,943
Justice	44	1,528	0	1,528
Police Forces	29	1,239	17	1,256
Waste	7	537	0	538
Home Office	6	73	0	73
CPS	7	14	0	14
Autumn Statement Additional funding		0	7,000	7,000
Total	728	238,471	263,778	502,249

Source: https://www.gov.uk/government/publictions/national-infrastucture-pipeline-2016

Among the leading sectors, investment is focused on:
- communications: the digital economy (£11.5 billion up to 2020/21);
- energy: electricity generation (£40 billion up to 2020/21 and £102 billion thereafter), nuclear decommissioning (£3 billion before and £26 billion after) and £34 billion on oil and gas before 2022;
- transport: HS2 high speed rail £55 billion (£15 billion before 2022 and £40 billion after), other rail developments (£33 billion before and £6 billion after) and roads (£7 billion up to 2020/21 and £6 billion later).
- utilities: electricity transmission and distribution (£40 billion up to 2020/21 and £10 billion later) and water and sewerage (£21 billion up to 2022).

There is no provision in the current pipeline for major infrastructure investment which is to be funded wholly from sources other than the UK Treasury (e.g. Hinkley Point C nuclear power station) or a third runway at Heathrow, the government's preferred option for the expansion of airport capacity in the South East.

The remainder of this chapter focuses on the largest infrastructure projects in energy with an overview of renewables, and in transport on airport expansion and high speed rail.

THE UK ENERGY SECTOR

The UK's civil nuclear programme dates back to 1956 when its first nuclear power station, Calder Hall at Windscale, opened. At its peak in 1997, 26% of the UK's electricity was generated by nuclear power. Since then, some older reactors have closed and by 2012 the nuclear power share of electricity generation had been reduced to 18.5%. Today there are 15 operational nuclear reactors at seven plants of which 14 are advanced gas-cooled reactors (AGR) and one pressurised water reactor (PWR). The older AGR reactors have been life-extended and further AGR life-extensions are expected.

The overseeing authority for all UK nuclear installations is the Office for Nuclear Regulation. All seven reactor sites currently operating are owned and managed by EDF Energy, a wholly-owned subsidiary of the French state-owned Électricité de France, with a combined capacity of 9,000 megawatts.

By 2011, the Government had identified and confirmed eight nuclear sites already having power stations at which future reactors could be accommodated. The Fukushima I nuclear accident of 2011 cast doubts on the willingness of the private sector to invest in new nuclear plants and caused controversy among government authorities and politicians on their viability.

In March 2012, two of the big six international power companies RWE and E.ON, who had previously planned to build 12.5 GW of new nuclear capacity in the UK, announced that they were pulling out of developing new nuclear power plants, echoing the Scottish Government's 2010 decision to ban the construction of any new plants in Scotland.

The need to build new capacity for England and Wales was underscored by the future operating life of eight current reactors managed by EDF, some of which have been extended to enable further generation beyond their original closure dates. Four of these, all AGR plants, are scheduled for closure by 2024, three more by 2030 and the eighth IPR plant by 2035. The last of eleven old Magnox plants which began commercial operation between 1959 and 1972 was closed in 2015.

The economics of nuclear power plan investment

There was no consensus in the UK about the cost/benefit advantages of nuclear energy investment up to 2011 with an unresolved debate between those arguing that energy security is paramount and those more concerned about environmental impact. The long lead-time of ten years or more between proposal and operation also deterred many investors, especially while energy market regulation and nuclear waste policy remained undetermined. As a result, no new nuclear reactors have been built since Sizewell B in 1995.

Since the national strategy for nuclear power plan development aimed at building 128 G of new nuclear energy capacity has been in place, and with the focus on securing private investment, the government has recognized that a key determinant for private investors is a guaranteed fixed price (a 'strike price') for electricity generated by each plant. This issue came to the forefront in negotiations with EDF Energy for its investment in Hinkley Point C. As the projected construction cost has escalated from £16 billion in 2012, to £18 billion in 2015 and in July 2017 to between £19.6 billion and £20.3 billion, the agreed strike price for Hinkley Point C electricity has been driven up to £92.50/MWh (in 2012 prices were inflation-linked during the construction and subsequent 25 years tariff period).

Current approved construction projects

The following five nuclear power stations are in varying stages of planning, development and construction:

Hinkley Point C
- capacity: 3,200 MWe with two EPR reactors and a projected plant lifetime of 60 years;
- financing: construction costs of £19.6 - £20.3 billion to be funded by state-owned CGN of China with a stake of 33.5%;
- cost to consumers under the strike price estimated at £29.7 billion (strike price could be reduced to £89.50 if a new plant is approved at Sizewell);
- operational opening date 2025-2027;
- EPR reactors are a new design with four under construction at Flamanville (France), Olkiluoto (Finland) and two at Taishan (China).

Oldbury and Wylfa
- Horizon acquired both installations from E.ON and RWE and was sold on in 2012 to Hitachi which intends to build me ABWR reactor at their Wylfa (Anglesey) and then Oldbury sites;
- the development is subject to a Generic Design Assessment by the Office of Nuclear Regulation following the retirement of Magnox reactors in 2011 at Wylfa and then at Oldbury;
- recently state-owned Korea Hydro & Nuclear Power (KHNP) has been named as potential investor in the Wylfa plant with a minority stake in Horizon. Other possible minority investors in Horizon are the UK government and the Japanese state arms JBIC and NEXI.

Moorside
- KPPC is also trying to buy the planned NuGen nuclear station in Moorside, Cumbria, involving the construction of three reactors;
- Toshiba, the present Japanese owner, is said to be a willing seller.

Bradwell
- as a part of its overall planned investment of £43.5 billion in UK energy infrastructure between 2014 and 2025, an agreement has also been made for Chinese-designed reactors to be built on the site of the approved Bradwell nuclear power station;
- the old Bradwell Magnox reactor was retired in 2002.

RENEWABLES

The capacity of renewable sources and electricity generated in 2015 is reported to have been as follows:

Table 1.3.2 – Renewables capacity and generation

	Installed capacity MW	Generation GW/h
Wind: onshore	9,188	22,887
offshore	5,103	17,423
Solar photovoltaics	9,187	7,561
Hydro: small scale	282	975
large scale	1,477	5,314
Bioenergy & waste	5,219	29,388
Landfill gas	1,061	4,872
Sewage sludge digestion	216	882
Energy from waste	925	2,782
Animal biomass	111	648
Anaerobic digestion	286	1,429
Plant biomass	2,619	18,587
Co-firing with fossil fuels	-	183
Total	30,465	83,550

Source: www.gov.uk/governement/sttiics/electricity-section-5-energy-trends (Dukes 6.4)

The generation and capacity of renewable energy continues to grow. In 2017 quarter 1 generation excluding non-biodegradable wastes rose 5.1% on 2016 quarter 1 and 4.6% on the previous record in 2015 quarter 4. Renewables' share of total generation reached 26.6% in 2017, quarter 1 of which bioenergy accounted for 9.6%, onshore wind for 7.2%, offshore wind for 5.9% and hydro for 2.3%, with the remaining 1.6% from solar photovoltaics (PV).

Renewables' capacity at the end of 2017 quarter 1 stood at 36.9 GW, an advance of 12% on a year earlier and 3.3% up on the end of 2016. At 12.2 GW, solar PV now has 33% of all capacity, followed by onshore wind (32%), bioenergy (16%) and offshore wind (15%).

Project finance

Most renewable energy projects in the UK are financed privately with some government incentives and support. The Clean Energy Pipeline (CEP) recorded £16.7 billion project finance in 2015 which represented a 37% increase on the £12.3 billion invested in 2014 and 85% on the £9.03 billion invested in 2013. The aggregation of individual projects into larger portfolios is a more recent trend and was a root cause of a decrease of deals reported in 2015 to 200 from 233 deals in 2014.

The high number of solar projects funded and brought online from 2013 onwards, until March 2016 when the grace period of the section 1.3 ROC subsidy regime expired, created a large pool of de-risked assets that attracted acquisitions from institutional and other low-risk investors. Funding activity in solar PV is highlighted in Table 1.3.3

Table 1.3.3 – UK project finance in renewable energy 2015

	Deal numbers	Deal value
	%	%
Solar PV	47	29
Onshore wind	34	22
Biomass	15	13
Offshore wind	4	36

Source: UK Renewable Energy Finance 2016
Solar PV deals

Notable solar investment and M&A deals in 2015 and 2016 quarter 1 include:
- £400 million acquisition package arranged by RBS and Investec to finance Octopus' acquisition of 74 solar projects from Lightsource Renewable Energy;
- £84.6 million package for SunEdison and TerraForm Power's 97 MW consented solar project portfolio in the UK;
- £264 million refinancing of Lightsource Renewable Energy's 101 MW portfolio of 33 operating solar PV projects;
- Blue Solar Income Fund's £149 million acquisition of a 105 MW solar portfolio from Primrose Solar Management;
- Hedge Fund Elliott Capital Advisors' £100 million investment into six UK solar projects;
- Canadian investment fund Fengate Capital's acquisition of a 45.1 MW portfolio of two solar projects.

Offshore wind

A record £6 billion was invested in offshore wind farms in 2015, an increase of 33% on 2014. Two major projects reported funding representing £5.2 billion investment in offshore wind in the first quarter of 2016:
- DONG Energy confirmed its decision to invest in the large 1.2 GW Hornsea Project One offshore wind farm scheduled to come online in 2020, at a total investment of £3 billion.
- Scottish Power Renewables finally decided to invest in the £2.5 billion 714 East Anglia ONE offshore wind farm.

In the same timeframe, after a year of low M&A activity in offshore wind, 2016 started on a higher note with a number of projects which matured in the first quarter at a total disclosed value of £1 billion, of which the following were notable:
- Repsol's sale of its 100% stake in the Inch Cape and its 25% interest in the Beatrice offshore farms off the Scottish Coast to SDIC of China for £186 million;
- SSE's sale of its 10% stake in the 558 MW Burbo Bank Extension offshore wind project to its Copenhagen partners;
- DONG Energy's £600 million divestment of its 50% stake in 258 Burbo Bank Extension offshore wind project to Danish pension fund PFA and KIRKBI, the parent company of LEGO Group.

Onshore Wind

Project finance in onshore wind farms peaked in 2015 with £3.7 billion invested, more than double the £1.5 billion invested in 2014. There was an urgency to secure financing to ensure that they were operational before the end of March 2017 when the ROC subsidy regime expired. Notable deals include:

- senior debt facility secured by Blue Energy with KW IPEX-Bank to fund construction of the Beinneun wind farm in Scotland in June 2015;
- £83 million project finance facility for Infinis to fund construction of the Galashiels offshore wind farm in June 2015, arranged by Santander and Barclays;
- project finance package for Invenergy Wind's 69 MW Corriegarth wind farm in Scotland in October 2015;
- Greencoat UK Wind and GUL's £365 million acquisition of a 49.9% stake in the Clyde wind farm in March 2016. GUL is an infrastructure joint venture between Greater Manchester Pension Fund and London Pension Fund Authority.

Biomass

Investment in biomass projects increased by 25% in value in 2015 to £2.3 billion. CEP reported that in the first quarter of 2016 a further £295 million was invested in biomass projects. Notable deals announced in the period from 2015 to 2016 quarter 1 were:

- European Investment Bank's £110 million investment in Viridor's Cardiff Energy recovery facility. The £223 million project will treat waste from local authorities and businesses to generate 30 MW of electricity;
- Finance package to include equity investment from Bioenergy Infrastructure Group, Israeli investor Noy Fund, John Hancock and others for the £200 million Energy Works Hull project. The project, which also secured a £20 million grant from the European Regional Development Fund, will have an output capacity of 25 MW;
- Czech utility EPH's acquisition of the Lynemouth Power station from RWE Supply & Trading. Currently running on coal, the plant will be fully converted to biomass with a gross capacity of 420 MW;
- Irish utility ESB and the Green Investment Bank's £70 million investment in the 60 MW Tilbury Green Power biomass plant through a combination of equity and shareholder loans.

TRANSPORT

Airports

The Heathrow third runway

After a two and a half year analysis of aviation capacity in the UK at a cost of £20 million, and having considered more than 50 alternative proposals during the process, the Airports Commission delivered its final report on 1 July 2015. The Commission recommended Heathrow expansion as the best option, citing up to £211 billion in economic benefits and up to 180,000 jobs across the UK that could result.

Heathrow is the UK's hub airport and has operated at 98% capacity for more than a decade. A third runway will create space for an additional 260,000 flights essential to UK economic growth and boosting passenger numbers to 130 million annually. Post-Brexit Heathrow will need to compete more than ever with other mainland European hubs.

On 25 October 2016, the Government confirmed its acceptance of the Commission's recommendation and gave a clear direction that allows Heathrow to further develop its plans for a third runway . A National Policy Statement is now awaited in order to establish the necessary policy framework, in relation to which the third runway proposal will be considered and consented

There are issues to be resolved about investment cost, increased landing charges to airlines and passenger fares to service the funding. The current estimate for construction of a new runway and terminal is £17.5 billion. The airport management plan has been challenged by a local hotel tycoon, whose alternative proposals for changing the design of terminal buildings and taxiways and reducing the amount of land used are estimated to save £5.2 billion. It is claimed that a possible shift of the runway to avoid any impact on the M25 and M$ motorways could achieve additional savings of £1.2 billion.

Most recently, the chief executive of IAG, the parent company of British Airways, has pledged to knock 'several billion' pounds off the cost by abandoning facilities such as an additional terminal which would require a major underground baggage handling system and a subsurface passenger metro system, which alone are estimated to cost £1billion. The plan now is to expand Terminal Five and subsequently Terminal Two. These economies would help to limit increases in landing charges and, in turn, ticket prices which were originally calculated to add £21.75 to the price of each ticket.

Before proceeding further, the revised plan has to pass a parliamentary vote in 2018 and be approved by planners in the early 2020s. The original 2025 target date for an operational third runway may now be ambitious.

Gatwick

Gatwick's long fought battle to construct a second runway with a rail link to Heathrow, as an alternative to Heathrow expansion, appears to be over. Merits of the Gatwick expansion proposal include a lower investment cost, private funding and more balanced and widespread economic growth for London and the South East. The future expansion of Gatwick to increase the UK's passenger traffic capacity is still a possibility.

Birmingham airport

Currently handling 12 million passengers annually, Birmingham serves 120 direct global destinations and a further 340 one-stop long haul routes with 50 airlines. By the end of 2017, it will have completed a £450 million programme of infrastructure developments with completion of air traffic control upgrades, a new hold-baggage screening system, a doubling of self-service check-in and bag drop desks and additional car parking. High-speed rail is a core attraction of the airport's appeal to airlines, which will be greatly enhanced by HS2. With the start of Phase 1 and the prospect of being the UK's first and only high-speed connected airport in 2026, Birmingham now faces the challenge of scoping out how use of the current airport site can be maximised.

Manchester airport

The owners of Manchester Airport have embarked on a 10-year investment plan to more than double the size of its Terminal Two and link it to an improved Terminal Three. The original Terminal One, which was constructed in 1962, will be phased out by 2022. The overall airport Transformation Programme has been prompted by the approved second phase of HS2 and further outline government plans to improve east-west rail connections with HS3 as a part of the Northern Powerhouse strategy. Manchester Airport Group forecasts that by 2050 passenger traffic will increase from the present 23 million to 55 million annually.

Glasgow airport

Opened in 1966 with flights operating only within the UK and to Europe on a limited basis, Glasgow airport now classifies informally as an international airport. In 2016 the airport handled 9.4 million passengers, a 7% annual increase, with a total of 98,217movements. Today, Glasgow serves destinations throughout Europe, North America and the Middle East. The largest aircraft to operate regularly there are the Boeing 777-300ER and the Boeing 747-400. Airlines having bases at Glasgow range from Jet2, Ryanair and EasyJet to Thomas Cook Airlines, Thomson Airways and Loganair. Emirates flew an Airbus A380 to Glasgow to celebrate the 10th anniversary of its Glasgow-Dubai route.

Future growth is constrained by the airport's location, having the M8 motorway to the south, Renfrew town to the East and the Clyde to the north. The Scottish Parliament has no approved plans for expansion of Glasgow or Edinburgh airport, which has a wider range of European destinations but more limited transatlantic and long haul routes. At the end of 2014 Heathrow Airport Holdings sold Glasgow, together with Southampton and Aberdeen airport, to a consortium of Ferrovial and the Macquarie Group for £1 billion.

RAILWAYS – HS2

Having gained parliamentary approval, development of the UK's second high-speed railway is now underway with construction contracts for the first phase awarded on 17 July 2017. The long-awaited HS2 railway development programme dwarfs all other UK rail projects currently in various stages of planning, such as the Oxford to Cambridge direct link. It is the Government's keynote infrastructure project to expand economic activity in the Midlands and North of England by accelerating physical communications with London and the south. The first phase is construction of the railway between London and Birmingham with the second phase of HS2 extending the link from Birmingham to the north-west, East Midlands and Yorkshire. The new line is projected to carry 300,000 passengers a day, enabling extra space for more trains on the existing network.

The big construction contracts for stages one and two are valued at £6.6 billion and are expected to support 16,000 jobs. Although it will be 10 years before the railway even opens, it will act as a catalyst for investment and rebalancing of the economy. Construction of the full HS2 route to the north-west and Yorkshire will create 25,000 jobs and 2,000 apprenticeships with 3,000 people operating HS2. Growth around the new HS2 stations is expected to create another 100,000 jobs.

Having now identified the phase two route, the government intends the second stage to begin in 2019, bringing forward the opening of the complete line – subject to parliamentary approval – to 2027. The complete programme is expected to generate 7,000 contract opportunities in the supply chain, of which SMEs are expected to secure about 60%. The total investment cost is currently budgeted at £55 billion within the Infrastructure Pipeline but inflation alone is certain to increase the Government's expenditure commitment.

1.4 SCIENCE PARKS AND BUSINESS INCUBATORS

Nick Hood, Carter Jonas

THE INVESTMENT RATIONALE FOR SCIENCE PARKS

In our opinion Science Parks should be considered as a separate sector within the property investment market. Factors for investors to consider include:

- consistently high occupancy rates leading to reduced void costs for investors;
- new opportunities for investors to enter the market with the pressure on public sector investment into the sector;
- tenants often willing to take long leases leading to security of income;
- a key source of growth is derived from existing tenants who prefer to remain on the Science Park, moving to larger premises as they grow;
- technology companies which perform well at different times within the wider economic cycle, diversifying the risk;
- preliminary evidence that investment returns have been better than office parks over one, three and five years.

These issues and the importance of Incubators are discussed in greater detail in this chapter.

SCIENCE PARKS

The Science Park movement in the United Kingdom is now over 40 years old and many Parks are celebrating 25 years or more. The United Kingdom Science Park Association (UKSPA) itself is over 30 years old and now has over 120 members plus affiliates. The Parks vary in size and composition but all contribute to the promotion of the 'knowledge based economy' in the United Kingdom. UKSPA provides a useful definition of a Science Park:

> *"A Science Park is essentially a cluster of knowledge-based businesses, where support and advice are supplied to assist in the growth of the companies. In most instances, Science Parks are associated with a centre of technology such as a university or research institute."*

The UK Government recognises the importance of Science and Technology and while the Catapult Centres make a contribution to the commitment to transform the UK's capability for innovation, there is still a lack of support for the important contribution to be made by the UK's Science Park sector. The Catapult Centres have helped forge closer links between academia and industry and supported growth for innovation in SMEs and larger companies, a role Science Parks have been actively pursuing for years. Many Parks interact with the Catapult Centres in their region or within their technology sector.

Science Parks are all different and what will work in one region will not necessarily work in another, but what is common between them is the human activities in the promotion of business support and interaction, coupled with the proximity and links to a centre of technology, which is the principal differentiator between a Science Park and a more conventional business park. The cluster effect is important and extends beyond the boundaries of an individual park. It is not therefore surprising that the more successful and prosperous Science Parks are located in cities with strong universities and research organisations. Edinburgh, Birmingham, Cambridge, Manchester and Oxford all have strong Science Parks.

Some of the important characteristics of these clusters are:

- Strong academic base in science
- Skilled workforce
- Effective research and development networks in the region
- Entrepreneurial culture
- Attractive environment so people wish to live in the area
- Good local schools
- Good local support infrastructure; access to finance, legal teams, accountants etc.

BUSINESS INCUBATORS AND INNOVATION CENTRES

Most Science Parks, but not all, will have a Business Incubator or Innovation Centre as part of their model. A Business Incubator or Innovation Centre does not necessarily need to be on a Science Park but where it is, it will often be considered a generator of tenants for the wider Science Park. The terms Business Incubator, Innovation Centre or Enterprise Centre are widely used but they vary considerably in terms of what they seek to provide and some are actually no more than managed work space.

A Science Park, Business Incubator or Innovation Centre will provide small business suites with units of normally less than 100m2 (1,000 sq ft) on short term 'easy in easy out' agreements with common services and meeting rooms, as with most business centres. Space will normally be let at market rates but there will be additional business support services provided either directly or through third party partners at often minimal or low cost to the recipient. Indeed, a good Innovation Centre will be delivering these services to a wider area so that tenants do not need to be in the Centre or even on the Park and this will contribute to the marketing of the Park. The Centre will interact with the local business community and regional higher education institutes and research organisations to provide a catalyst for the growth of new and early stage business opportunities in their region. This activity will sometimes be supported by the local authority but some Parks will see this activity as the pipeline for future tenants not only for the Incubator/Innovation Centre but also for the Park. A good Innovation Centre or Incubator will act as a flagship in terms of generating activity and publicity for the benefit of the wider Science Park and will usually be focused on a particular sector or sectors of the technology market place, reflecting the region in which it is located.

While Incubators have differing models, they tend to take businesses at an earlier stage, often before a full business model has been developed, to establish viability. They will often invest time and expertise into the business, possibly in exchange for equity, and would expect to have established a viable route to market within three to six months, after which the business will be expected to move on. If within that period the business is deemed unviable, it will be closed down. This requires a different business model and can be more closely akin to investment into a business rather than a property investment.

The majority of Incubators and Innovation Centres will provide basic workshop or office specification space, with good high speed internet connectivity. A few will offer more specialised space for biotechnology or other laboratory users. Some have been established in response to the closure of a research organisation, such as Pfizer in Kent or Roche in Welwyn Garden City, but the Babraham Institute in Cambridge has been building small laboratories in response to demand. The availability of specialised laboratory space at low or reduced cost, coupled with a skilled workforce, can provide a unique opportunity to create a new broader business base at a time when potential job losses in the local market place are seen as a major problem.

In contrast, managed workspace will provide simple offices or workshops for small businesses without any additional management support or advice and while they may well serve a useful local need they are not Incubators or Innovation Centres. Business centres provide an additional level of service and provide active support to their tenants and seek to create a business community within the centre but will not be actively looking to promote economic activity. They are often supported by local authorities and well run centres can thrive in private ownership within a vibrant local economy but are unlikely to be actively supporting business incubation.

Innovation Centres are considered high risk investments given the short term nature of their agreements and the comparatively poor covenant strength of their tenants. However, they generally charge inclusive rental packages and in well managed centres can, once established, achieve consistently high occupancy rates with the opportunity to generate additional revenue from other activities such that the net rent to the investor can often match or better the income from conventionally let buildings over time. In over thirty years the occupancy of the St John's Innovation Centre in Cambridge has very rarely fallen below 90% and then usually only when unfortunate timing means more than one larger tenant matures and moves onto new premises. If this can generate leads to the wider Park, both from indirect marketing and tenants expanding, the centres can provide a positive contribution to a Park.

OWNERSHIP

The Science Park movement is now reaching maturity and should be considered an investment sector in its own right. The original Science Parks were often funded by academic institutions seeking to promote the growth of businesses utilising the technologies within academia and to foster links between academia and the wider business communities. In general, while they were not considered on strict investment criteria, they were expected to deliver a return to their promoters in the longer term. These parks are generally found close to the major universities; the Surrey Research Park or Heriot Watt would be typical examples.

The success of these first Parks encouraged others into the field and the public sector saw the potential benefits in the growth in knowledge based businesses. Local authorities started to encourage Incubators and Science Parks in association with their local higher education institutes and a number of publicly funded research organisations also saw the benefit of promoting businesses alongside their own research. A number of leading Science Parks are joint developments between various stakeholders, including local authorities and academic institutions such as Manchester Science Parks whereas Birmingham Science Park at Aston is a local authority initiative.

Over 50% of Science Parks have a direct investment from an academic institution and a further 20% from publically funded research organisations and over 50% also have some aspect of funding from local authorities and development agencies. It is difficult to see significant further public sector initiatives, other than through the Catapult Centres, though the Local Enterprise Partnerships (LEPs) are beginning to become engaged. It is a concern that there are relatively few investment and development companies who have taken an interest in the Science Park movement. At present only about 20% of Parks are controlled by the private sector and while some of these will also have public sector funding, they are expected to provide an economic return to their investors. These investment or development companies, such as Aviva, MEPC or Palmer Capital, have appreciated the potential of Science Parks and can see that proactive management of their Parks, coupled with knowledge of the sector(s) in which they are investing, can improve investment performance. Unfortunately there are too few private sector companies who understand the sector or are perhaps even aware of the opportunities it presents.

Innovate UK is the UK's national innovation agency and has established ten Catapult Centres in response to a report by Herman Hauser in 2010. The Centres themselves have a physical presence but are primarily a catalyst for innovation and development in their specific sector. Through them Innovate UK will deliver other services to support business using their Knowledge Transfer Network and other initiatives. Science Parks are working with the Centres operating in their region for the benefit of their tenants.

SECTORS

Science Parks encompass a wide variety of uses and the building specifications will reflect this. Many technology companies are engaged in computing and software for which a standard office specification is appropriate, though possibly with enhanced cooling systems for server rooms, and most investment companies or developers would be entirely comfortable with this specification. At the other extreme, a fully fitted biotechnology building will have an extensive fit out, probably costing rather more than the basic shell and core building. This requires a different approach by the developer/investor who may choose to simply provide a shell and core building, leaving the occupier to fund the fit out, usually on the basis of a 20 or 25 year lease with a rent geared to a proportion of an office rent. The basic shell and core will itself potentially be more expensive than a similar shell specification for a straightforward office use due to the requirement for the capacity for additional plant and equipment which might include an extra floor just for plant.

A more creative approach by a limited number of developers has been to split the package with a basic rent related to the shell and core building and a further 'rent' related to the fit out of the laboratory, where the deal will be more related to a financial package than a traditional property one. Again, the package may have different elements relating to the different elements of the fit out and the potential life expectancy of the components. This may give the occupier greater flexibility to modify the fit out as requirements change over time. Churchmanor Estates Company and Aviva Investors at Chesterford Research Park near Cambridge have successfully developed laboratory buildings and recently completed a 60,000 sq ft building pre-let to Biofocus, where they assisted with the fit out.

The strength of the tenant covenant will play an important part in the negotiations as a specialised fit out may have limited value should a tenant vacate, necessitating an expensive refit before the building is capable of occupation by another company.

Technology companies operate in growth markets often with higher margins than companies in more traditional markets. They are prepared to pay a premium for the right premises in the right location with the appropriate facilities to attract and retain their employees. Company failure rates on Science Parks are reputedly lower than average but this needs substantiation.

Science Park users are historically considered to come from the pharmaceutical sector but increasingly there is a confluence of life sciences and technology to the extent that physical and materials engineering are becoming inextricably linked to health care solutions. MEPC have acquired land adjacent to Silverstone race track and are developing buildings for technology rich enterprises whose work in motorsport leads to innovations that are applicable to med tech and all research and development activities.

FUNDING

The majority of existing Science Parks have been established through public sector funding in various forms, often working together and including universities, local authorities, the former regional development agencies and research organisations. While in some instances the initiative may have been in response to economic deprivation, in others it has been to exploit the economic potential of research within the local institutes. In the latter case the private sector can be involved in supporting the initiative as development can be economically viable.

Larger property investment funds will have an exposure to 'out of town business parks' and through these probably already have an exposure to science based tenants. These tenants will possibly have located to an area based on the potential 'cluster effect' and parts of the London market, the M4 corridor and Cambridge are typical.

The companies are looking for the right environment for their employees and their business and the criteria that make a good business park are equally valid for a science based company, including crèche facilities and good transport links. Larger companies will generate their own links with academia and research organisations and will therefore look for the best premises and terms to meet their requirements within a general geographical location. Science Parks should be seeking to provide a better environment to attract these businesses through the provision of services tailored to the specific needs of technology companies.

Technology companies will tend to be in growth sectors and, in our opinion, can often operate on slightly different economic cycles to the remainder of business in a region. If so, they should also be considered as a separate asset class offering an opportunity to spread risk within the property sector. However, data is required to support this contention and at present, partly due to the nature of the ownership of a significant number of the Parks, this is not available. With Parks which are in private ownership, or even where funds own an individual building on a Science Park, they will be assessing the performance of their assets by reference to the performance of other assets and, in particular, other property funds and as such are likely to provide information to the most widely used benchmark, the Investment Property Databank (IPD) Index. At present there is no IPD Index covering the Science Park sector.

CONCLUSION

As part of their 30th birthday celebrations in 2014 UKSPA carried out a study to support their assertion of their catalytic role in supporting growth in the UK economy. The study provided an overview on the impact of Science Parks on the commercialisation of research, start-ups and the growth of technology based firms, also their contribution to creating high quality employment in a local area, the growth of exports and the attraction of foreign investment. The need for that role remains with Science Parks well placed to participate in the integration of the whole innovation ecosystem to further investment in science and technology. Parks are not generally in competition with each other and can work together with Catapults, tech cities and smart cities to better enhance collaboration between government, large corporates, entrepreneurs and academics. To do so Science Parks must promote themselves as a complementary sector capable of offering competitive returns to investors and further spreading their risk from regional offices and business parks whilst offering job creation for local and national government.

Part Two

The Business Environment

2.1 MAKING THE MOST OF IP IN YOUR BUSINESS

Guy Robinson, UK Intellectual Property Office

All businesses have some intellectual property (IP), whether they realise it or not. For some, it is the very cornerstone of their business; for example, the hugely successful British company ARM which licensed the manufacture of its silicon chips. For others, it can be incidental to their core activities.

Since the early 2000s levels of investment in intangible assets, that is ideas and knowledge, have outstripped investment in tangible assets such as buildings and machinery. Our research shows that in 2014, UK firms invested £133 billion in intangible assets, 7 per cent higher than investment in tangible assets (£121 billion). Of this investment, more than £70 billion (53 per cent) was protected by IP rights. It is clear that the knowledge-based economy is of increasing importance to the UK, but business knowledge of IP does not meet these growing demands.

Our business surveys tell us that knowledge of IP, throughout UK businesses, is generally very low. For example, nearly 80 per cent of companies surveyed did not know that telling people about your invention could lead to an unsuccessful patent application. Fewer than one in ten firms has any formal IP training for staff and, unsurprisingly, 96 per cent of them had not valued their IP. However, of real interest to us was that 94 per cent of businesses we spoke to thought protecting IP was important and one in five firms license its IP for others to use for a fee.

At the Intellectual Property Office (IPO) we want to help businesses, of all shapes and sizes, to understand their IP better so they can make informed and strategic decisions to support the running and development of their business.

IP is an investment and, like any investment, a business needs to weigh up the pro and cons of spending money on one thing and not another. The resource required to apply for an IP right needs to be considered in the context of all of the other decisions that need to be made to keep a business running. We routinely direct firms to seek expert advice when applying for IP rights, especially patents, to help to navigate the technical and legal processes. We know that of the unrepresented individuals that apply for patents only around 5 per cent of their applications are granted. And, despite the great advances improving access to low cost and effective justice, a business should still consider the impact of having to defend its rights. On the other hand a lack of understanding about the value of your IP assets and how to exploit them, may mean many a firm might be missing a trick.

So, how do we go about changing this situation? Over the last decade the IPO has developed an increasingly sophisticated business outreach programme. We have chosen to focus our efforts on face to face engagement, mainly because engaging firms on IP is not simple and straightforward. We attend around 300 events a year, from conferences to seminars, working in partnership with other government organisations such as Companies House, where we meet and speak to around 60,000 people annually. In addition to that we have built a business advisers network, providing them with information and training including our successful IP Masterclass. We know that increasing the understanding of IP among the professional community that directly supports businesses will always reach more people than we can.

But, we are always alive to new ideas and the latest developments in the way we communicate. As our face to face work has matured, so we have developed our digital content and social media activities in parallel. We have built a suite of online tools that aim to build more detailed knowledge and its application, IP Equip, (available on the GOV.UK website as well as downloadable as an app) takes you through basic learning modules to help understand the different IP rights, whether they are relevant to your business and how best to access them. Our IP Healthcheck is a more thorough questionnaire-based tool that produces a tailored, confidential report for your business. It makes specific recommendations, provides guidance on how to implement them and points you to useful sources of further information.

We support this offering through a range of other rich content to get a complex message across. We have a series of video case studies of companies that have had a positive business experience by making informed decisions about their IP. We have also produced a series of animated films called IP Basics which areaccessible on YouTube and we provide a series of podcast discussions, a highly regarded blog through GOV.UK and LinkedIn and Facebook Live events to cater for the widest audience possible on as many aspects of IP practice as we can manage. We are taking on the challenge of trying to bring IP to life, making it relevant to everyday business practice. We want to get creators, companies and investors to think about IP as part of their whole approach to business, as an integrated business process just like planning an investment strategy.

Year on year we know we are reaching more businesses; in 2016-17 we estimated that we directly and indirectly reached more than 200,000 business across the country.

In the coming years we will build our understanding about what decisions businesses take after we engage with them so we can improve our offering further.

Engaging with firms, assisting them to identify, understand and better manage their IP, does not sit in isolation. By drawing insight from our existing customers and our well established stakeholder community we have a well-developed and strategic approach to business support. This support is also integrated into the Government's wider approach to making the UK the best place to start and grow a business by focusing on driving growth across the whole country, encouraging investment in research and innovation and supporting trade and inward investment.

At the heart of this is helping firms understand the value of their IP and then providing hands-on tools to help them commercialise it. Your IP could be as valuable as your plant, premises or stock. It could even be your single most valuable asset which you could use to secure finance for company growth. You may also need to know the value of your IP assets when looking for more funding, thinking of joint ventures, mergers and acquisitions and, in the worst case, during bankruptcy. But not all IP is valuable. Unless your IP assets help to create, maintain or increase cash flow they may have no financial value.

But valuing IP is not an easy task. How much is your brand name worth after years of marketing? Does your patent protect your product or is it redundant?

IP rights might change in value for a variety of reasons. A patent may begin its life as a unique solution to a problem, but in time other solutions to the problem may be found which reduce its worth. Alternatively, successfully marketing your product can ensure your patent is very valuable. Trade marks generally gain value as they become better known.

There are a number of ways to value IP rights. They all have their limitations and no method is appropriate in every case. The stage of development of the IPR, the availability of information and the aim of the valuation all have a bearing on the method used. We provide some detailed information on methods that can be used, such as the cost, market value and income or economic benefit methods, and support this with a useful checklist and skeleton licence to guide you through the process of exploiting your IP.

Being able to easily value IP may well lead to better commercialisation and trade. Unfortunately there is no universally agreed methodology for the valuation of IP. We know that IP rich businesses struggle to secure lending against their IP due to the opaque nature of the asset and this can be one of the things preventing them from scaling up. Over the past few years we have been working closely with the investment community to help them understand better the nature of IP as an asset and facilitate the development of the market in IP. For a number of years we have worked with partners across government to identify high growth potential businesses and offer them IPO part-funded IP audits. This has helped them get a better grip on the value of their IP assets and supported the development of a proper business strategy to develop and exploit their value to the business.

This work has a knock-on beneficial effect in supporting better collaboration between research institutes and businesses and, in turn, driving innovation. In 2016 we reviewed and refreshed a set of tools, known as the Lambert toolkit, designed to help facilitate negotiations between potential partners, reduce the time, money and effort required to secure agreement and provide examples of best practice. The toolkit consists of a decision guide, model agreements and guidance notes to walk you through the process and address a wide range of situations.

Closely tied to better valuation and commercialisation of your IP is better protection. Setting up and running a business can be a risky business. In the same way you can protect your physical assets from a variety of risks you can also insure your intangible assets. Much of this insurance (but not all) is aimed at businesses who have already secured IP rights. However, you can also protect yourself against inadvertently infringing the rights of others. We provide a range of information on types of insurance that are available and how they can be used to protect your investment. As with all other aspects of business decision-making, expert advice should be used to help make the best choices for your circumstances.

In the same way, we work with business advisors to help spread our message through our outreach activities, so we work with other business representative and support organisations to extend and improve our reach. We are putting increasing emphasis on driving growth across the whole of the country by putting IP representatives in key regional areas to enhance existing regional networks. By the end of 2017 we will be running pilot approaches in the North West and West Midlands.

As the trend for greater investment in knowledge and ideas continues to grow it is apparent that the ability to use your IP more effectively is a key business advantage. By bringing together our efforts to help businesses, through targeted information and support and a creative approach to outreach and engagement, we are building a better informed business community ready to face the challenges of a more complex and challenging global marketplace.

The Intellectual Property Office
The Intellectual Property Office (IPO) is the official UK government body responsible for intellectual property (IP) rights including patents, designs, trademarks and copyright. The IPO is an executive agency of the Department for Business, Energy & Industrial Strategy.

2.2 COMPANY FORMATION – METHODS AND LEGAL IMPLICATIONS

Helen Harvey, Mazars LLP

INTRODUCTION

The UK has an open and transparent system for setting up companies. No permission is required to set up a business, although some industries, such as financial services, may require specific authorisation before they can commence trading. This chapter looks at the options available to investors wishing to set up a new enterprise in the UK or expand an existing one.

COMPANY TYPES

In the UK, there are four main types of company that can be separated into two categories:

Unlimited Liability
The owners of organisations having unlimited liability are personally liable for all the debts that the business may incur. Should the enterprise fail, the owners may have to liquidate some (or all) of their personal assets in order to pay the enterprise's outstanding debts. Examples of such businesses are sole traders, unlimited companies and partnerships.

Limited Liability
The owners of these types of business are only liable for the amount that they originally invested in the company. Should the business fail, investors in the failed company will only lose the original value of their investment or the amount they agreed to contribute, as set out below.

In the UK, there are three main types of Limited Liability Company:

1. A private company limited by shares – the liability of members is limited to the amount unpaid on shares they hold.
2. A private company limited by guarantee – members are only liable for the amount they agreed to contribute to the company's assets should the company be wound up.
3. A public limited company – these companies are permitted to sell shares to the general public, and their liability is limited to the amount unpaid on shares they hold.

FORMING A COMPANY

The majority of businesses setting up in the UK register as limited companies and are therefore subject to the Companies Act 2006. This Act sets out the rules governing the setting up and day-to-day running of companies.

To set up a company in the UK, you can use a company formation agent, arrange for your professional adviser (solicitor or accountant) to form the company, or you can incorporate a company yourself by using the web incorporation services operated by Companies House.

Companies House is the government agency responsible for incorporating, dissolving and registering companies, and making company information available to the public.

Eligibility for Company Directorship
Any company setting up in the UK must have formally appointed officers. The number of officers depends on the type of company that is being set up:

*   A private company must have at least one director and may have a company secretary. The company's sole director can also be the company secretary.
*   A public company must have at least two directors and the company secretary must hold a formal professional qualification.

Procedure to Incorporate a Company
To register a private or public limited company, the following documents must be sent to Companies House:

*   A Memorandum of Association
*   Articles of Association
*   Form INO1

The Memorandum of Association is a document that sets out the company's name and the names of the subscribers (first shareholders) who agree to become members of the company.

The Articles of Association set out the standard rules and procedures that state how the company runs its internal affairs. A company can either adopt the model articles in their entirety as prescribed by the Companies Act 2006, the model articles with amendments or an entirely bespoke set of articles.

Form IN01 provides details of the first director(s) and company secretary (if appointed), the address of the company's registered office, a statement of the issued share capital on incorporation, the names and addresses of the subscribers and similar details of the those persons deemed to be able to exercise significant influence or control over the company. The directors must also include personal details such as their address, date of birth, occupation, nationality and country of residence.

PERSONS OF SIGNIFICANT CONTROL

From 6 April 2016 Companies and LLPs are required to keep a register of People with Significant Control ('PSC') as part of the government's pledge to improve transparency over who owns and controls UK companies and will help inform investors when they are considering investing in a company. It will also support law enforcement agencies in money laundering investigations.

The PSC requirements mean that the company must keep information of any individual or legal entity who could directly or indirectly have significant influence or control in the business. Initially, this information is required upon incorporation and lodged with Companies House and then any changes to the details of a PSC must be updated on the register and at Companies House as and when they occur.

The legislation regarding the notification of PSC changes to Companies House came into force on 26 June 2017. It states that the company has 14 days to update its own PSC register from the date of the receipt of information regarding a change and a further 14 days to notify Companies House.

CAPITAL FOR PRIVATE AND PUBLIC LIMITED COMPANIES

When first registering, the first members of the company must each agree to take at least one share and their names must also be included on the memorandum. Shares have a par value, which can be of any amount. The value of the shares held by the shareholders (number of shares multiplied by their par value) is the company's 'Issued Share Capital'.

The amount of share capital required differs depending on the type of company you are setting up and the requirements of the business. A private limited company has no maximum or minimum issued share capital required in order to commence trading, save that it must have at least one share in issue unless the regulatory requirements of its particular industry require a specific minimum. The rules for public limited companies are more complex.

Capital for Public Limited Companies

For a public limited company to trade, the requirement is that it must have at least £50,000 or Euro equivalent of issued share capital, of which 25% must have been paid up and the whole of any premiums (that is the amount investors are asked to pay for the shares less the par value) on these shares. As with private companies a company operating in a particular industry may be required to have a significantly higher issued share capital.

Once the share capital has been paid the company will need to send the relevant information to the Registrar of Companies, who will then issue a 'Certificate to commence business and borrow'. Without this certificate the company cannot trade or carry on business.

MANAGEMENT OF COMPANY

A private limited company must have at least one director, and a public limited company must have at least two directors. In both types of company, the directors are responsible for the day-to-day running of the business, and are personally responsible for any decisions made. The main responsibilities include:

* Producing the annual accounts and making sure that a copy of these are sent to Companies House (a legal requirement for both public and private limited companies);
* Making sure any other information required by Companies House is sent there (for instance, notification of a change in address of the company's registered office or a change in the directors of the company).
* Ensuring that all tax returns and tax payments are made and that other legal and regulatory matters are complied with.

Some of these responsibilities are required by law and, as such, any breach by the directors is a criminal offence for which the penalties can be severe (prosecution, fines, and/or imprisonment).

OTHER FORMS OF COMPANY

Sole Traders

Sole traders are businesses set up by individuals. They are typically small and usually financed by the individual. They are unlimited liability businesses, so the owner is responsible for meeting all the debts of the business. Sole traders are not required to publish annual accounts, although they must keep financial records for tax purposes.

Partnership

Regarded as a step up from a sole trader, this is where a group of two or more individuals set up a business together. Partnerships are regulated by the Partnership Act 1890 (as amended). Normally, a partnership agreement is drawn up before trading commences and this agreement usually contains information on the names of the partners of the business, how profits and/or liabilities will be shared, how the partnership will be run, and the procedures for dissolving the partnership.

As with a sole trader, partnerships have unlimited liability, with the partners jointly and severally liable for all debts, that is, if one or more of the partners is unable to meet these debts, then the remaining partners will become liable for them. A partnership in England and Wales does not have a separate identity from its partners, as a company has from its members. Partnerships are not required to publish their annual accounts, although they must keep financial records for tax purposes.

Limited Partnership

It is still possible to register a limited partnership under the Limited Partnership Act 1907, although they have been superseded in the main by the Limited Liability Partnership (see below). Limited partnerships are very similar to partnerships with these exceptions:

- There are two types of partner: general partners, who are liable for all the businesses debts, and limited partners, who have limited liability up to the amount of money they have invested as capital in the business. Limited partners cannot take back any money invested in the business during the partnership's lifetime, nor can they have a management role in the business.
- By law, limited partnerships must be registered at Companies House by sending a form signed by all partners giving the name of the business, what the business does, and details of all the money invested by the limited partners.

Limited Liability Partnership (LLP)

The Limited Liability Partnerships Act 2000 created a new business vehicle, the Limited Liability Partnership (LLP) which combines the organisational flexibility and tax status of a partnership with limited liability for its members.

Members of limited liability partnerships benefit from limited liability because the partnership, rather than its members, is liable to third parties. However, where the members of an LLP are professional people, a negligent member's own personal assets may still be at risk because under general law, a professional person owes a duty of care to his or her client. While the Government originally intended to restrict the use of LLPs to members of regulated professions, the LLP Act makes LLPs available to two or more persons carrying on any trade or profession. In view of this, as the LLP combines the tax/NIC (National Insurance Contributions) advantages of partnerships with incorporation and limited liability, it may well become a popular vehicle for small businesses.

LLP profits are taxed as if the business were carried on by partners in partnership, rather than by a body corporate. There are no special tax treatments, or reliefs, available to LLPs or members of LLPs beyond the treatments or reliefs available to partners and partnerships.

The European Public Limited Liability Company

The European Public Limited Liability Company or 'Societas Europaea' (SE) is available to businesses operating in more than one member state. It has been possible to set up this type of legal entity in the UK since October 2004.

The purpose of the SE is to make it easier for businesses to structure and carry out cross-border activities within the EU. In practice, however, they are probably of more value for presentational purposes, although the ability to change the domicile of an SE by an administrative procedure can prove to be useful in certain circumstances.

The SE European Public Limited Liability Company

An SE may be created on registration in any one of the Member States of the European Economic Area (EEA). Member States are required to treat an SE as if it is a public limited company formed in accordance with the law of the Member State in which it has its registered office. UK national laws that apply to public limited companies also apply, in many respects, to SEs registered in the UK.

Overseas Companies Carrying on Business in the UK

Some companies might still want to do business in the UK without registering a company in the United Kingdom. This can be done by setting up a branch.

A branch is part of an overseas limited company that employs local representatives in the UK to carry out its trading activities. To register a branch with Companies House, the company must complete a OSINO1 Form (this lists details such as the company's name and directors, and details of the branch being set up), the most recent set of audited company accounts, and a certified copy of their constitutional documents (both these must be in the home language of the company). If these are not in English, then a certified translation made in the country where the company was incorporated must also be submitted. A non-UK company can establish one or more branches and must register each one separately, but it is only necessary to file the constitutional documents once.

Overseas companies may also wish to set up a joint venture with a UK firm, usually through a partnership or a limited company.

2.3 THE UK IMMIGRATION REGIME FOR STARTING UP IN THE UK

Alison Hutton, Mazars LLP

The UK Government are keen to attract the 'brightest and best' talent to the UK and to encourage overseas businesses and entrepreneurs to invest here. Companies choose to expand or move their businesses to the UK because it's an ideal location. Aside from the attraction of it being a multi-cultural environment and the benefits of English being the main language, the UK can offer a skilled talent pool, a competitive tax rate system, first class educational institutions, and a transparent regulatory system making it easier to do business. The current immigration regime offers a number of visa options to foreign nationals wishing to do business in the UK which cater for short term business visitors, startups and entrepreneurs looking to set up in business, as well as routes for larger businesses who already have an established entity in the UK.

The following two chapters provide a high level overview of the key immigration options and how they operate in practice.

BUSINESS VISITORS

The Standard Visitor visa category is the immigration category now used for people who are based abroad but who intend to visit the UK for a short time to do business on their own or on their employer's behalf. It encompasses various business related visitor activities that were previously treated as separate types of visitor application including the Business Visitor visa (including visas for academics, doctors and dentists), Sports Visitor visa, Entertainer Visitor visa and the Prospective Entrepreneur visa.

A business visitor must be genuinely seeking entry to the UK for a period not exceeding six months and must:

- Leave the UK at the end of the visit;
- Maintain and accommodate themselves without using public funds;
- Not be paid or employed in the UK (subject to the exception below);
- Meet the cost of the return or onward journey; and
- Be at least 18 years old.

PERMITTED ACTIVITIES

The activities that business visitors are permitted to undertake in the UK are very restricted and ultimately must not result in them undertaking 'productive' work.

PERMITTED ACTIVITIES	ACTIVITIES WHICH ARE NOT PERMITTED
Attend meetings, conferences and interviews, providing such arrangements are made prior to arrival in the UK. If the visitor is a board-level director who wishes to attend board meetings in the UK they can do so, providing they are not employed by a UK company (although they can be paid a fee for attending the meeting).	Take employment. Produce goods or provide services within the UK. Undertake hands-on/on-the-job training. Undertake a course of study except in limited circumstances.
Attend trade fairs for promotional work only, provided the visitor is not directly selling.	Project management.
Arrange deals, or negotiate or sign trade agreements or contracts.	
Carry out fact-finding missions or conduct site visits.	
Attend classroom based training and/or undertake observation and familiarisation.	

Speak at a one-off conference which is not organised as a commercial concern, and is not making a profit for the organiser. Service or repair the company's products for a UK based customer within the initial guarantee period. Be briefed on the requirements of a UK customer, provided this is limited to briefing and does not include work involving use of the applicant's expertise to make a detailed assessment of a potential customer's requirements. Act as an adviser, consultant, internal auditor, trainer or trouble shooter to the UK branch of the same group of companies as the applicant's overseas company.	

RECEIVING PAYMENT IN THE UK

As a general rule a business visitor to the UK must not receive payment from a UK source. However, there are several exceptions to this:

1. Where the individual is the employee of a multi-national company who, for administrative reasons, handle payment of all their employees' salaries from the UK; or
2. Where the applicant is engaged in a Permitted Paid Engagement (PPE), provided the applicant holds a visa or leave to enter as a PPE visitor; or
3. Where the individual is a board member attending a board meeting and receives a fee in this respect.

Often there is a fine line between what a 'business visitor' activity is and what 'work' is. Ultimately, there will be an element of judgement exercised by the visa issuing officer or Immigration Officer at the port of entry as to whether they feel the activities fall within the permitted activities or not. Other aspects that will be taken into consideration are where lengthy or frequent visits are undertaken which may lead the officer to have concerns as to whether the individual is a genuine business visitor.

The Standard Visitor visa is usually valid for six months, and if you can satisfy the decision maker that you have the genuine need to visit the UK regularly over a longer period of time, you can also apply for longer-term multiple entry visit visas which last two, five or even ten years. However, the maximum duration you can stay in the UK on each visit is still six months.

DO I NEED A VISA?

Certain nationals travelling to the UK will require a visa in all instances, regardless of the reason for their travel. This includes travelling to the UK temporarily as a visitor. They are known as visa nationals. Non-visa nationals (which includes European nationals and 56 other nationals who are visa exempt) do not require a visa to enter the UK as a visitor in most instances. The UK government reviews the visa national list periodically and so it is wise to check whether you require a visa or not before travelling.

If a visa is required, this will necessitate an application being made to the British diplomatic post in the individual's home country or country of main residence to obtain the visa (known as entry clearance) prior to travel. For non-visa nationals no application is required to travel to the UK as a visitor, but the Immigration Officer at the port of entry will assess the individual against the visitor criteria prior to granting entry.

It is important to note that the UK is not a party to the Schengen agreement and so it is not possible to travel to the UK using a Schengen visa (a Schengen visa allows an individual to travel freely across certain other EU countries who are party to the Schengen agreement for up to 90 days in a 180 day period). Nor is it possible to travel into other EU countries on a UK visitor visa.

EUROPEAN NATIONALS & BREXIT

In June 2016, the UK voted to leave the EU and on 29th March 2017 the Prime Minister triggered Article 50, which means that during the intervening two years up to March 2019, negotiations will take place regarding Britain's departure from the EU. It is difficult at the current time to comment on how the UK immigration landscape will look after that date. It is clear that the UK Government, in addition to looking at how European Economic Area (EEA) nationals will be treated for immigration purposes post Brexit, will also take the opportunity to review UK immigration policy as a whole.

In the meantime, nothing has changed in respect of the rights of EEA nationals travelling into or living and working here in the UK. EEA nationals still have full and free movement rights into the UK and are entitled to exercise Treaty rights here, which means that they can study, work, look for work, set up in business or be self-employed or indeed reside here as a self-sufficient individual. They do not require a visa to enter the UK and although it is possible to obtain an EEA Registration certificate or Permanent Residence Card to evidence status, these documents are not mandatory (note that for Croatian nationals, as new members of the EU, the immigration position is currently different and work permission may be required).

START-UPS AND ENTREPRENEURS

If you are looking to do more than just visit the UK, then there are a number of visa options, depending on what you plan to do in the UK and your future intentions. This next section sets out the main options that work best for start-ups and individuals.

TIER 1 INVESTOR VISA

This visa route is for high net worth individuals who wish to obtain long-term residence in the UK for themselves and their family members by making a substantial financial investment to the UK. This can be achieved by investing £2 million into UK government bonds, share capital or loan capital in active and trading companies registered in the UK. The one exception to this is that is it not acceptable to invest in companies mainly engaged in property investment, property management or property development.

The applicant must have money of their own, under their control, held in a regulated financial institution, and which is already in the UK or transferrable and disposable in the UK, amounting to not less than £2 million. They must also be able to show that they have opened an account with a UK regulated bank for the purposes of investing not less than £2 million in the UK. There is now also a new requirement that overseas applicants and adult dependants obtain a criminal record certificate from any country they have lived in for 12 months or more in the last 10 years to submit with their application.

Following a change in the rules from 6 November 2014, it is no longer possible to apply with funds acquired via a loan from a financial institution. However, it is possible to apply with funds held jointly with, or solely by, a spouse, civil partner, unmarried partner or same sex partner. Gifts, wills, deeds of sale, divorce settlement, evidence from a business and financial awards and prize winnings may all be considered as acceptable sources of funds, providing certain criteria are met.

Maintaining the £2 million investment is vital for applicants to secure an extension of leave to remain after three years and to also apply for indefinite leave to remain (settlement) in the UK after five years.

Tier 1 Investors can also take advantage of the accelerated route to settlement if they can make a greater investment:

- £5 million investment – settlement after three years,
- £10 million investment – settlement after two years.

The Tier 1 Investor visa allows a person to take up self-employment and employment in the UK (certain exceptions apply) as well as to study if they wish. It is not necessary to meet the English language requirements (as it is for many other visa categories).

English language	No
Initial visa grant	3 years 4 months
Extension	2 years
Indefinite leave to remain	After 5 years (or after 3 years/2 years via accelerated route)
Dependants	Spouse and children under 18
Dependant activities	Spouses and partners can work or study if they wish and children of school age can attend school.

TIER 1 ENTREPRENEURS

For those with the intention of setting up their own business or investing in an existing UK business, the Tier 1 Entrepreneur category might be an option worth considering. Unlike the Tier 1 Investor category discussed above, a Tier 1 Entrepreneur must have the intention of being a registered Director and actively involved in the running of the business.

Individuals wishing to apply under this category will qualify if they can provide evidence to show that:

- They have access to at least £200,000; or
- They have access to £50,000 through a venture capital firm registered with the Financial Conduct Authority (FCA), a UK entrepreneurial seed funding competition endorsed by UK Department for International Trade (DIT) or a UK Government department making funds available for the purpose of setting up or expanding a UK business.

The funding rules are different if the applicant is changing ('switching') from certain UK visa categories, such as a Tier 1 Graduate Entrepreneur visa, Tier 1 Post-study work visa (closed now to initial applications), Tier 1 General visa (also closed now to initial applications) or a Tier 4 Student visa and additional criteria apply in these circumstances.

The applicant can also qualify if they have already made the investment into the UK business. In these circumstances, the investment must have been made in the 12 months leading up to the application.

Two business partners can qualify for Tier 1 Entrepreneur status together relying on the same investment funds, known as an 'Entrepreneurial Team', provided that they have equal access and control over the funds and will both be actively involved in the running of the business.

Similar to the Tier 1 Investor visa, applicants (and adult dependants) who apply from overseas will need to obtain the suitable criminal record certificate(s).

It is necessary to meet the English language requirements for this visa category. This can be done by the applicant in one of 3 ways:

- Showing that they are a national of a majority English speaking country;
- Demonstrating that they have passed an approved English language test to the prescribed level in reading, writing, speaking and listening; or
- By having an academic qualification that was taught in English and is recognised by UK NARIC as being equivalent to a UK Bachelors degree, Masters degree or PhD.

It is also necessary for the applicant to meet the maintenance requirements to show that they have sufficient personal funds to support themselves and any accompanying family members. This means having a certain level of funding held in personal bank accounts for at least 90 days leading up to the submission of the application.

Key criteria must be met regarding the investment of the funds and the creation of two full-time jobs in the UK in order to meet the requirements for an extension of leave to remain in the UK.

It is important to note that applications are subject to a 'Genuineness Test', meaning that the UK Visas & Immigration will take into account all evidence submitted, with a particular focus on assessing the viability and credibility of the source of the funds, and the business plan, as well as the applicant's previous educational and business experience and immigration history before making the decision.

Tier 1 Entrepreneurs will also be able to settle in the UK after three years via an accelerated process if they create ten jobs or turn over £5m in the initial three year period.

English language	Yes
Initial visa grant	3 years 4 months
Extension	2 years
Indefinite leave to remain	After 5 years (or 3 years under accelerated route)
Dependants	Spouse and children under 18
Dependant activities	Spouses and partners can work or study if they wish and children of school age can attend school.

Tier 1 Graduate Entrepreneur

This route is designed for graduates who have been endorsed as having a genuine and credible business idea which has been endorsed by either:

- UK DIT as part of the elite global graduate entrepreneur scheme (Sirius); or
- A UK higher education institution (HEI) providing it is an authorised endorsing body.

Every year the Tier 1 (Graduate Entrepreneur) route has a limit of 2000 places (beginning on 6 April and ending on 5 April the following year). 1900 places are allocated to the HEIs with the remaining 100 allocated to the UK DIT. Applicants can apply for leave (permission to stay in the UK) under the Tier 1 (Graduate Entrepreneur) route for an initial period of one year. If their endorsing body agrees to sponsor them after this, they can apply again and they may be granted further leave for another year. Applicants are only allowed a maximum of two years under this route and it does not lead to settlement, but of course they can switch from this route to the Tier 1 Entrepreneur route in certain circumstances.

It is necessary to meet the English language requirements for this visa category as detailed above. It is also necessary to meet the maintenance requirements to show that the applicant has sufficient personal funds to support themselves and any accompanying family members.

English language	Yes
Initial visa grant	1 year
Extension	1 year
Indefinite leave to remain	No
Dependants	Spouse and children under 18
Dependant activities	Spouses and partners can work or study if they wish and children of school age can attend school.

REPRESENTATIVE OF AN OVERSEAS BUSINESS (ALSO KNOWN AS SOLE REPRESENTATIVE)

A remnant of the immigration system prior to the Points Based System being introduced, this visa category is designed to allow businesses based outside of the UK to send a senior employee into the UK to set up its very first commercial presence (a wholly owned branch or subsidiary of the parent company overseas) in the UK.

The application is a personal one, made by the individual who intends to be the sole representative, but is supported by the company. The company's track record and business plans for the UK entity will be assessed as part of the application process, as well as the skills and experience of the applicant themselves.

Unlike the Tier 1 Investor and Tier 1 Entrepreneur options, it does not require any level of financial investment in the UK and so is a popular choice for businesses. However, there are certain other specific criteria to be met which include that the applicant:

- Has been recruited and employed outside the UK by a company whose headquarters and principal place of business are outside the UK;
- Has extensive related industry experience and knowledge;
- Holds a senior position within the company (but is not a majority shareholder) and has full authority to make decisions on its behalf;
- Intends to establish the company's first commercial presence in the UK, e.g. a registered branch or a wholly owned subsidiary.

It is very important that the company does not yet have a legal entity in the UK that employs staff or transacts business. If it does, then unfortunately this route cannot be used . In addition, only one sole representative is allowed, so if the parent company overseas wishes to send other employees to the UK to staff up the UK business they must come in under the Tier 2 Skilled Worker route (see below).

Unlike the Entrepreneur route there are no set deadlines as to when the set-up of the business must be achieved, providing that this has been done in advance of any extension application. Indeed, initial time spent on this visa can be used to undertake market research and market testing before any firm corporate roots are established.

The sole representative must be able to meet the basic standard in English language for this type of visa and although there is no minimum salary criteria, the applicant must be able to show that he/she can maintain themselves and any accompanying dependants without recourse to public funds. They cannot take employment with another company whilst in the UK and must work full time.

English language	Yes
Initial visa grant	3 years
Extension	2 years
Indefinite leave to remain	After 5 years
Dependants	Spouse and children under 18
Dependant activities	Spouses and partners can work or study if they wish and children of school age can attend school.

TURKISH NATIONALS

Specific options are available to Turkish nationals by virtue of the Ankara Agreement which facilitates Turkish entrepreneurs and business people, as well as Turkish workers in certain circumstances.

The Turkish Businessperson visa allows Turkish nationals to come to the UK to start a new business or to join and help in the running of an existing business. An initial one year visa will be granted, which can be extended for a further three years. It is also possible to apply for settlement after four years in the UK.

Initial visa grant	1 year
Extension	3 years
Indefinite leave to remain	After 4 years
Dependants	Spouse and children under 18
Dependant activities	Spouses and partners can work or study if they wish and children of school age can attend school.

The Turkish Worker visa is an option open to Turkish nationals who have legally worked in the UK for at least one year as the spouse of a British or settled person, the holder of a work visa (such as a Tier 2 visa) or as a student who has been allowed to work 20 hours a week during term time and full time during vacation periods. How long the individual can stay in the UK and what work they can do will depend on how long they have already been legally working in the UK.

Initial visa grant	1 year
Extension	Up to 3 years
Indefinite leave to remain	No
Dependants	Spouse and children under 18 if already in the UK
Dependant activities	Spouses and partners can work or study if they wish and children of school age can attend school.

2.4 THE UK IMMIGRATION REGIME FOR ESTABLISHED BUSINESSES

Alison Hutton, Mazars LLP

For established businesses and where the Tier 1 or Sole Representative options aren't suitable, then the Tier 2 Sponsor Licence/Skilled Worker routes ought to be considered. In some instances, even where the Sole Representative option may be viable, a business may decide that since its long term plan is to bring more than just one migrant into the UK, that the sponsor licence route makes more sense both administratively and financially. A popular route that has been adopted by many overseas established businesses is to send one senior employee to the UK first with the Sole Representative visa to set up the UK entity and then apply for the Tier 2 Sponsor Licence for this entity in order to bring more skilled workers to the UK to further develop the operation here.

TIER 2 SPONSOR LICENCE

As an established business in the UK, before it is possible to hire a migrant worker from outside the European Economic Area (EEA), the company must apply for a sponsor licence. Once approved, the licence will enable the employer to issue a Certificate of Sponsorship (known as a CoS, but essentially a work permit) to the migrant in question to allow them to apply for their work visa to the UK. In order to be granted the licence the business needs to satisfy the Home Office that it is a genuine trading entity in the UK and that it will be able to meet the duties and responsibilities of being a licence holder. This means that the business has to put in place robust HR systems and processes to ensure that they can track and monitor the migrants that they sponsor and report in to the Home Office any changes to the migrant's work as required.

There are broadly two main visa categories under Tier 2:

- Tier 2 Intra-Company Transfer (ICT) – for multi-national companies who wish to transfer employees to the UK from part of the group overseas for any period up to five years (with the exception of high earners earning at least £120,000 gross per annum who can remain in the UK for up to nine years).
- Tier 2 General – usually for permanent hires and high earners (those earning over £159,600 per annum). With the exception of high earners it is usually necessary for the sponsor to show that they have tested the Resident Labour Market and that they have not been able to find a suitably qualified resident worker for the role. The maximum period of stay in this category is six years and it is possible to apply for settlement after five years.

In both categories, dependant family members (spouse/partner/children under 18) can accompany the main applicant. Spouses and partners can work or study if they wish and children of school age can attend school.

TIER 2 INTRA-COMPANY

Changes introduced in November 2016 and April 2017 mean that short term options under the ICT route are now limited, with the Short-term staff route (for assignments up to 12 months) and the Skills Transfer route no longer open to new applicants. The remaining ICT routes include:

Tier 2 Graduate Trainee: This category caters for graduate transfers into a structured graduate training programme with defined progression towards a managerial or specialist role within the organisation. The applicant will need to be a recent graduate with at least three months' employment with the company overseas. The maximum period of stay in the UK is 12 months and there is a limit of 20 migrants that can use this route per company per year. The graduate trainee will also need to be paid at least £23,000 gross per annum or the appropriate rate for the role on offer as dictated by the Standard Occupational Codes published by the Home Office, whichever is higher.

Tier 2 ICT – Long Term staff: This category allows for an assignment period of up to five years in total (or nine years in circumstances where the individual earns more than £120,000 per annum, as mentioned above). A minimum of 12 months pre-transfer employment with the company is required unless the assignee is going to earn at least £73,900 gross per annum. Otherwise, the assignee will need to be paid at least £41,500 gross per annum or the appropriate rate for the role on offer as dictated by the Standard Occupational Codes published by the Home Office.

English language	No
Initial visa grant	Graduate Trainee 1 year, Long-term ICT up to 3 years or 5 years
Extension	Long-term ICT up to 2 years (High-earners also a further 2 years), subject to the maximum duration allowed under this visa category as aforementioned.
Indefinite leave to remain	No
Dependants	Spouse and children under 18
Dependant activities	Spouses and partners can work or study if they wish and children of school age can attend school.

TIER 2 GENERAL

For permanent hires and high earners, this category allows UK employers to sponsor and employ migrants in the UK on a permanent basis to fill a vacancy within the UK business.

In most instances (with the exception of high earners, those in roles on the shortage occupation list and those switching from Tier 4 Student status) employers will need to show that they have advertised the role in accordance with the Resident Labour Market Test requirements and that they have not been able to find a UK settled worker to fill the position.

If the migrant is coming from overseas, the application is deemed to be a 'Restricted' one and it will fall under the annual cap, currently set at 20,700 per year (6th April to 5th April). This is the only instance where the employer must seek approval from UK Visas & Immigration first before being able to issue the certificate of sponsorship. If the request is approved, the employer is then able to issue the certificate of sponsorship to the migrant who can then proceed to apply for their visa to the UK at the British diplomatic post in their home country or country of residence.

Where the migrant is already in the UK in another immigration category which allows them to switch status to Tier 2 General without having to leave the UK first (with the exception of dependants of Tier 4 students), then this is deemed to be an 'Unrestricted' application and the employer can issue the certificate of sponsorship in the usual way.

The migrant will need to be paid at least £30,000 gross per annum or the appropriate rate for the role on offer as dictated by the Standard Occupational Codes published by the Home Office, whichever is higher. They cannot own more than 10% of the company's shares (unless they earn more than £159,600 a year).

English language	Yes
Initial visa grant	Up to 3 years
Extension	Up to 3 years
Indefinite leave to remain	After 5 years
Dependants	Spouse and children under 18
Dependant activities	Spouses and partners can work or study if they wish and children of school age can attend school.

OTHER ROUTES

For completeness sake, it must be mentioned that there are other categories outside of the Points Based System that will enable a foreign national to work in the UK, although some aren't strictly deemed to be work visa categories. These include the UK Ancestry route for Commonwealth nationals who have a British born grandparent, Tier 5 Government Authorised Exchange Schemes and the Tier 5 Youth Mobility scheme for nationals of Australia, Canada, Japan, Monaco, New Zealand, Hong Kong, Republic of Korea and Taiwan based on reciprocal schemes overseas. Similarly, partners of British nationals are entitled to work in the UK, as are family members (and in certain instances extended family members) of EEA nationals.

STAYING ON IN THE UK

Indefinite leave to remain

With the exception of visitors, graduate entrepreneurs, Turkish workers and Tier 2 intra-company assignees, all of the categories discussed above lead to settlement in the UK, usually after five years. There are also accelerated routes to settlement for Tier 1 Investors and Entrepreneurs as detailed in the previous chapter.

Key points to note in the lead up to settlement is that the main applicant's absences from the UK will be taken into account as part of the consideration. Current rules require that the applicant has no more than 180 days absence per visa year in order to qualify for settlement. It is also now required that in addition to the applicant taking and passing the Life in the UK test, they must also meet the English language requirements for settlement.

Where family members have been treated in line with the main applicant for the full five year period they too will be eligible to apply, including children who are at that stage over 18 providing they are still part of the family unit.

Once settlement has been granted there are no conditions or time restrictions placed on the individual which means that they can live and work in the UK for as long as they wish. Children born to parents who hold indefinite leave to remain or British citizenship at the time when the child was born automatically acquire British citizenship.

However, it is important to note that despite the name, indefinite leave to remain can be lost if the holder spends two years or more outside of the UK in one go.

British citizenship

Once settlement has been acquired and held for at least 12 months (with the exception of spouses of British nationals), it is possible to apply to naturalise as a British citizen if desired. Applicants must be over 18 and of 'good character'. They must also meet the Life in the UK test and English language requirements if they did not have to at the point they acquired settlement. Residence requirements also come into play although the rules are somewhat different to those that apply at the settlement stage. For citizenship the applicant must show that they have not spent more than 450 days outside of the UK during the five years preceding the citizenship application and that they have not spent more than 90 days outside of the UK in the 12 months leading up to the application. Where absences are for business purposes, discretion can be exercised in respect of these thresholds.

Children under 18 can apply to be registered as British citizens.

Although the UK allows its citizens to hold dual citizenship, some countries, such as India and China for example, do not and in these circumstances if British citizenship were to be acquired then the original citizenship may have to be renounced. It is therefore important that individuals check the position with the relevant authorities in this respect before applying for British citizenship.

The above information is correct at the time of writing but readers are advised to check the current position before taking any action as the UK Immigration Rules are subject to frequent change.

2.5 COMPLYING WITH THE UK'S MONEY LAUNDERING REGULATIONS

Jac Berry, Mazars LLP

The current UK Money Laundering Regulations came into force in December 2007, replacing and updating the existing regulations; their purpose is to protect the UK financial system. Any business covered by the regulations must implement controls to prevent it being used by criminals or terrorists for money laundering activities. Failure to comply with the law could have serious consequences.

WHICH BUSINESSES ARE COVERED BY MONEY LAUNDERING REGULATIONS?

Regulations apply to a number of business sectors, including:

- Most UK financial and credit businesses such as banks, currency exchange offices,
- cheque cashers or money transmitters;
- Independent legal professionals;
- Accountants, tax advisers, auditors and insolvency practitioners;
- Estate agents;
- Casinos;
- 'High Value Dealers' – businesses that accept cash payments for goods worth 15,000 Euros or more either in a single transaction or in instalments;
- Trust or Company Service Providers.

If your business falls into one of these business sectors there is a requirement for it to be monitored by a supervisory authority. It may be the case that your business is already monitored, for example by a professional body, such as the Law Society, or by the Financial Conduct Authority, but if it is not you will probably need to register with the UK Revenue & Customs (HMRC).

To register with HMRC under Money Laundering Regulations you must complete an application form (MLR100) to register each place where you carry on business activities that require supervision. There is a fee for registering each business premises and a subsequent annual renewal fee.

If your business is a Money Service Business or a Trust or Company Service Provider, you are also required to apply for the 'fit and proper' test (form MLRlOl) in addition to registering with HMRC. The 'fit and proper' test must be taken by all those people who are involved in the running of the business.

CRIMINAL OFFENCES UNDER THE ANTI-MONEY LAUNDERING LEGISLATION

Money Laundering is the term used for a number of offences involving the proceeds of crime or terrorist funds. It includes possessing, or in any way dealing with, or concealing, the proceeds of any crime. It also involves similar activities in relation to terrorist funds, which include funds that are likely to be used for terrorism, as well as the proceeds of terrorism.

Someone is engaged in Money Laundering if they:

- Conceal, disguise, convert, transfer or remove (from the United Kingdom) criminal property;
- Enter into or become concerned in an arrangement which they know or suspect facilitates (by whatever means) the acquisition, retention, use or control of criminal property by or on behalf of another person;
- Acquire, use or have possession of criminal property.

Criminal Property is very widely defined, but, in summary, property is Criminal Property if it:

- Constitutes a person's benefit in whole or in part (including pecuniary and proprietary benefit) from criminal conduct; or
- Represents such a benefit directly or indirectly, in whole or in part; and
- The alleged offender knows or suspects that it constitutes or represents such a
- benefit.

Criminal Conduct is conduct that constitutes an offence in any part of the United Kingdom or would constitute an offence in any part of the United Kingdom, if it occurred there (subject to the exemptions listed below). This includes tax offences committed abroad if the action would have been an offence were it to have taken place in the United Kingdom. There is no need for there to be any consequential effect on the United Kingdom's tax system.

However, no offence is committed in any of the following circumstances:

- Where the persons involved did not know or suspect that they were dealing with the proceeds of crime;
- Where the act is committed by someone carrying out a law enforcement or judicial function;
- Where the conduct giving rise to the criminal property was reasonably believed to have taken place outside the UK, and the conduct was in fact lawful under the criminal law of the place where it occurred, and the maximum sentence if the conduct had occurred in the UK would have been less than 12 months (except
- in the case of an act which would be an offence under the Gaming Act 1968, the Lotteries and Amusements Act 1976 or under sections 23 or 25 of the Financial Services and Markets Act 2000, which will fall within the exemption even if the relevant sentence would be in excess of 12 months).

It is a general rule that an element of intent is required before many criminal offences can be committed. For example, theft can only be committed where the offender is dishonest and has intent to deprive permanently. In some cases, where the monetary proceeds of a suspected theft or tax fraud are small, it may be that the perpetrators were acting in error or in the mistaken impression that they had permission to act as they did.

It is also important to note that for indirect tax, section 167(3) Customs & Excise Management Act 1979 provides that a wide range of innocent/accidental errors are criminal offences (although they are in practice generally dealt with under the civil penalty regime).

For the avoidance of doubt, Criminal Property includes (but is by no means limited to):

- The proceeds of tax (direct or indirect) evasion including the under declaring of income and the over claiming of expenses.
- A benefit obtained through bribery and corruption (including both the receipt
- of a bribe and the profits earned from a contract obtained through bribery or the
- promise of a bribe).
- Benefits obtained through the operation of a cartel.
- Benefits (in the form of saved costs) arising from a failure to comply with a regulatory requirement, where that failure is a criminal offence, e.g. a breach of health and safety regulations.
- Property, even of minimal value, acquired by theft (including, for example,

not telling a customer that they have erroneously paid twice or an overdrawn director's current account in a relevant company).

The following can constitute a criminal offence:

- Providing assistance to a money launderer to obtain, conceal, retain or invest funds if you knew, or in some cases, if you should have known that the funds were the proceeds of serious criminal conduct. Making a report precludes a charge of assisting a money launderer.
- Tipping off a person, or any third party, in connection with an investigation into money laundering. This could include, for example, informing someone of your money laundering suspicions.
- Failing to report a suspicion of money laundering if the suspicion was acquired in the course of your employment (or, as the case may be, your profession). It is a criminal offence not to comply with the Regulations and a criminal offence may also be committed by anyone who has consented to or connived at non-compliance with the Regulations, including where such non-compliance is attributable to their neglect.

There are thousands of criminal offences in the United Kingdom that, if committed, are likely to result in a person benefiting from an offence and thereby having Criminal Property. The key point to note is that the Proceeds of Crime Act (POCA) introduced an 'all crime' reporting regime. That is, Money Laundering offences can relate to the proceeds of any criminal activity, not just, for example, drug trafficking.

In addition to the offences under the POCA, there is also an obligation for businesses to report belief or suspicion that finance proceeds from, or is likely to be used for, terrorism, or its laundering, based on information which came to them in the course of their business or employment.

MONEY LAUNDERING CONTROLS AND PROCEDURES

Businesses covered by the Money Laundering Regulations must put controls in place to prevent them being used by criminals or terrorists for money laundering purposes. The controls include:

- Assessing the risk of the business being used by criminals to launder money;
- Appointing a 'nominated officer;'
- Implementing a procedure to check the identity of customers and 'beneficial
- owners' of corporate bodies and partnerships and keeping all relevant documents;
- Ensuring employees are aware of money laundering regulations.

The 'nominated officer' must be a person in the business; they cannot be an external consultant. As it is an important role, it must be undertaken by a person who:

- Has access to all customer records and documentation;
- Can make the decision, without reference to others, whether or not to report suspicious activities;
- Can be trusted with the responsibility.
- If you are a sole trader in a regulated business with no employees, you must act as the
- 'nominated officer' yourself.

The duties of the 'nominated officer' include:

- being the first point of contact for reports of suspicious activity from any
- employee in the business;
- considering all information and assessing whether evidence of money laundering
- or terrorist financing exists;
- reporting any suspicious activities or transactions to the National Crime Agency (NCA);
- requesting permission from NCA to continue with any transactions that they have reported, and ensure that no transactions are continued illegally.

All employees, particularly those in customer-facing positions, must receive regular training to ensure that they are aware of the money laundering laws, understand how the business's procedures affect them and appreciate the penalties of non-compliance. They should also be able to recognise suspicious activity and know what to do about it.

WHAT ARE THE PENALTIES FOR NOT COMPLYING WITH THE MONEY LAUNDERING REGULATIONS?

If you do not comply with Money Laundering Regulations there are various measures that can be taken, from warning letters to criminal prosecution. Although criminal prosecution is a last resort, the penalty may be harsh; depending on the severity of the offence, the courts can impose penalties ranging from unlimited fines to lengthy imprisonment, or both.

FUTURE CHANGES

The requirements of the EU's Fourth Anti-Money Laundering Directive are expected to be transposed into UK law in 2017. Key changes are expected to include the following:

- changes around customer due diligence requirements to ensure the focus is on a risk-based approach;
- the extension of the requirements around Politically Exposed Persons (PEPs) to cover domestic PEPs, as well as those based overseas;
- member states to establish a directory of ultimate beneficial owners; and
- a reduction in the one-off transactions limit.

INVESTING IN THE UK –
MAZARS, YOUR INTERNATIONAL PARTNER

Mazars provides specialist advice to businesses like yours every day. From setting up your company, choosing the most effective tax structure, paying your staff and setting up the back office, our international experts support you so you can stay focused on your business.

For further information please contact:

Toby Stanbrook
Head of Accounting and Outsourcing

T: +44 (0)20 8661 4120
E: toby.stanbrook@mazars.co.uk

www.mazars.co.uk

We can help with:

- Company formations
- Corporate and personal tax
- Governance and risk
- Immigration advisory
- Management accounting and reporting
- Payroll and pensions
- Transaction services

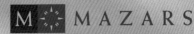

SIMPLY BETTER ADVICE

&COMMERCIAL PROPERTY

———————

When it comes to commercial property, it pays to have Carter Jonas on board. Our experienced experts offer commercial property advice in agency, development, investment, valuations, landlord and tenant, property management and building consultancy.

With a network of 38 offices across the UK, we employ more than 700 people, we are renowned for the quality of our service, the expertise of our people and the simply better advice we offer our clients.

Commercial • Planning & Development • Residential • Rural

www.carterjonas.co.uk/commercial
Offices throughout the UK

Carter Jonas

Inspire Improve Impact

Are you looking for R&D grant funding opportunities?

PNO Consultants

PNO Group is Europe's largest independent public funding advisory, employing more than 230 staff across 12 European countries. Supporting small businesses, large enterprise and universities across all research disciplines and sectors, PNO has extensive experience of all principal national and European funding programmes with a service model that covers the entire grant acquisition process. This includes the identification of grant funding opportunities to support project ideas and company activities, a comprehensive but flexible writing service that includes full writing support through to peer review guidance and support in the post award reporting process to ensure that the full draw down of a grant is achieved once an individual project is underway. PNO also offers an extensive range of project services including project management, technology intelligence, development of exploitation strategies and dissemination. With a client base of more than 15,000 organisations throughout Europe, PNO can also help with finding suitable project partners as well as identifying potential projects for our clients to join.

Our Services:

1. Initiate
    -   Assessment of projects for grant potential
    -   Linking with potential partners/ projects
    -   Grant education and training
2. Apply
    -   Bid writing support: Full support, co-writing and peer review
    -   Development of project budget
    -   Contract negotiation with Grantor Body
3. Comply
    -   Advice on administrative requirements
    -   Project management assistance
    -   Support to ensure full draw down of grant
    -   Managing project spend against project deliverables

Grant Schemes

There are a range of funding programmes available for UK businesses that aim to help take projects from research to as close to commercial viability as possible to support the development of new products, processes or services. Key national funding programmes include:

-   **SMART -** a single applicant scheme open to all R&D performing UK SME's from any sector
-   **Collaborative R&D** – supports industrial and research collaborations in strategically important areas of science, engineering and technology
-   **Catalyst Programmes** - a form of research and development funding which focuses on a specific priority area. Current areas include Industrial Biotechnology, Energy, Agri-Tech and Biomedical
-   **Small Business Research Initiative (SBRI) -** supports the engagement of the public sector with industry during the early stages of development across a range of industry sectors.

Key European R&D funding programmes include **H2020** and **Eureka Eurostars.**

Contact Us:
Olaf Swanzy, Director
Telephone: 07810 837479 / 0161 488 3488
Email: olaf.swanzy@pnoconsultants.com
Web: www.pnoconsultants.com

INNOVATION PLACE
Projects, networks and funding
Sign up to our free online innovation portal
www.innovationplace.eu

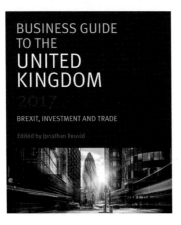

Published: 30 September 2017
ISBN (Paperback): 9781785079139
ISBN (Ebook): 9781785079122
Rights: World

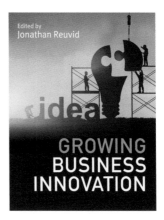

Published: 31st October 2017
ISBN (Paperback):
9781787198937 ISBN (Ebook):
9781787198920
Rights: World

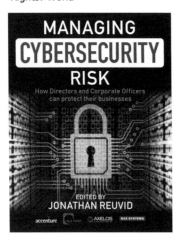

Published: 30 November 2016
ISBN (Paperback): 9781785079153
ISBN (Ebook): 9781785079146
Rights: World

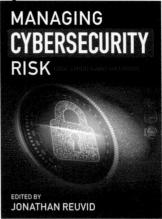

Published: 30 November 2017
ISBN (Paperback): 9781787198913
ISBN (Ebook): 9781787198906
Rights: World

Published: 30 April 2016
ISBN (Paperback): 9781785079320
ISBN (Ebook): 9781785079337
Rights: World

Published: 28 May 2011
ISBN (Paperback): 9781907756382
ISBN (Ebook): 9781908248169
Rights: World

BRITISH EXPORTERS ASSOCIATION

The British Exporters Association (BExA) is an independent national trade association representing the interests of the export community. Our membership is drawn from a wide cross section of companies; Large and SME Exporters, Banks, Credit Insurers and Brokers, Legal firms and other service providers – giving us an excellent perspective of the issues that matter to UK exporters.

BExA is a valued contributor to, and is engaged with, many Government departments and committees to drive export policy forward. These include meetings with the Minister for Trade and Investment, the Department for International Trade and UK Export Finance, and attending the APPG for Trade & Industry, House of Commons Select Committees and EGAC.

Membership is open to all companies and other organisations resident in the United Kingdom who export goods or services, or who provide assistance to such companies in the promotion and furtherance of export activities.

Benefits of membership include:

Representing members
BExA represents members interests on day to day and policy issues relating to UK export and trade policy and on other specific trade related issues raised by members. We meet ministers and Government officials, participate in UK and EU consultations, liaise with other trade associations and obtain press coverage.

The Exporters' Forum
Members meet, exchange views, discuss trade-related problems and update themselves on developments at periodic meetings of BExA's Industry Committee, Banking Committee and SME & Micro Exporters Committee. These Committees report to BExA's Council.

BExA Seminars
BExA holds an export seminar each year.

Networking events
Our Annual Lunch, held in the autumn at the Mansion House, City of London, and our Spring Reception at the House of Commons are prestigious networking events in exporters' diaries.

Information dissemination
Members receive informative minutes of Council and other meetings, focussed e-mailings on specific topics, and newsletters.

BExA Guides
The Association has published seven guides 'by exporters for exporters' on key trade issues. The guides are available to download at http://www.bexa.co.uk/bexa-publications/

GTR BExA Young Exporter of the Year Award
This annual award brings recognition to a particularly capable young exporter. For award parameters and to download a nomination form, please visit www.bexa.co.uk/export-award

Discounts for export events
Discounts are available to members on many leading trade-related seminars.

Applications for membership can be made online at **http://www.bexa.co.uk/join**
Membership is an annual subscription and based on the number of employees in the UK.

For further information please visit **www.bexa.co.uk** or contact:
Michelle Treasure – BExA Secretariat – michelle.treasure@bexa.co.uk – Tel. +44 (020) 7222 5419

Legend 📖 Press

Who are we?

Legend press was founded in 2005 and is focused primarily on publishing literary fiction, crime thrillers, women's fiction, historical fiction, and young adult novels.

Visit our website for information on events and new releases as well as blog posts from authors and details on how to send your manuscript to our submissions department: www.legendtimesgroup.co.uk/legend-press

Passionate about books?

The Legend 100 club is a group of bloggers and reviewers who hear about our upcoming titles, receive free ebooks ahead of publication and post reviews on blogs, Amazon, Goodreads, netgalley and other literary publications.

If you'd like to join or find out more about becoming a Legend 100 reviewer, get in touch at imogenharris@legend-paperbooks.

Legend 📖 Press
Upcoming Releases

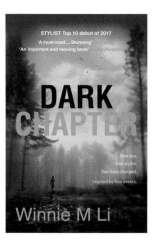

The Magician's Lie, Greer Macallister
Magic, Murder & Mystery
Paperback out 2nd October

A historical mystery following the most famous female illusionist of her day, The Amazing Arden. Arrested for the death of her husband, Arden reveals a spellbinding tale that she hopes will prove her innocence.

Dark Chapter, Winnie M Li
Inspired by True Events
Paperback out 1st November

A hard-hitting thriller inspired by the author's own sexual assualt. This debut explores not only the aftermath of the attack but the events that led to it from the perspective of both the perpetrator and the suvivor.

The Winter's Child, Cassandra Parkin
Haunting Story of Grief & Hope
Paperback out 16th October

A family tale with a psychological twist. Susannah's life begins to unravel when a fortune-teller predicts that her son - who has been missing for five years - will return to her by Christmas Eve.

The Visitors, Catherine Burns
Dark & Graphic Suspense
Hardback out 3rd october

With echoes of real cases like Josef Fritzl and Natacha Kampusche, this is one psychological thriller you won't be able to put down - even if you want to. When Marion's brother dies suddenly she is forced to face the gruesome secret he keeps locked in their cellar.

Support business growth with us

Introducing COBCOE
Council of British Chambers of Commerce in Europe

COBCOE is the membership body for British business organisations across Europe.

Our members are present in almost all European countries, representing around 12,000 businesses. Another 40 business organisations in the UK and around the world are affiliated to COBCOE.

We're on a mission to break down the barriers to international trade and investment. through new initiatives to help businesses succeed in new markets.

How to get involved

Find out about the corporate and business organisations working with COBCOE through partnerships and affiliations.

Support our Brexit Ambition project by following us or joining our mailing list.

We recently introducing new corporate partnerships starting at £1,500 pa. Please contact us for more informatiion:

Visit: www.cobcoe.eu
Contact: info@cobcoe.eu info@cobcoe.eu

We believe that trust is the most important aspect of a successful business relationship

Trusted business contacts around the world, matched to your needs

Join now for a free trial: https://cobcoe.tiao.world/signup

2.6 COMPETITION LAW AND POLICY IN THE UK

Jeremy Robinson, Watson Farley & Williams LLP

INTRODUCTION

When engaging in many common business transactions in the UK or having an effect in the UK, it is sensible to consider whether competition law may apply. Failure to abide by the rules can be costly: civil and indeed criminal penalties may be enforced; damages (including collective damages) actions are possible and there can be severe consequences for an individual's career.

Here are some common situations (although this list is certainly not exhaustive):

- You are attending a meeting of your trade association and the question of industry prices and volumes is raised;
- You receive – without asking – information about a competitor's future pricing intentions;
- You learn that your major supplier may have been involved in a price-fixing conspiracy that could have raised your costs substantially;
- The supplier of your main input, who is dominant, is charging customers in the downstream market in which you operate little more than it is charging you for the input, leaving you with no margin to be competitive;
- Two of your suppliers merge and you face having less choice (and perhaps higher costs) in future;
- You and your nearest competitor decide to merge and wish to implement the deal quickly;
- You are buying a company which has received a grant from a public body;
- You are nervous about entering a new market without knowing your competitor's future conduct in that market; and

- In response to an invitation to tender, you have received some peculiar bids.
- In some of these situations your business may face competition law liability; in others, you may be the "victim" of possible anti-competitive activity and wish to claim redress.

It pays therefore to have a basic understanding of the rules both to avoid liability and to protect your business.

A book chapter cannot replace in-depth consideration of your specific circumstances nor does it replace a proper compliance programme. This chapter is instead designed to raise awareness and provoke questions.

COMPETITION LAW, THE EU AND RELATED AREAS OF LAW

Competition law in the EU seeks to address several problems:

- Anti-competitive agreements between two or more "undertakings" (Article 101 of the Treaty on the functioning of the EU – TfEU – and chapter I of the Competition Act 1998);
- The abuse by one or more undertakings of a dominant position (Article 102 TfEU and chapter II of the Competition Act 1998);
- Mergers, acquisitions or – in some cases – joint ventures above a particular size (the EU merger regulation – Regulation 139/2004; the Enterprise Act 2002);
- State Aid (Articles 107-109 TfEU); and
- Public procurement (regulated by Directive 2014/25 in the Water, Energy, Transport and Postal Services, by Directive 2014/24 in other sectors, and by Directive 2014/23 for concession contracts.

The EU competition rules form part of the broader body of EU law, the goals of which include the creation and development of an internal market within the EU. The free movement of capital, services and workers and the freedom of establishment are fundamental principles of EU law which at times overlap with the application of competition law.

Competition law is not an isolated discipline: it may overlap or share common principles with other forms of regulation, and this alone makes it exceptionally important for any business operating in the EU and in the UK; in particular:

- *Sector regulation:* in addition to competition law, many industries are subject to specific regulation, which may serve economic, consumer, environmental or other purposes. These industries include: financial services, payment systems, communications and the traditional utilities, such as energy (gas pipelines, storage facilities and electricity transmission and distribution networks); airports

(Heathrow and Gatwick are subject to a price cap on their overall returns); the railway network; and water (and water and sewerage) companies.

- *Consumer law*: one of the main objectives of competition law is the protection of consumers; consumer law (both EU and UK) complements this objective and some consumer law investigations are carried out by the same institution as competition law investigations (e.g. the Competition and Markets Authority);
- *Fraud and criminal law*: in the UK, it is a criminal offence for an individual to make or implement (or cause to be made or implemented) arrangements that could result in price fixing, limiting or prevent supply or production; or bid rigging – this is known as the "Cartel Offence" and it carries a maximum penalty of five years in prison or an unlimited fine. Either the Serious Fraud Office or the CMA can prosecute and in some cases of market abuse activity the question may arise whether they are to be prosecuted as fraud or as a cartel.

Businesses operating in an IP-rich environment, particularly where the industry creates common standards (for example, in the IT or comms sectors), should mind the interface between competition and intellectual property law.

Consequently, you must consider competition law compliance in your business activities as a priority.

ANTI-COMPETITIVE AGREEMENTS

The most obvious example of an anti-competitive agreement is a price-fixing or market-sharing cartel, but the scope of the EU's legal prohibition is broader.

The law prohibits agreements, decisions of associations of undertakings or concerted practices (a form of understanding falling short of an agreement) which have as their object or effect the prevention, restriction or distortion of competition and which may affect trade between EU Member States. The UK rules are the same, except that the requirement to affect trade is directed towards trade within the UK.

There is an important distinction between agreements which are anti-competitive by object and those which are anti-competitive by effect. Simply put, an agreement which is anti-competitive by object is by its nature so serious that there is no need to prove that it has actually had an anti-competitive effect. "By object" infringements encompass the most serious anti-competitive agreements, such as cartels, but in practice, competition authorities and businesses have argued over the threshold at which an anti-competitive agreement can correctly be considered a "by object" infringement. This argument – which at first sight appears to be a pure "lawyers' point" - can have very significant effects for the ability of a business under investigation to defend itself.

The law then provides that agreements (etc) falling within the prohibition are void (and therefore unenforceable), but that certain agreements may be exempt from the prohibition if they meet four cumulative criteria, which may – at the risk of oversimplification – mean that the pro-competitive aspects outweigh the anti-competitive aspects. An agreement may be exempt either because – individually – it meets the criteria for exemption, or because it fulfils the criteria for "block" exemption, that is, an exemption for agreements belonging to a defined class. The EU competition law recognises several types of agreement as capable of being block exempt, and these are set out in Appendix 1.

In practice, the law often needs to be considered in the context of a range of common business agreements, from licensing distribution and supply arrangements, non-compete clauses/restrictive covenants, joint venture arrangements, to research and development agreements and more, but in many cases the prohibition may not apply, or if it does, the agreement is exempt.

The greatest concern for competition authorities – and the target of substantial enforcement time and resource – are the cartels, which are considered the most serious infringements of competition law, because they cause the greatest consumer and economic harm. They attract the highest penalties.

The EU as a whole has not criminalised infringements of competition law. However, some Member States have chosen to criminalise cartels: for example, Ireland, the UK, Hungary and Romania.

There are two ways in which competition authorities learn about cartels: intelligence gathering (this includes information it may learn through carrying out market studies, or even through using covert human intelligence sources) or whistle-blowers. The main form of whistle-blower is the corporate leniency applicant. Leniency programmes have been a highly effective way for competition authorities to detect cartels, because they promise substantial reductions in corporate fines in return for information on the cartel. Such reductions extend to complete immunity for the first to reveal the cartel to the authority. The second form of whistle-blower in the UK is the individual corporate informant, who can receive up to £100,000 in return for informing the CMA about a cartel.

THE ABUSE OF A DOMINANT POSITION

Competition law prohibits the abuse by one or more undertakings of a market dominating position. Again, where trade might be affected determines which rules – EU or UK – apply.

A dominant position allows a business to behave in a way that impedes competition, or as one case put it, in a manner "to an appreciable extent independently of its competitors and customers and ultimately of the consumers." The law does not prohibit having a dominant position, but only its abuse. That said, it is also possible for the abuse to take place in a non-dominated market, if such market is sufficiently closely related to a dominated one.

There are many established forms of abuse (and these have grown over time). Broadly, we can distinguish between "exclusionary" abuses – those which tend to exclude competitors from the market and so harm competition – and "exploitative" abuses – those which seek to take advantage of customers or suppliers.

Exclusionary abuses are sometimes described as "price-based" and "non-price based" abuses. Price-based abuses include predatory (below cost) pricing, margin squeeze (where a supplier competes with the customer in the downstream market and distorts competition in the downstream market); and certain discounts. Non-price abuses include refusal to supply and tying/bundling.

MERGER CONTROL

Merger control rules make the conclusion of structural business deals involving parties above a certain size threshold – mergers, acquisitions, structural joint ventures – subject to a competition review. There are two ways a business can be affected by these rules: as a party to the deal, or as supplier, customer or competitor, affected by the deal.

In practice, it is essential to distinguish between the "jurisdiction" rules and the "substantive" rules. The jurisdictional rules determine whether – and if so where – merger notifications may be required or advisable (if not otherwise required). The substantive rules determine whether a merger subject to review may proceed, and if so on what terms. For example, some complex cases may be granted permission to proceed, but only subject to the combined group divesting certain assets to preserve competition.

The distinction between jurisdictional and substantive rules is an important one: many mergers are required to be notified and pre-cleared each year even though they are harmless to competition.

Jurisdictional tests

Jurisdictional tests set out (a) the types and (b) the size of the parties brought together which the merger control rules cover. In EU law and practice, the first stage is normally to assess whether the EU rules (contained in the EU merger regulation) will apply. The types of transaction covered by the EUMR are broad: these are "concentrations", which include mergers, acquisitions (including acquisitions of minority stakes where these allow the acquirer to exercise decisive influence over the target) and structural ("full function") joint ventures. The size of the parties brought together by the transactions is determined by two alternative sets of turnover information, set out in Appendix 2.

The advantage of a concentration falling within the EUMR is that with few exceptions, the national merger control rules of the EU Member States will not apply. This is known as the "one stop shop" principle. The risk of multiple concurrent competition authority timetables as well as the overall administrative burden are thereby reduced.

That said, deals may also be subject to merger review outside the EU as over 100 jurisdictions worldwide now operate some form of merger control. It is important to remember that the rules are not harmonised globally, and it will be important in some cases to take local law advice.

For deals falling outside the EUMR, national EU Member State rules may apply. In the UK, the rules operate slightly differently in three relevant respects: the definition of the transactions covered; and the size threshold at which the rules are engaged; and the requirement to obtain clearance.

The UK rules apply when two enterprises cease to be distinct, as a result of merger, or one party acquires legal control, de facto control or material influence over the other. The target enterprise must achieve an annual UK turnover over £70 million; or, as a result of the transaction, the parties will together supply at least one quarter of the relevant goods or services in the UK, or in a substantial part of the UK (and this means there must be an increment in that share of supply).

Unlike many other jurisdictions, the UK still operates a voluntary filing regime, which means that in principle, the parties are not required to obtain clearance from the CMA before implementing the deal. However, the CMA can investigate all mergers (before or after implementation) and force divestments if necessary. In practice, the CMA may intervene to prevent a completed merger being implemented while it is carrying out its investigation. Consequently, merging parties should carefully consider the risks involved in implementing a deal without first having obtained clearance.

MARKET INVESTIGATIONS

Where the CMA considers that particular features of a market may give rise to anti-competitive effects which may not be caught by the prohibitions on anti-competitive agreements and the abuse of dominant positions, it may investigate these markets where it considers that consumer harm may result. Note that the focus here is on industry practices, rather than the actions of specific firms, although in one notable investigation, into BAA Airports, the market under investigation was also one single firm.

Following a market study, the CMA may refer the case for more detailed investigation by the CMA Panel if it has reasonable grounds for suspecting that any feature, or combination of features, of a market in the UK for goods or services prevents, restricts or distorts competition in connection with the supply or acquisition of any goods or services in the UK, or a part of the UK. The reference period is 18 months, extendable to 24 months where there are special reasons for doing so, and a timetable of six months (extendable to ten) for implementing any remedies. The sector regulators may also make references to the CMA Panel for issues within their own sectors. If a market is found not to be working well, the CMA can impose significant regulatory or structural reforms.

THE ENFORCEMENT OF COMPETITION LAW

Competition compliance is important. Consider the CMA's powers:

- In cases of suspected infringement of the rules on anti-competitive agreements and the abuse of dominance, the CMA may make surprise inspections ("dawn raids") to gather information, interview employees and block access to email accounts (to prevent tampering with evidence). In practice, these investigations can be exceptionally disruptive to the operation of a business as well as marking the start of what could be lengthy investigative proceedings. The CMA can also submit lengthy questionnaires for the business to complete. These take time and care to complete properly.
- The CMA can impose "interim measures" where it considers that "significant damage" is likely to result from the alleged anti-competitive behaviour. Although there has been only one example of the UK competition authorities imposing interim measures (in the London Metal Exchange case, where the measures were later withdrawn), reforms have lowered the threshold for imposing interim measures from "serious and irreparable harm" to "significant damage." Interim measures are most likely to be sought (and applied) in cases where an abuse of a dominant position is alleged.
- A price-fixing case may see the CMA conducting parallel civil and criminal law proceedings. The threshold for sending individuals to prison has been lowered by reforms which have removed the requirement for a jury to find that the individual was "dishonest". Under the old law, which required a finding of dishonesty, four individuals received prison terms between six and thirty months.
- The CMA can impose fines of up to 10% of worldwide turnover for infringing competition law;
- The CMA can also seek to have a company director disqualified for up to fifteen years;
- In the UK, individuals may be extradited if their actions breach both the cartel offence in the UK and competition rules in another country, for example, the USA.

There are numerous competition regulators in the UK. If you are operating in certain regulated sectors, other bodies will have powers to apply competition law alongside the CMA – this principle is known as "concurrency" and the sector regulators are said to have "concurrent" competition law powers. These bodies, and their remit as competition authorities, are as follows:

Regulator	Responsibilities
Ofcom	Communications and post
Ofgem	Gas and Electricity markets
ORR	Rail
OFWAT	Water Services
Utility Regulator NI	Northern Ireland energy, water and sewerage
CAA	Airport Operation Services and Air Traffic Services (but not air transport providers such as airlines, or tour operators)
Financial Conduct Authority	Financial services firms
Payment Systems Regulator	Payment systems

PRIVATE ENFORCEMENT OF COMPETITION LAW

For many years it has been possible in principle to seek damages to compensate for losses suffered as a result of anti-competitive behaviour. The mechanism exists for the victim to begin a case in the High Court for damages, or – following a decision by the CMA or the European Commission that competition law has been infringed – in the Competition Appeal Tribunal. The latter route is seen to be more attractive for the victims of anti-competitive behaviour, at least in principle, because the competition authority has already established the infringement.

For some, this right was more apparent than real, as those often harmed by anti-competitive behaviour – consumers – were often unmotivated and unable to enforce their rights. It is the policy and intent of both the European Commission and the UK Government that more consumers be able to enforce the law. To that end:

- The EU Damages Directive (Directive 2014/104) aims to harmonise the EU Member States' national rules and procedures for damages cases, and the EU Member States were required to implement the directive by 27 December 2016.

At the time of writing, only 17 Member States (including the UK) have fully transposed the directive.

- The UK's Consumer Rights Act 2015 provides for enhanced consumer rights to enforce competition law, particularly (a) allowing for a form of class action lawsuit (known as a representative action) to be brought on an opt-out basis – i.e. all the consumers within the class would be included unless they specifically chose to opt-out (b) allowing damages claims to be concluded with a collective settlement between business and consumers; and (c) allowing infringing businesses to set up a collective redress scheme as a partial or full alternative to court action, by which consumers can be compensated.

Table 2.6.1 Competition enforcement institutions

UK Institutions	
Competition Markets Authority (CMA)	• The CMA is responsible for enforcing the Competition Act 1998, carrying out merger control functions and conducting in-depth market investigations with a primary duty to promote effective competition. • The key sectoral regulators in Tab 2.2.1 above also have concurrent powers with the CMA in Competition Act cases and in-depth market investigations in their sectors. The sectoral regulators do not have the leading role in merger control cases in their sector.
Financial Conduct Authority (FCA)	• Regulates financial firms providing services to consumers and maintains the integrity of the UK's financial markets. • It focuses on the regulation of conduct by both retail and wholesale financial services firms. Powers include regulating conduct related to the marketing of financial products. • Responsible for regulating the consumer credit industry from 1 April 2014, taking over the role from the Office of Fair Trading.
Payment Systems Regulator (PSR)	• The PSR is responsible for promoting competition and innovation, and ensuring that payment systems are developed and operated in the interests of service-users, working alongside the Financial Conduct Authority and Competition and Markets Authority, thus creating a more competitive banking industry.

Competition Appeal Tribunal (CAT)	• hears appeals on the merits of decisions made under Competition Act 1998 – appeals against decisions of the CMA or other sector regulators; • hears actions for damages on a stand-alone or follow-on basis, including collective actions; • can approve collective settlement of claims in collective proceedings • reviews mergers and market references; appeals against regulatory decisions of Ofcom.
High court	• Claimants can bring private actions for damages to the High Court. Claims can follow on from an adverse finding by the CMA or CAT or can be brought directly to the High Court.

EU Institutions	
European Commission (DG Competition)	• enforces competition rules of the TfEU; • reviews mergers with a European dimension (phase I and phase II); • publishes guidelines on the application of competition rules for consumers, industry and national competition authorities.
General Court (was Court of First Instance (CFI))	• Hears appeals against decisions of Community institutions, including DG Competition.
Court of Justice of the EU (was European Court of Justice (ECJ))	• hears references for preliminary rulings – the Court of Justice provides decisions or reasoned orders on specific points of law referred from national courts; • hears appeals against decisions of the General Court.

BREXIT AND UK COMPETITION LAW

Brexit will change UK law, including competition law, in ways that depend on the UK's post-Brexit relationship with the EU. Before the referendum and in the immediate aftermath, many speculated about future "models" for this relationship, whether the "Norway" model (EEA), the "Swiss" model (EFTA), the Canada or the Turkey models. After the UK government stated that it was prepared to leave the single market and the customs union, talk of different models ceased in favour of a bespoke UK-EU deal, or no deal at all. The UK's June 2017 General Election did not give a clear majority to the ruling Conservative Party, which has led to speculation that "softer" Brexit models may again be open for consideration.

Even assuming – as the rest of this chapter does – a "hard" Brexit (UK leaves the EU Single Market and Customs Union), the EU competition rules will continue to apply to agreements or conduct of UK businesses that have an effect within the EU, in the same way as agreements or conduct of non-EU businesses are currently subject to EU competition law where their agreements and conduct affect EU markets. A UK participant in a global cartel will therefore continue to face investigation and fines by the European Commission.

Following Brexit, however, the European Commission will lose its power to carry out dawn raids in the UK and will no longer be able to ask the CMA to do so on its behalf. Although the CMA is part of the European Competition network and works closely with the European Commission and other national competition authorities of the EU Member States, it is likely that over time there will be some divergence in the two authorities' strategies post-Brexit. This could even lead to the two authorities investigating the same competition law issue, resulting in added legal costs and an increased administrative burden for businesses.

Furthermore, after Brexit, the UK is likely to lose the benefit of the "one stop shop" principle of EU merger control, and the merging parties could potentially be required to notify their transaction both to the European Commission and to the CMA where the transaction meets both the EU and the UK thresholds. This could lead to increased transaction costs, both in terms of adviser costs and merger filing fees. It could also increase uncertainty for companies, as separate notifications to the European Commission and the CMA may lead to conflicting decisions from the two authorities.

Similarly, Brexit may harm the UK's status as a premier destination for bringing private competition damages claims but this will not become clear until the post-Brexit relationship between the UK and the remaining EU Member States has been established.

SUMMARY CHECKLIST

Activities in the contexts of:

a. Negotiating with customers
b. Cooperation with competitors
c. Mergers/joint ventures
d. Information gathering
e. Unilateral action by "dominant" companies

Activities which are likely to be permitted and those which are likely to be prohibited under EU Law are listed in Table 2.6.2 below.

The main block exemptions at the time of writing are identified in Appendix I and threshold for European notification under merger control are listed in Appendix II.

Table 2.6.2 Activities likely to be permitted and prohibited

LIKELY TO BE PERMITTED	LIKELY TO BE PROHIBITED
A. NEGOTIATING WITH CUSTOMERS OR SUPPLIERS	
• Checking aggregated industry-wide statistical data. • Offering discounts to customers based on the suppliers' costs. • Setting recommended retail prices ("RRPs") for distributors, provided that there is no explicit or implicit pressure on the distributor to follow the RRPs and that you are not dominant.	• Agreeing minimum or fixed resale prices with a distributor or a supplier. • Preventing a distributor from exporting a product to another EU member State. • Charging a distributor prices that vary according to whether the goods are to be resold in a specific country or exported to another EU member State. • Preventing a distributor from selling a product to a customer because they intend to export the product to another EU member State. • Preventing manufacturers of components from selling these components as spare parts.

LIKELY TO BE PERMITTED	LIKELY TO BE PROHIBITED
B. CO-OPERATION WITH COMPETITORS	
<ul><li>Attending meetings of trade association.</li><li>Discussing health and safety.</li><li>Discussing proposed regulatory changes.</li></ul>	<ul><li>Bid-rigging, i.e. allocating tenders between competitors.</li><li>Agreeing production quotas with competitors.</li><li>Agreements or arrangements with the effect of dividing product or geographic markets with competitors.</li><li>Warning a competitor to stay away from "our territory" or specialist field.</li><li>Discussing prices, profit margins, rebates or discounts with competitors.</li><li>Discussing the cost of key raw materials with competitors that also source similar materials.</li><li>Agreeing to boycott particular suppliers or distributors.</li><li>Discussing prices or profit margins with competitors.</li><li>Agreeing current or future prices with competitors.</li><li>Discussing terms of sale or supplier/customer business relationships.</li><li>Discussing strategic plans, such as pricing strategy or product/territorial expansion.</li><li>Agreeing with a competitor to fix the timing for the introduction of a new technology that has been developed independently.</li><li>Delaying quoting a price until you know a competitor's price.</li></ul>

LIKELY TO BE PERMITTED	LIKELY TO BE PROHIBITED
C. MERGERS / JOINT VENTURES	
• Entering into a research & development co-operation agreement with a competitor, where both parties are free to exploit the results independently.	• Agreeing with a competitor to fix the timing for the introduction of a new technology that has been developed independently.
D. INFORMATION GATHERING	
• Obtaining information on competitors' sales and prices from publicly available sources or from customers in the ordinary course of business. • Giving historical sales data to a third party which distributes aggregated, industry-wide sales figures to participants.	• Contacting customers specifically to gather competitors' pricing information ("fishing trip").
E. UNILATERAL ACTION BY "DOMINANT" COMPANIES	
	• Excessively high pricing, i.e. where the price has no reasonable relation to the economic value of the product. • Selling goods below cost in order to foreclose competitors from the market. • Offering discounts to customers in a discriminatory manner, e.g. offering discounts to customers if they source all or most of their supplies from you. • Suggesting recommended retail prices to a distributor. • Refusing to sell a product to a purchaser with an existing business relationship. This will be permitted only if there are sound commercial reasons for refusing to sell, such as poor credit history. • Refusing to sell a particular product unless it is purchased with another non-essential product from your dominant market. • Insisting that a distributor must stock the whole range of your products.

APPENDIX 1

Block Exemptions
The main EU block exemptions in force at the time of writing are listed below:

Block exemption	Council Regulation
Vertical agreements – agreements between non-competitors – new block exemption	Regulation 330/2010 Expires 31 May 2022
Specialisation/production agreements – unilateral specialisation; outsourcing; reciprocal specialisation; joint production agreements	Regulation 1218/2010 Expires 31 December 2022
Research and development – joint R&D and joint exploitation of findings	Regulation 1217/2010 Expires 31 December 2022
Motor vehicle distribution – purchase, sale and resale of motor vehicles or spare parts; repair and maintenance services	Regulation 461/2010 Expires 31 May 2023
Technology Transfer Block Exemption Regulation – certain patents, knowhow and software copyright licensing agreements	Regulation 216/2014 Expires 1 May 2026
Insurance – joint establishment of calculations and tables; establishment of non-binding standard policy conditions for direct insurance	Regulation 267/2010 Expires 31 March 2017
Road and inland waterways groupings	Regulation 169/2009 Indefinite duration
Liner consortia – joint operation of liner shipping transport services	Regulation 906/2009 25 April 2020

The *Commission's Notice on Agreements of minor importance (de minimis notice) 2001/C368/07* applies to agreements where the combined market share of competing/ potentially competing undertakings ("horizontal agreements") is less that 10% and less than 15% for non-competitors ("vertical agreements"), provided they do not contain any hardcore restrictions.

APPENDIX 2

Merger Control:
Thresholds for European Notification

Issue	Primary test	Alternative test
Combined worldwide turnover	> €5,000 million	> €2,500 million
Individual EU-wide turnover	At least two parties > €250 million	At least two parties > €100 million
Presence in three member States		Combined turnover of all parties in at least three member States > €100 million AND Individual turnover of two or more of the parties in three of the member States referred to above > €25 million
Exception	A merger will not have a Community dimension if each of the parties achieves more than two-thirds of its EU-wide turnover in one and the same member State.	

The European Commission can refer the merger analysis to a national authority where the concentration would affect competition in a distinct market of a specific member State (Art. 4(4) or Art. 9 EUMR).

Part Three

Operating a Business in the United Kingdom

3.1 FINANCIAL REPORTING AND ACCOUNTING: AN OVERVIEW

Stephen Brown, Mazars LLP

INTRODUCTION

All limited and unlimited companies in the UK, regardless of whether they are trading or not, are required to keep accounting records throughout the period. This chapter sets out the key financial reporting and accounting requirements for companies trading or investing in the UK.

GENERAL PRINCIPLES

Where formal financial statements are required, in particular for limited companies, these must include for accounting periods commencing after 1 January 2016:

- A Strategic Report signed by a director (if applicable);
- A Directors' Report signed by a director or the company secretary;
- An Auditor's Report signed by the auditor (if required);
- An Income Statement;
- A Statement of Financial Position signed by the director;
- Statement of Changes in Equity;
- Statement of Cashflows (if applicable); and
- Notes to the financial statements.

The financial statements would need to be consolidated financial statements (if applicable – please refer to size limits).

In general, all private and public limited companies are required to send a full copy of their financial statements to Companies House every year.

Once received, all financial statements filed and held at Companies House are available to the general public on request. For this reason the option to file abridged/filleted financial statements is attractive to some small companies.

Small companies are entitled to certain disclosure exemptions in relation to the financial statements they must send their shareholders, and can, in addition, file abbreviated financial statements with the Registrar of Companies. Medium-sized companies can also send abbreviated financial statements to the Registrar but the reduction in disclosure in these financial statements is negligible. For both small and medium-sized companies, the production of abbreviated financial statements is entirely voluntary.

A company/group filing small reduced disclosure financial statements does not need to file a Directors' Report, or Income Statement and can include fewer notes to the financial statements.

For a company or group to qualify as small, at least two of the following conditions must be met:

- Turnover must be less than £10.2 million;
- Gross assets must be less than £5.1 million; and
- Average number of employees must be less than 50.

For a company/group to qualify as medium-sized, again, at least two of the conditions below must be met:

- Turnover must be less than £36 million;
- Gross assets less than £18 million; and
- Average number of employees less than 250.

The time normally allowed for companies to deliver their financial statements to Companies House is:

- Nine months from the ARD (Accounting Reference Date) for a private limited company.
- Six months from the ARD for a public limited company.

The ARD is the period-end date to which all financial statements are prepared and normally covers a period of 12 months, although this can be extended to a maximum of 18 months. Filing of financial statements for a first year entity must be within 21 months of incorporation. Late delivery of financial statements to Companies House will result in a late filing penalty, which is, technically, a criminal offence for which Directors can be prosecuted.

ACCOUNTING

Regulations regarding the presentation of the primary financial statements in the UK are found in several sources such as UK company law and UK and international accounting standards. Branches or places of business of overseas firms have special registration procedures.

Accounting Principles

All financial statements in the UK are prepared in accordance with two fundamental accounting concepts:

- Going concern – the financial statements are prepared as if the company will be trading in the foreseeable future (at least 12 months from the date of signing the financial statements);
- Accruals basis – income and expenditure should relate to the period in which it occurred, not the period in which it was received/paid.

Whichever accounting policy is selected, they must be transparent and reflect industry and sector norms.

Financial Reporting

Until recently, Financial Reporting Standards were developed solely by the Accounting Standards Board (ASB). These standards, in conjunction with the requirements of UK companies legislation (principally the UK Companies Acts), helped make up what is known as UK GAAP, which gives guidance to companies and auditors on how UK financial statements should be prepared to give a 'true and fair' view of the company's financial position.

However, due to increasing globalisation in the world economy, it became necessary to produce a set of International Financial Reporting Standards (IFRS) so that potential investors can compare firms on a global scale.

EU firms with securities that are publicly traded on a regulated stock exchange are required to apply EU-adopted IFRS when producing consolidated financial statements. In the UK, this means any company listed on any of the markets of the London Stock Exchange. Individual subsidiary companies are not required to prepare financial statements under IFRS.

At present, only the types of company detailed above are required to adopt IFRS. However, even companies not required to do so can choose to adopt these new standards.

A company that chooses to use IFRS to produce its financial statements for one financial period cannot change back to UK standards in the following year. There are limited exceptions to this, such as if the company becomes a subsidiary of a group that uses UK standards as opposed to IFRS, in which case the company can revert back to using UK standards.

Listed and AIM companies must use IFRS in their group financial statements – AIM companies because the listing rules require it and full listed companies because regulations require that all companies listed on an EU regulated market use IFRS, as adopted in the EU, in their group financial statements.

Other entities that are not required to use IFRS have the following choices:

- IFRS – any entity, except a charitable one, can adopt IFRS if they wish;
- FRS 101 – ('IFRS' with reduced disclosures) This is only available to subsidiaries of parent companies who have adopted IFRS, and it allows the subsidiaries to adopt IFRS but with reduced disclosures;
- FRS 102 – the standard that has replaced UK GAAP;

  * FRS102 – for smaller companies (which is an amendment to FRS102 by way of a new section 1A for small entities) requires entities to apply the full recognition and measurement principles contained in FRS102, but retain presentation and disclosure requirements that are appropriate to a small company.

- FRS103 Insurance contracts is a fourth standard added to the framework which is relevant to entities that are applying FRS102 and have insurance contracts;

  * FRS103 should be applied by an entity that applies FRS102 and issues insurance contracts and/or holds reinsurance contracts. This FRS should also be applied to financial instruments (other than insurance contracts) that it issues with a discretionary participation feature.

- FRS105 – the financial reporting standard applicable to micro entities.

Companies that meet the 'micro' criteria have the choice of applying FRS105 for micro entities. For a company to qualify as micro-sized, at least two of the conditions below must be met:

- Turnover must be less than £632,000;
- Net assets less than £316,000;
- Average number of employees less than 10.

For a company to be eligible to apply FRS105 it cannot meet any of the following criteria:

- Companies excluded from the small companies regime;
- Financial institutions including credit, insurance and banking institutions;
- Charities;
- Small parent companies who choose to prepare consolidated financial
- statements;
- Companies that are included in consolidated financial statements; and
- Public companies.

FRS105 is effective for accounting periods commencing on or after 1 January 2016.

FRS105 requires only two primary statements and the information contained on these primary statements will be condensed. Amongst other simplifications assets cannot be measured at fair value or at revaluation under FRS105.

As before, FRS105 and FRS102 for smaller companies are not mandatory and a company could instead use full FRS 102 or indeed IFRS if it so desired.

Other entities that are not 'small' or 'micro' and are not required to use IFRS end up with various choices, depending on their situation. Charitable companies are expected to use FRS 102 and a new Charities SORP (SORP 2015) was issued to update the changes to UK GAAP in line with the adoption of FRS 102 for accounting periods commencing on or after 1 January 2015.

AUDIT

Audits must be carried out by someone authorised to provide an audit, by:

- Being a member of a Recognised Supervisory Body (RSB); and
- Having the necessary qualifications/eligibility of that RSB to be an auditor.

An RSB can be a professional body such as the Institute of Chartered Accountants for England and Wales. UK companies are required to be audited unless they are designated as 'small' in size (and can satisfy two out of the three criteria), or are dormant.

This 'small' exemption is subject to a number of detailed conditions which must be met in order for it to apply.

If a UK small company is part of a group of companies (UK or worldwide), the group in its entirety must meet the definition of 'small', otherwise the small UK company will be subject to an audit regardless of its individual size unless there is a parent company guarantee.

There are circumstances where a parent company registered in an EEA state can guarantee the liabilities of a UK trading subsidiary and this can allow it to take advantage of an exemption from audit regardless of its size.

If a group of companies (UK or worldwide) contains a listed entity with its shares traded on a recognised stock exchange anywhere in the world, then any UK company which is part of that group will require an audit regardless of its own individual size unless there is a parent company guarantee.

Note here that exemption from the audit requirement does not exclude the company from having an audit if it so wishes.

Auditors are normally appointed in the following ways:

- They are appointed by a newly formed company, or by an existing company that requires a new auditor;
- They are reappointed by a company for which they are already existing auditors; or
- They are ordered to be auditors of a firm by the Secretary of State.

This last case occurs when a company requiring an audit fails to agree to appoint an auditor.

The company's auditors are appointed/reappointed each year by either majority vote of the shareholders, or for a private company the provisions of deemed re-appointment of an existing auditor may apply. Directors have the authority to fill a vacancy that arose during the year but this will need to be later confirmed by the shareholders before the new auditor may continue in office for subsequent financial years.

Upon appointment, the auditor should send the company an engagement letter confirming their appointment as auditors, and setting out other items relating to the audit, such as the work they will carry out, confirmation of their independence and payment of audit fees. The auditor should also seek professional clearance from the previous auditors before accepting any audit appointment.

An auditor ceases to audit a company in the following ways:

- They resign from the post of auditor of the company; or
- They are removed by the company.

If an auditor resigns they must provide a written notice to the company and a statement of circumstances in return to their resignation to the Registrar of Companies and anyone else entitled to copies of the company financial statements.

If the members of a company wish to remove the existing auditor, the auditor has the right to have written circularisation to all members and the right to be seen and heard at the company's general meeting at which their removal is proposed.

3.2 BUSINESS TAXATION

Andrew Ross, Mazars LLP

INTRODUCTION

This chapter is divided into the following parts:

- The key forms in which an overseas company could set up in the UK with a view to carrying on business.
- The basis of taxation in the UK, summarising the key taxes an investor needs to be aware of.
- Setting out the basis of calculation of taxable profits, noting the key rules on tax deductibility of expenditure and certain important tax reliefs and anti-avoidance provisions.

VEHICLES FOR DOING BUSINESS IN THE UK

There are several different vehicles that could be used when doing business in the UK, each with their own legal and commercial peculiarities. When considering the most suitable form of vehicle to use, investors would be recommended to consider such factors in addition to taking account of the differing tax treatment of each.

Representative Office

It is important to distinguish between 'trading in' and 'trading with' the UK. An overseas person will not be subject to UK tax on profits simply because they are transacting with UK entities, even if the goods are delivered to UK locations or services are carried out within the UK.

This can be the case even if the overseas investor has set up an office within the UK, although this will depend on the nature of the activities carried out by that office.

If, however, those activities cross a certain line, this could result in the creation of a taxable branch or permanent establishment.

In this context, it should be noted that in 2013 the OECD commenced a project referred to as 'BEPS' – Base Erosion and Profit Shifting. The objective of this project is to review the current rules on allocation of taxable profits between territories, including the extent to which profits are allocated to locations which differ from where the actual business activity takes place. The UK Government supports the introduction of BEPS and changes are already being made to UK tax law as a result (e.g. in relation to tax relief for interest expense and in relation to cross-border hybrid tax structures). This will be particularly relevant to overseas companies intending to set up operations in the UK via a representative office or branch/permanent establishment.

In addition, for profits arising on or after 1 April 2015, the diverted profit tax (DPT) applies, under which a 25% tax is charged on profits relating to UK activities of multinational enterprises which are diverted (avoiding the UK tax net) using 'contrived' arrangements. One example of this might be where a non-UK resident company operates in the UK in such a way that whilst it earns (significant) profits from the UK, its operations are structured in such a way as to avoid the creation of a taxable permanent establishment (on which, see below).

Branch / Permanent Establishment

The UK branch (referred to for tax purposes as a 'permanent establishment' or PE) of a foreign company will be subject to tax in the UK on profits that are attributable to the branch. UK domestic legislation gives a definition of a PE which is broadly similar to that contained in many double tax treaties. Typically, a foreign company will have a UK PE if:

- it has a fixed place of business in the UK through which the business of the company is wholly or partly carried on; and/or
- an agent acting on behalf of the company has and habitually exercises in the UK authority to do business on behalf of the company (except where that agent is of independent status acting in the ordinary course of his business).

There are exceptions to this where, for example, the fixed place of business is for the storage of goods or purely for purchasing or information-gathering functions. In such a situation, the foreign company may not have a UK taxable presence.

Subsidiary

A UK incorporated subsidiary will be subject to UK tax on all of its trading profits, wherever those profits are earned (subject to the possibility of claiming an exemption from UK tax for profits within overseas branches).

A non-UK incorporated company can also be treated as UK tax resident (and so taxable in the UK on its worldwide profits) if its 'central management and control' is located in the UK. Therefore, care needs to be taken where a non-UK company is operating in the UK to ensure that the company as a whole does not become UK tax resident.

Branch v Subsidiary
From a UK tax point of view, there is generally little difference in the basis of taxation between a branch and a subsidiary. UK corporation tax is charged at the same rates on branch or subsidiary profits and no withholding tax is charged on the remittance of funds by a branch to its head office or on dividends paid by a subsidiary to its parent company.

Therefore, a decision on the most appropriate form will generally need to be based on commercial & legal factors and the non-UK tax implications.

One potential tax advantage of using a UK branch (particularly in start-up ventures) is that tax losses of the branch may (depending on the law of the relevant overseas country) be available to offset non-UK profits arising in the same foreign company. At the same time, those tax losses can also be carried forward to shelter future profits of the branch from UK tax (although the flip-side of this is that there may be less double tax relief to shelter those same future profits from tax in the overseas country).

Joint Ventures
Where an investor wishes to enter into a UK joint venture-type arrangement with a 3rd party, the parties will likewise need to agree on the form of the joint venture, for example:

- Contractual joint venture: Each party (through its own legal entity) enters into a contract with a view to carrying out a business transaction or a project.
- Partnership: This is a more formal legal structure involving the carrying on of
- a business in common with a view to profit. Each party (again through its own legal entity) will enter into a formal partnership agreement. The basis for sharing profits will be set out in this partnership agreement.
- Company: A company is set up to carry out the joint venture business, with the joint venture parties owning shares in that company. The relationship between the joint venture parties may also be governed by a shareholders' agreement.

Again, commercial and legal considerations must be taken into account in determining the most appropriate vehicle. The tax treatment of each will also vary.

BASIS OF TAXATION

The main taxes payable in the UK may be summarised as follows.

Tax on Company Profits

Corporation tax is payable on the taxable profits (both income and capital) of a UK subsidiary or the UK branch of an overseas company. The rate of corporation tax is the same for both a branch and subsidiary.

Tax is calculated based on the profits of an 'accounting period', which will normally coincide with the period for which the company prepares its financial statements.

Historically, there were two rates of corporation tax – the main rate and the 'small profits rate', although these rates have now converged, resulting in a single rate of tax applicable to all companies.

The current and proposed future rates of corporation tax are:

Profits arising in year from 1 April to 31 March:	2017/18	2018/19 and 2019/20	2020/21
Rate of corporation tax	19%	19%*	17%*

It was previously announced that the corporation tax rate would reduce to 19% for the years starting 1 April 2018 and 2019 and to 17% for the year starting 1 April 2020. However, these reduced rates for are yet to be formally legislated.

In charging corporation tax on companies with year ends other than 31 March, a proportionate part of profits for an accounting period is taxed at each of the applicable rates. For example, the rate of tax on taxable profits of a company with a 31 December 2017 year end is 19.25% (given that the 2016/17 corporation tax rate was 20%).

From 1 April 2013 a new 'Patent Box' regime was introduced, giving reduced corporation tax rates which ultimately result (from 1 April 2017) in a 10% corporation tax rate for 'patent derived profits' (including royalties) for both new and existing patents.

The original patent box regime was closed to new entrants from June 2016, following which companies with IP which already qualified (patents which are already registered) may continue to apply the reduced 10% tax rate until June 2021. A modified patent box regime (which gives similar benefits but which is more restricted in its application) was introduced for new entrants with effect from 1 June 2016.

In the past, rates of corporation tax were impacted by the number of associated companies. Post 1 April 2015, the number of associated companies only really impacts on whether a company is required to pay its corporation tax liability by quarterly instalment payments (QIPs). A company must make QIPs during the accounting period where it is 'large,' i.e. its profits exceed £1.5m (divided by the number of associated companies) and it was either large in the previous accounting period or its current period profits exceed £10m (again, divided by the number of associated companies). From 1 April 2015, an associated company arises where one company is a 51% subsidiary of another, or both companies are 51% subsidiaries of a third.

From 1 April 2017, the precise timing of payments under QIPs will depend on the profitability of the company. Companies with annual taxable profits over £20m in an accounting period will have to pay quarterly instalments earlier than other large companies to whom QIPs applies. (This £20m limit is likewise reduced proportionately depending on the number of companies in the group.)

For large companies (as defined above) the corporation tax liability for an accounting period is due and payable quarterly, the first instalment being six months and 14 days after the beginning of the period (and hence estimates of the forecast tax for a particular year will need to be made for at least the first two quarterly payments). However, for companies with profits above the £20m threshold, the first quarterly instalment is due in month 3 after the beginning of the period. For companies not within the quarterly payment obligation, tax is due in a single payment, nine months after the end of the company's accounting period. Interest is payable to/receivable from HMRC on any under/over and late/early payment of tax.

Tax on individuals

Individuals are liable to income tax on trading profits, employment income, interest, dividends and other income and are subject to capital gains tax on capital gains. The rates for the tax year commencing 6 April 2017 are:

Taxable income (£)	Tax rate on income	Effective tax rate on UK/overseas dividends	Tax rate on capital gains* **
up to 33,500	20%	7.5%	10%
33,501 - 150,000	40%	32.5%	20%
over 150,000	45%	38.1%	20%

A reduced rate of 10% is payable on the first £10m of gains made in a taxpayer's lifetime, on the disposal of qualifying business assets ('Entrepreneurs' relief').
** An 8% surcharge applies on the sale of residential property and carried interest.

Only the first £5,000 of dividend income will be tax-free for basic rate tax payers (it is likely that this will reduce to £2,000 from 6 April 2018, although the relevant legislation has not yet been enacted). Above this level, a basic rate tax payer will pay tax at 7.5% and a higher rate tax payer will be subject to tax at 32.5%. Over £150,000 of income, dividends will be subject to 38.1% income tax.

An individual who is trading in partnership is assessed for income tax on their share of the tax-adjusted trading profits for the accounting period of the partnership ending in the tax year. The basis of calculation of taxable trading profits is broadly the same as for a company.

The rules for the calculation of individuals' capital gains differ from the rules for companies in that 'indexation allowance' (an allowance for inflation) is not available to individuals, whilst there are other reliefs available to individuals that are not available to companies (e.g. Entrepreneurs' relief).

Interest income is taxable when received. In most cases, UK interest is paid to individuals net of basic rate income tax. The gross income is taxable, with credit given against the tax liability in the tax year for the tax deducted. Where the tax liability is less than the tax deducted, the excess withholding tax is repayable.

Income tax on trading and other income that is not subject to PAYE (see below) is due in two instalments – on 31 January within the relevant tax year and 31 July following the end of the tax year.

Payroll Taxes/National Insurance Contributions
An employer is obliged to make deductions from pay for employee income tax and employee national insurance contributions (NIC), using the 'pay as you earn' (PAYE) system.

Employer NIC is an additional cost payable by the employer based on each employee's wages plus benefits in kind. The rates of employer NIC vary depending on whether the employer offers a final salary pension scheme and has contracted out of the state earnings related pension scheme. The rates for the year commencing 6 April 2017 are:

Weekly earnings	Monthly earnings	Rate
Up to £157	Up to £680	Nil
Excess over £157	Excess over £680	13.8%

The employer has to make monthly remittances to HMRC (by mandatory electronic funds transfer) of the amounts they deduct for employee income tax and NIC, along with the employer NIC. All employers are required by law to report to HMRC on a real-time information basis (RTI). This means that the employer files a RTI notification to HMRC via the Government Gateway every time an employee is paid. The RTI return is filed either in advance o,f or along with, the remittance to HMRC.

VAT

All businesses investing or trading in the UK must register for UK VAT if they have a business establishment or usual place of residence in the UK. This test differs from the corporation tax tests of residence and it is therefore possible for an overseas investor to be required to register for UK VAT even though it may not have a branch that is liable to corporation tax.

A business will be required to register if it has VAT taxable turnover of more than £85,000 in a 12 month period.

VAT registered businesses are generally required to file VAT returns quarterly by way of electronic returns and therefore any VAT payable will usually be payable by not later than one month and seven days after the end of the relevant quarter. However, VAT-registered businesses with an annual VAT liability in excess of £2.3 million must make interim payments at the end of the second and third months of each VAT quarter as payments on account of the quarterly VAT liability. A balancing payment for the quarter is then made with the VAT return.

Stamp Duty Land Tax (SDLT)

SDLT is payable on the acquisition of any interest in land situated in the UK regardless of whether the acquirer is an individual, a partnership or a company or whether the acquirer is UK or non-UK resident.

When a capital sum is paid to acquire non- residential land or an interest in such land (whether the acquisition is ownership of the land or on the grant or assignment of a lease) the rate of SLT is:

TRANSFER VALUE	SDLT RATE
Up to £150,000	0%
The next £100,000 (i.e. the proportion from £150,001 to £250,000)	2%
Excess over £250,000	5%

There are exceptions for intra-group transfers.

Different rates of SDLT apply to the acquisition of residential land.

Care must also be taken, in particular, where residential land which was valued at 1 April 2012 (or at acquisition date, if later) at more than £500,000 is held by a company (or other collective investment vehicle). In this situation an Annual Tax on Enveloped Dwellings may also be payable.

On grant of a non-residential lease, in addition to the SDLT on any premium (at the above rates), the tenant is liable to pay SDLT based on the net present value of the total rent payable under the lease.

NET PRESENT VALUE OF RENT	SDLT RATE
Up to £150,000	0%
The portion from £150,001 to £5,000,000	1%
Excess over £5,000,000	2%

Stamp Duty

Stamp duty, at 0.5%, is payable by the person acquiring shares or convertible loan notes of a UK registered company. There are exceptions for intra-group transfers. No duty is payable on the transfer of ownership of other assets, for example loan notes, goodwill or trade debtors. There is no duty on the issue of shares or convertible loan notes.

Withholding Taxes

The UK does not impose withholding tax on dividends.

A 20% withholding tax is generally imposed on interest payments made :

1.   By a company
2.   By or on behalf of a partnership of which a company is a member;
3.   By a person to another person whose usual place of abode is outside the UK.

However, the rate may be reduced under an applicable double tax treaty or the EU Interest and Royalty Directive, provided that certain conditions and formalities are complied with prior to the payment of the interest.

There is no withholding from payments of interest by a UK company to UK companies or to UK branches of overseas companies (which will include, in particular, UK branches of overseas banks), or on payments of interest on certain quoted loan stock. Where securities are issued at a discount, no withholding is applied on the discount element.

For royalties, a 20% income tax withholding applies, subject to lower rates in the relevant applicable double tax treaty or under the EU Interest and Royalty Directive. Rent paid to a non-UK resident person in relation to a UK property is subject to a 20% withholding deduction, unless the landlord has met the requirements of HMRC's non-resident landlords' scheme.

Under the construction industry scheme, there may be a withholding requirement on payments made by contractors to sub-contractors in relation to building projects.

No withholding tax is applied on service fees, technical fees or management charges.

DETERMINATION OF TAXABLE PROFITS OF A BRANCH/SUBSIDIARY

The rules for the calculation of the taxable profits of both a branch and subsidiary are essentially the same. The key issue for a branch is the extent to which profits of the relevant overseas legal entity should be allocated to the head office or the UK branch.

Taxable Trading Profits
The taxable result from trading is based on the profits for the year, as shown in the company's financial statements (provided the financial statements are prepared in accordance with IFRS or UK GAAP).

Costs that are not deductible for tax purposes include entertainment expenditure, fines and penalties, expenditure of a capital nature and non-specific provisions. Depreciation, amortisation and gains/losses from the disposal of fixed tangible assets are not allowed or taxed. For tax depreciation, there is a statutory relief for certain classes of assets (see capital allowances, below).

From July 2015, no tax relief is available on the cost of the acquisition of purchased goodwill and customer related intangibles.

Remuneration paid to employees is deductible on an accruals basis, providing payment to the employee is no later than nine months after the year end. Remuneration paid more than nine months after the year end is tax deductible in the period when payment is made. Tax relief for payments made by the employer into a pension scheme is generally given when the payment is made (rather than on an accruals basis), although relief may be spread where there is a large increase (> £500,000) in the level of contributions from one period to the next.

Capital Allowances
Capital Allowances is the UK term for the statutory code for deducting the cost of capital expenditure from trading profits. The main class of asset that is eligible for capital allowances is plant and machinery. This includes plant within a building or structure (e.g. electrical, heating, water and air conditioning systems, lifts, escalators,

sanitary ware). No allowances are given for the cost of buildings.

Eligible expenditure on plant and machinery qualifies for tax relief at one of two rates. Certain specified expenditure can obtain allowances at a rate of 8% per annum and all others at 18% per annum. For both, allowances are calculated on a reducing balance basis.

Assets in the 8% expenditure category include:

- Those with an expected life when new of more than 25 years;
- Some plant within buildings;
- Cars with emissions of more than 130 g/km (from 1 April 2013) of CO2.

Up to £200,000 of a company's annual expenditure on eligible assets, other than cars or assets for leasing out, is subject to 100% tax relief in the year of purchase. This is known as the 'annual investment allowance'. Where the company is a member of a group only one annual investment allowance is given to the whole group.

Full relief is also available in the year in which it is incurred (100% tax allowances) for certain other expenditure, notably:

- Environmentally beneficial or energy saving plant (which includes cars with CO2 emissions of no more than 75 g/km;
- Plant for research and development activities.

On disposal of plant, the net sale proceeds, up to a maximum of cost, are deducted from the accumulated net pool of qualifying expenditure.

Interest and Finance Income and Expense

In general, interest is taxed or relieved in accordance with the treatment in the company's financial statements.

Until 31 March 2017, tax relief for finance expenses in 'large' (as defined) corporate groups could be restricted due to the worldwide debt cap. This restriction is considered after making any transfer pricing (thin capitalisation) adjustments (on which, see below). Broadly speaking, the intention of the worldwide debt cap is that the tax deductible finance expense relieved against a group's UK profits should be no greater than the external finance expense in the consolidated results of the group. However, this regime will not apply if the UK net debt is less than 75% of the group's consolidated gross debt.

New rules on corporate interest restrictions have been proposed which will replace the worldwide debt cap with effect from 1 April 2017 (assuming that the legislation is passed broadly as currently drafted). In general terms, a UK company/group will not be able to claim a tax deduction for its net interest expense in excess of 30% of EBITDA (calculated based on tax rather than accounting principles) although there are other tests that can be applied which might result in a higher tax deduction for interest. There is a de minimis whereby the rules only apply where the annual net interest expense exceeds £2m. This is a complex area on which further advice should be sought.

Transfer Pricing on Debt

The UK has transfer pricing rules, which substitute arm's length amounts to transactions with connected persons. These are broadly aligned to the OECD transfer pricing guidelines. The transfer pricing rules apply to both the interest rate (such that interest at a rate in excess of market value would not be deductible) and the amount of the borrowing (i.e. thin capitalisation, whereby a tax deduction will not be given for the whole of the interest on the element of debt in excess of that which would have been loaned by a 3rd party acting at arm's length).

Exemptions from transfer pricing rules or reduced documentation requirements apply to small and medium sized enterprises although in some circumstances, HMRC can issue a direction for medium sized companies to comply with transfer pricing legislation.

There are no safe-havens with regard to debt equity ratios or interest cover ratios (e.g. EBIT:interest or EBITDA:interest). Each has to be negotiated separately with HMRC. In order to be non-discriminatory with regard to the EU, the transfer pricing rules apply to all connected party transactions, including those between UK enterprises.

The transfer pricing rules can also apply to the provision of finance by lenders who do not control (or even have no shareholding in) the borrower where those lenders are acting together with other persons who between them have control over the borrowing company.

Dividends Received

The UK has a comprehensive dividends received exemption which applies to dividends a UK-resident company receives from UK or non-UK companies (although the exemption may not apply were a small company receives a dividend from a company based in a tax haven). Various conditions must be met, although there is no minimum holding period or minimum ownership percentage.

Sale of Capital Assets

The taxable gain on the disposal of a capital asset is calculated as net proceeds received less the acquisition cost and costs incurred on improvements. Indexation allowance (an allowance for inflation) may also be given to disposals by companies. Gains on certain assets can also be deferred by reinvesting the proceeds in certain replacement assets ('rollover relief').

The UK has a form of participation exemption, which can exempt from tax the gain or loss on the disposal by a company of shares in a trading company or trading sub-group; the exemption is called the Substantial Shareholdings Exemption (SSE). SSE, along with the dividends received exemption, are core features that make the UK an attractive location for holding companies.

The SSE rules contain several detailed requirements and therefore professional guidance should be sought as to whether it applies, not least because a group's non-trading activities do not necessarily need to be substantial for the group not to be regarded as a 'trading group' and hence not qualify for the relief. An advance clearance application can be made to HMRC where there is uncertainty as to whether SSE applies to a particular disposal.

Transfers of capital assets (including intangibles) between UK members of a group take place on a tax neutral basis regardless of the value of the asset or the price paid (see below in relation to tax groups). However, if the transferee subsequently leaves the group still holding the asset within six years of the transfer, this can create a 'de-grouping' tax charge based on a deemed disposal (and re-acquisition) of the asset at its market value at the date of the intra-group transfer. Depending on the circumstances, this de-grouping charge may be taxable either in the transferee company that leaves the group or in the company selling the shares in the transferee.

Reliefs may apply to the transfer of a trading business to a company (a business incorporation) and to corporate acquisitions effected by a share-for-share exchange.

Loss utilisation – utilisation of losses within the company

New rules have been announced for the treatment of tax losses, effective from 1 April 2017 (although the relevant legislation has not yet been enacted). As a result, there are two sets of rules, depending on when the losses arose. These are summarised below. Irrespective of whether the tax losses arose before or after 1 April 2017, there is now (from 1 April 2017) a restriction on the amount of brought forward tax losses that can be used to shelter taxable profits. The first £5m of a group's taxable profits may be sheltered in full using brought forward losses and the excess over £5m will be limited to 50% of annual profits. Thus, a company with taxable profits of £7m and brought forward losses of £10m will only be able to shelter £6m of its profits from tax (being £5m plus 50% of its profits above £5m).

Pre-1 April 2017 losses

- A company may claim to set a trading loss against all of its taxable profits within the same accounting period, and against the profits of the immediate preceding period, providing the company was carrying on the same trade in the previous period.
- A trading loss not applied to the current or previous accounting period and which has not been surrendered via group relief is carried forward and used against profits of the same trade arising in later periods, without time limit.

- Tax relief for a company's non-trading finance expense in excess of the company's profits for an accounting period may be claimed against financial profits of the previous year. Any unrelieved finance expense which has not been surrendered via group relief is carried forward, without time limit, to be used against future non-trading profits of the company.

Post-1 April 2017 losses:

- The rules for current year use of losses and the carry back of losses are unchanged.
- Carried forward losses of all kinds (excluding capital losses) can be used to offset total profits (including trading profits, non-trading profits and capital gains) of the company.

Loss utilisation – surrender of losses via group relief
The rules for group relief also now differentiate between pre and post 1 April 2017 losses. The 50% restriction on the maximum loss offset (described above) applies equally where there is a surrender of carried forward losses via group relief.
Pre-1 April 2017 losses
   All or some of a trading tax loss or non-trading finance expense arising in a UK company can be transferred to other UK companies within a 75% group, for use against the other companies' total profits within the same accounting period only. This is known as 'group relief'.

Post-1 April 2017 losses

- Losses of all kinds (excluding capital losses) arising within an accounting period can be used to offset total profits (including trading profits, non-trading profits and capital gains) of other group companies arising within the same accounting period, via group relief.
- Carried forward losses of all kinds (excluding capital losses) can be offset against future total profits of other group companies, i.e. group relief for carried forward losses.

Capital losses
Capital losses are set against chargeable (capital) gains of the company for the same period, with any excess being carried forward, without time limit, for use against net chargeable gains of subsequent periods. These rules are unchanged.

Loss anti-avoidance
There are several anti-avoidance provisions which may deny the use or carry forward of tax losses. For example:

- Losses will be forfeit when a group purchases a company with existing tax losses, and the main reason for the acquisition is to access these tax losses.
- A company with no assets capable of producing income cannot surrender carried forward losses. Thus a dormant company with tax losses will not be able to derive any value from any unutilised tax losses.
- Five year restriction on the group relief surrender of carried forward losses on the acquisition of a company with tax losses.

Research and Development Tax reliefs
Enhanced tax relief is available to companies which conduct Research and Development (R & D) for the purposes of resolving scientific or technological uncertainty with a view to achieving an advancement in science or technology, or an appreciable improvement in existing technology.

There are two schemes of relief – one for small and medium sized companies (SMEs), including so-called 'larger SMEs', and one for large companies.

For these purposes, an SME is broadly a company with less than 500 employees and not more than either €100m turnover or balance sheet total of €86m, taking into account certain linked and partner enterprises (e.g. group companies). An SME may claim an enhanced tax deduction of 230% of its qualifying R&D spend. If the SME is loss making, it may instead trade in losses for a cash rebate of 14.5% of the enhanced tax deduction (i.e. just over 33p in the £ of the actual qualifying spend), based on the rate applicable from 1 April 2015, thereby creating an additional source of cash-flow for the company.

With effect from 1 April 2016, large companies may claim under the Research and Development Expenditure Credit (RDEC) credit scheme. Under this scheme, in a large company's financial statements, the RDEC credit will be recognised as a reduction in R&D expenditure in the Profit and Loss Account. For tax purposes, the RDEC credit will be treated as a taxable receipt of the trade. For large companies with no corporation tax liability, or with a CT liability less than their RDEC credit, the key advantage of this new scheme is that such companies can claim an immediate benefit from their R&D claim through a payable credit of 11% of qualifying R&D expenditure. For large companies, RDEC operates instead of the super-deduction scheme.

A UK R&D tax relief claim must be made via the company's tax return and must be made within 24 months of the accounting year end of a company.

3.3 BUSINESS TAXATION AND PLANNING

Andrew Ross, Mazars LLP

INTRODUCTION

This chapter follows on from the overview of the UK business tax system set out in chapter 3.2 and covers various areas of UK tax planning that an investor should consider, both with a view to realising tax savings and also avoiding unnecessary tax costs. The chapter is divided into the following parts:

- Tax planning on the acquisition of a business (including the form of the acquisition, financing and exit considerations)
- Employee incentivisation and investor reliefs.

ACQUISITION OF A BUSINESS: ASSETS V SHARES

Asset Acquisitions

An asset (business) purchase could be effected using a UK company or a UK branch of an overseas company. As discussed above, a UK branch of an overseas company and a UK company are subject to UK tax on profits in broadly the same way. Therefore, an overseas investor wishing to purchase a business in the form of an asset purchase will need to take into account commercial, legal and non-UK tax factors in deciding a preferred route.

One of the key non-tax advantages of an asset purchase is that any liabilities or exposures within the selling company do not automatically transfer across to the purchaser.

Share Acquisitions

A company is a separate legal entity and, as such, when an investor acquires a company they are acquiring all of that company's history and liabilities. Therefore, any unknown or contingent liabilities (as well as those of which the purchaser is aware) will effectively be inherited by the purchaser. For this reason, a purchaser will normally seek to obtain from the vendor an indemnity against such liabilities, whether or not they had crystallised as of the date of the sale (together with warranties over the company's tax position).

One of the first questions an investor will need to address is the vehicle to be used to make the acquisition, i.e. should the acquisition be made:

- directly by the overseas investor;
- by an intermediate holding company set up in the UK; or
- by an intermediate holding company set up in a 3rd territory.

Each investor will have its own particular fact pattern that may influence the choice and, as such, specific advice should be taken. But examples of factors that could, from a tax point of view, influence a purchaser towards one or other of these acquisition vehicles include:

- Where overseas tax rates are higher than UK rates, there could be an advantage to making the acquisition using the overseas investing company in order to benefit from any financing tax deductions in that territory;
- Where the overseas investor does not have sufficient profits to offset financing costs, a UK debt-financed acquisition vehicle may be preferable;
- If the investor wishes to create a sub-group to facilitate the cross-border expansion of the target business, it may be appropriate to set up an intermediate holding company (either in the UK or elsewhere);
- Whether the overseas territory has a favourable tax regime for the holding of shareholdings and how any local 'controlled foreign company' rules may affect this.

Asset v Share Purchase

When acquiring shares in a company, the existing tax profile of the target company will remain and so the purchaser effectively inherits this.

From a buyer's point of view, the potential tax advantages of buying assets or shares include:

Assets

- Can claim capital allowances for plant & machinery and other qualifying
- fixed assets based on the consideration allocated under the Business Purchase Agreement rather than on the existing tax value of those assets within the target company (assuming the former is higher).

- Avoids 0.5% stamp duty (although stamp duty land tax would be payable if land is being acquired).

Shares

- Existing tax losses transfer across (but subject to anti-avoidance legislation aimed at preventing the acquisition of companies solely or mainly to enable the purchaser to benefit from these tax losses).
- If the current tax value of fixed assets is greater than the purchase price allocated to those assets, a share acquisition avoids a reduction in the amount on which capital allowances can be claimed.
- Avoids stamp duty land tax, which could be significant if there is valuable non-residential land within the target business (although there will be a 0.5% stamp duty charge on the consideration paid for the shares).
- Greater flexibility to enable the vendors to reduce or defer tax where the vendors are to retain a direct or indirect stake in the target business (e.g. by exchanging shares in the target company for new shares in the purchaser).

Historically, one advantage of an assets deal was the ability to obtain tax relief for the goodwill element of the deal price. However, with effect from 8 July 2015 tax relief is no longer available for the acquisition of goodwill or customer related intangibles. The Government's stated purpose of this change was to put assets and share deals on a level footing as regards tax.

There will often be a conflict between the interests of the sellers and the buyers and it is important that a buyer appreciates this when negotiating a transaction. Buyers may prefer to purchase assets in order to benefit from the advantages listed above. By contrast, sellers will often prefer to sell shares because:

- Individual sellers may be able to benefit from Entrepreneurs' relief, such that they only pay tax on the resulting capital gain at 10%;
- A corporate seller may be able to claim an exemption from tax on any gain (taking advantage of the 'substantial shareholdings' exemption);
- An assets sale could give rise to a double tax charge on the seller – a first tax charge crystallising within the company, making the disposal and a second tax charge on the shareholder when extracting the net proceeds from the company.

See below for exit considerations that a buyer will also need to take into account when investing.

ACQUISITION OF A BUSINESS: FINANCING

The funding for an acquisition could be sourced in a number of different ways –
e.g. existing cash resources within the investor, 3rd party borrowings, equity injection
by the ultimate shareholder(s) – and this will need to be taken into account when
determining the optimal financing structure from a tax point of view.

Likewise, a review will need to be carried out of the tax regimes of both the overseas
territory and the UK in determining the optimal place for locating interest deductions
if the funding is to be effected through loan finance.

Questions that may need to be considered include:

- Is the acquisition to be made by the overseas investor directly or by a UK
  acquisition vehicle? Clearly, if the investor is to make the acquisition directly,
  any external funding will need to be taken out by the investor (even if the assets
  of the target business are used as security, which has been possible over recent
  years following the relaxation of the 'financial assistance' rules).
- What capacity do the investor and the target company each have to utilise
  interest deductions against forecast taxable profits? No benefit will accrue from
  deducting interest in a territory in which there are insufficient taxable profits
  against which those deductions can be offset.
- Is the corporate tax rate in the investor's home territory higher or lower than
  the UK rate? The preference may be to locate borrowings (and hence interest
  deductions) in the territory with the higher tax rate.
- What restrictions apply to the deductibility of interest in the UK and the overseas
  territory? In relation to the UK, for example, transfer pricing/thin capitalisation
  considerations and the corporate interest restrictions will need to be taken into
  account even if all or some of the finance is being provided by a 3rd party (see
  above for more detail).
- Will the borrower be required to withhold tax on payment of interest? 3rd party
  lenders will often include a gross-up clause such that any withholding tax
- will effectively be a cost to the borrower rather than a lender. Therefore, the
  borrowing may need to be structured in such a form or location that avoids or
  minimises any withholding taxes.

Consideration will also need to be given to how interest payments are to be financed.
Where the acquisition is funded out of existing cash resources provided by the
investor, this may be less of an issue. But where 3rd party lenders are involved, the
investor will need to have a clear plan on how payments of interest are to be funded. A
UK company can remit cash to an overseas parent free of UK tax, whether by way of
dividend or an upstream loan (although such a loan should itself be interest-bearing in
order to meet transfer pricing rules), but the parent will need to consider the taxation

of such receipts under its local tax regime. In this regard, it should not be assumed that an upstream loan would be tax-free to the investor, as some tax regimes can treat such loans as deemed dividends.

TAX GROUPS

Where an investor has an existing UK business, there will be advantages to structuring the acquisition so as to create a UK tax group. The main advantages are:

- Current period UK trading profits of one company can be sheltered from tax by using current period or brought forward losses of another UK group company arising in the same accounting period, by way of 'group relief' (on which see above);
- Capital assets can be transferred between UK members of the tax group without crystallising a tax charge. This would enable the tax-neutral combination of two UK businesses, if commercially desirable;
- Capital gains arising in one company can effectively be offset against brought forward non-trading losses (including capital losses, expenses of management and non-trading loan relationship debits) of another company in the UK group.

Where investors are part of a consortium, it is also possible in certain scenarios to use some of the current period tax losses arising in the consortium-owned company to shelter taxable profits arising in one of the consortium members (or vice versa).

The definitions of group relief groups and capital gains groups differ and so care must be taken where companies are not 100% owned, since in some situations not all of the above benefits of tax grouping will be available.

Group relief group: Comprises companies in which a shareholding of at least 75% is held directly or indirectly by the parent company (provided that the shareholder is also entitled to at least 75% of profits available for distribution and assets on a winding up). Non UK resident companies can be taken into account when tracing 75% ownership. In Figure 3.3.1, tax losses can be surrendered between UK 1 (owned 80% directly) and UK 3 (owned 81% indirectly). However, UK 2 is owned only 72% by Overseas Co. and therefore cannot surrender losses to UK 3 (or vice versa).

FIGURE 3.3.1 – EXAMPLE OF HOW GROUP RELIEF MAY BE APPLIED ACCORDING TO LEVELS OF OWNERSHIP

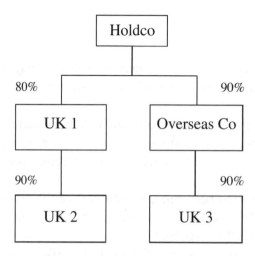

Capital gains group : This comprises companies which are held at least 75% by their immediate parent and which are indirectly held more than 50% by the top company in the group (provided also that the top group company is also entitled to more than 50% of profits available for distribution and assets on a winding up). Thus, in the above diagram UK 1, UK 2 and UK 3 are all part of the same capital gains group.

A tax group cannot be formed unless there is a common corporate parent company. Therefore, if an individual investor directly owns a number of UK companies, that investor will need to interpose a common holding company (which need not be a UK company) in order to create a tax group as in Figure 3.3.2:

FIGURE 3.3.2 – CREATING A TAX GROUP

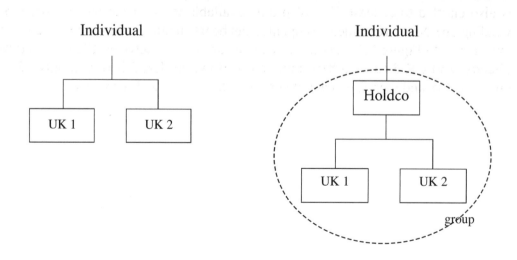

Even where there is no tax group in place, i.e. the individual holds both companies directly, the relationship between the two UK companies is such that they may still be regarded as associated or connected with each other for certain UK tax purposes. Hence:

- Transfer pricing rules can still apply to transactions or dealings between the two companies, to ensure that they are taxed on an arm's length basis;
- Transfers of assets must be for an arm's length consideration, failing which HMRC can substitute an arm's length value for the actual consideration.

EXIT CONSIDERATIONS

When structuring an acquisition, an investor should also be mindful of the likelihood of a future exit, what form that exit might take and the tax implications of such an exit event.

Business Held via a UK Branch of an Overseas Company

- The disposal would need to be effected via an asset sale (assuming that a sale of the overseas company would not be feasible).
- This will trigger a UK tax liability, with any gains on the sale of chargeable assets being taxed at the prevailing corporation tax rate. Overseas tax may also be payable (subject to double tax relief for UK tax paid, depending on the tax regime in the overseas territory).
- The branch could be packaged up into a new UK company, with the overseas investor selling that new company. This is a more complex area and could give rise to both UK tax charges in the new company and overseas tax charges in the overseas company.

Business Held within a UK Company

- Gives the flexibility to sell via a sale of assets or sale of shares.
- A sale of shares would generally not give rise to a UK tax liability within the target company (although a 'de-grouping charge' could arise if the UK company holds assets that were transferred into it from another UK group company within the preceding six years). If the overseas parent company benefits from a 'participation exemption' regime, this could enable a sale of the business, by way of a sale of shares, free of both UK and overseas tax.
- A sale of assets would generally be less tax effective, since a UK tax charge would arise in the UK company on any gains and an overseas tax charge could arise on a subsequent remittance of the disposal proceeds by the UK company.

EMPLOYEE INCENTIVISATION

Where an investor wishes to incentivise or recruit/retain key employees by means of the issuing of shares in the target business, there are a number of different share plans that can assist in achieving this objective in a tax efficient way. Ultimately, the most appropriate plan will be dependent on commercial requirements and the characteristics of the investors (e.g. UK v overseas; company v individual).

The area of share options and employee incentivisation is a complex one on which specialist advice should be sought.

INVESTOR TAX RELIEFS

There are also incentives aimed at encouraging UK resident individuals to invest in smaller, higher-risk trading companies, by offering tax relief for the purchase of new shares in such companies. So far as direct investment in companies is concerned, the main schemes are as follows:

Enterprise Investment Scheme (EIS) – Under EIS, an investor can claim income tax relief (i.e. a reduction in their income tax liability) of up to 30% of the amount invested (up to a maximum investment of £1,000,000 in a single tax year). The investor can also use the amount invested to defer other capital gains (whether or not on shares), with the deferred gain crystallising when the EIS shares are disposed of. In addition, disposals of EIS shares after three years may be free from capital gains tax. EIS is aimed at smaller, unquoted companies and enables such companies to raise up to £5m in any 12 month period.

Seed EIS (SEIS) – An individual subscribing for shares that qualify for SEIS can claim income tax relief of up to 50% of the amount invested (up to a maximum annual investment of £100,000). In addition, disposals of SEIS shares after three years may be free from capital gains tax. There is also a relief equal to 50% of capital gains tax payable on gains realised from the disposal of other assets, where the gains are reinvested in SEIS shares within the same tax year. This relief is also subject to the same £100,000 annual investment limit. SEIS is targeted at companies whose trade is less than two years old and whose assets (pre-subscription) do not exceed £200,000.

3.4 UK TAXATION FOR FOREIGN NATIONALS

Paul Barham, Mazars LLP

This chapter gives a brief overview of the UK tax considerations for a foreign national coming to the UK to work. By necessity, it only highlights the areas to consider and gives some indication of the current law. Advice should be sought in all respects, preferably before coming to the UK.

BASIS OF TAXATION

There are two concepts which need to be understood with regard to taxation in the UK. These are:

1. Residence
2. Domicile

Residence

Up until 5 April 2013, the question of residence in the UK was always a matter of case law and interpretation by the UK tax authorities, being broadly the number of days a person spends in the UK and their connections to the UK.

A new statutory residence test was introduced from 6 April 2013. The legislation contains three parts detailing rules which will result in conclusive non residence, conclusive residence and a list of 'connecting factors' which will determine residence for the individuals who do not fall within the conclusive tests.

The tests are looked at in a certain order and only if a test is not satisfied do you move on to the next test.

The new rules are extensive and exhaustive but generally if a person comes here to work full time they will be resident in the UK for tax purposes. Although the tests are meant to give certainty, HMRC have issued substantial interpretation and guidance which indicates they are not necessarily as straightforward as they first look. There are also anti avoidance rules to ensure that the rules are not used in a way that the UK Government did not intend.

'Overseas workday relief' is available if certain conditions are satisfied. It only applies to non UK domiciled individuals (see below) and will, in limited circumstances, give the 'remittance basis' to foreign employment duties.

Domicile

Domicile is a concept of general law, not a tax law and it is determined in a different way to residence.

At the time of writing, there are three types of domicile relevant to Income Tax (IT) and Capital Gains Tax (CGT). These are:

- Domicile of origin: An individual will normally acquire a domicile of origin from their father at birth. An individual's domicile of origin need not be the country in which the individual was born. This is determined by the relevant parent's domicile at the child's birth;
- Domicile of choice: An individual has the legal capacity to acquire a new domicile at the age of 16. Whilst it is possible to acquire a domicile of choice, this means much more than simple residence and a person must settle in another country permanently and sever ties with the country of origin. It is extremely difficult to acquire a domicile of choice;
- Domicile of dependence: A child under 16 cannot have a domicile of choice. Whilst under 16 their domicile will follow that of the person on whom the individual is legally dependent.

In addition, there is a concept of 'deemed domicile' which currently applies for Inheritance Tax (IHT) purposes only. This means that, where a person who is not domiciled in the UK under general law has been a UK resident in at least 17 of the last 20 tax years, they will be treated as being domiciled in the UK from the start of the 17th year.

In the 2015 Summer Budget, it was announced that changes would be made to the taxation of non-UK domiciled individuals who have been long term UK residents. These rules were due to be introduced in the Finance Act 2017 but were removed following the announcement of the general election in June 2017.

At the time of writing it is expected that the rules will be included in a subsequent Finance Act, and it is likely that they will be retrospectively introduced from 6 April 2017.

Under the measures that were due to apply from April 2017:

- The concept of being deemed domiciled in the UK being extended to cover IT and CGT as well as IHT for non-UK domiciled individuals who have been tax resident in the UK for 15 out of the last 20 tax years. From the start of the 16th year of residence, the individual will be treated as UK domiciled for all UK tax purposes.

- Reversion of a domicile of origin if an individual who has established a domicile choice outside the UK subsequently returns to the UK and becomes a UK resident again.
- All UK residential property held by non-UK domiciled individuals, whether directly or indirectly, including UK residential property held by offshore companies, offshore trusts and non-UK partnerships will be subject to UK IHT.

UK Taxation
In general, individuals resident in the UK will be liable on all their worldwide income and gains, known as the 'arising basis' of taxation. This means that they will pay UK tax on all of their income as it arises and on their gains as they are realised, wherever that income and those gains arise in the world.

Whilst an individual is non-domiciled he can choose whether to use the 'remittance basis' of taxation which is discussed later in this chapter.

Personal Allowances
In general, individuals resident in the UK are entitled to an income tax personal allowance. This is set at £11,500 for the 2017/18 tax year and is the amount of income each individual can receive before they are liable for tax. For individuals with income over this amount, tax is only charged on income in excess of £11,500.

However, a personal allowance will not be available in certain circumstances, and so the individual will be chargeable for tax on all of their income. The allowances are withdrawn either where the income is in excess of £100,000 (and it is withdrawn gradually), or where the remittance basis is being claimed under certain circumstances.

There is also a CGT annual allowance available to reduce chargeable gains, which is currently set at £11,300 for the 2017/18 tax year.

UK Tax Rates
Most forms of income are chargeable to tax at the following rates for the 2017/18 tax year:

£0 - £11,500	0%*
£11,501 - £45,000	20%*
£45,501 - £150,000	40%*
£150,000 +	45%

* If the personal allowances are still available.

Generally the rate of CGT for individuals is either 10% or 20% depending on the level of the individual's income and gains for the year. The lower rate is charged where income and taxable gains are less than the higher (40%) rate threshold (currently £45,000 – see above). When income exceeds the higher rate threshold, the 20% rate of CGT will apply to all gains. Where gains straddle the higher rate threshold, gains up to the threshold will be taxed at 10% and the remainder at 20%. If the gain arises on the disposal of residential property the rates increase by 8% to 18% and 28% respectively.

Access to the Remittance Basis

Where an individual is resident in the UK, but not domiciled in the UK, they will have a choice whether to use the arising basis of taxation and therefore be taxed on their worldwide income or gains as they arise or to use the remittance basis of taxation.

If a claim for the remittance basis is made then the individual will only be liable to tax on income and gains arising in the UK and any overseas income and gains remitted (i.e. brought to or used to benefit the individual) in the UK.

Where an individual has been in the UK for less than seven years, he/she can claim the remittance basis without paying for the privilege; however, this will result in the loss of his/her personal allowance and CGT allowance.

Long term residents in the UK (broadly resident seven out of nine years) must pay a £30,000 remittance basis charge (RBC). Furthermore, where an individual has been in the UK for 12 out of the last 14 years, this RBC is increased to £60,000 per annum. From 6 April 2015, a higher charge of £90,000 per annum applies to individuals who have been UK resident for 17 out of the last 20 years. Under the proposed rules which were due to be introduced from 6 April 2017 (but have not as yet), the remittance basis of taxation would no longer be available to individuals who would be deemed domiciled in the UK for IT and CGT purposes.

This is a particular area which needs specialist advice and would require a whole book to cover the rules, planning and anti-avoidance in sufficient detail.

ON ARRIVAL

There are no specific tax forms which need to be completed on arrival in the UK, other than to register with HMRC as necessary. There are likely to be two registrations, one to obtain a National Insurance number and one to register with HMRC for tax purposes. Both of these are discussed briefly below.

National Insurance Contributions

Both employers and employees, including self-employed people, make compulsory National Insurance Contributions (NIC) to HMRC in order to pay for a number of social benefits including the state pension and jobseeker's allowance. An individual is exempt from NIC once they reach State Pension Age (which differs depending on age and gender). For employees, their employers will calculate their NIC and deduct this from their gross pay using PAYE; self-employed persons must work out their contributions themselves.

All UK residents over the age of 16 must have a National Insurance number if they wish to work in the UK and have their contributions credited to their 'account'.

So, before working in the UK, an individual will need to obtain a National Insurance number. This can be obtained by contacting HMRC and arranging for either an 'Evidence of Identity' interview or agreeing to submit a postal application in limited circumstances.

If an employee is being sent to the UK by his employer, the position in respect of social security will vary depending on the country from which the employee is being sent. It may be possible for the employee to continue paying social security in their home country or it may even be compulsory. Either way, agreement will need to be obtained from the tax authorities to ensure the appropriate compliance requirements are met.

In some circumstances, a 52 week NIC holiday may be appropriate, where the employee continues to pay social security in their home country for the first 52 weeks and then commences paying NIC in the UK.

National Insurance rates for 2017/18 are 12% for employees up to the threshold of the higher (40%) rate of income tax and 2% thereafter, and for employers they are 13.8%. There is a small exemption (equivalent to £157 per week).

UK Tax Return Requirements

The UK tax year runs from the 6 April one year to 5 April of the next. The UK operates a self-assessment system, meaning that the responsibility to ensure the correct amount of tax is paid rests with the individual taxpayer. A UK tax return is likely to be required where the following circumstances apply:

- the individual is the director of a company in the UK; or
- chooses to make a claim for the remittance basis; or
- has income which is subject to tax (or a further tax liability) in the UK.

If an individual needs to be within the self-assessment system he/she need to complete a form on HMRC's website (www.hmrc.gov.uk) or a form SA1 (obtainable from HMRC) in order to register.

HMRC does not generally assist an individual in the preparation of his/her tax return but they can ask questions and challenge certain items on the return. In general they are able to do this for up to a year after the return has been filed, though in certain cases this can be extended for up to six years (or even 20 years in cases of deliberate misconduct).

HMRC may request that a return is prepared, but if they do not request a return, the individual is responsible for notifying HMRC that he/she is required to prepare a return for a particular tax year.

Completed tax returns need to be filed with HMRC by 31 October following the tax year end, when the individual files a paper tax return. In most cases tax returns should be filed online as this provides a much more efficient service from HMRC and in addition, this extends the filing deadline to 31 January following the end of the tax year.

If the tax return is filed late, an automatic penalty of £100 will be charged which may be increased if the delay in filing is extended beyond three months.

Any additional tax liability will need to be paid to HMRC by 31 January following the end of the tax year. Provided the return has been processed by this time the taxpayer should receive a reminder from HMRC, providing details of how to pay and a payslip to use when making the payment.

If the individual's return has not been processed by this time, he/she is still liable to pay their tax by 31 January.

If the tax is paid late, interest will be charged from the day after the due date. In addition, if the tax has not been paid within a month of the due date, a surcharge of 5% of the outstanding balance will be levied. Further charges may be raised if the tax liability remains unpaid after this date.

For an individual coming to the UK, the date of arrival and some brief details on their individual intentions should be disclosed in the annual income tax return for the tax year of arrival.

OTHER TAXES

Capital Gains Tax

Mention has been made earlier of CGT with regard to the annual exemption amount and the tax rates at which it is charged. CGT is broadly charged on any gain made on disposals of assets, such as shares or property.

There are several valuable exemptions, the most important one being an exemption for an individual's main residence. In addition, there are certain tax breaks which are available to encourage business investment. One of those is Entrepreneurs' Relief, described below.

Entrepreneurs' Relief

Entrepreneurs' Relief (ER) is available for 'qualifying business disposals'. The effect is to reduce the rate of Capital Gains Tax from a maximum rate of 20% to 10%, for total lifetime gains of £10 million.

A claim for ER can be made more than once, but the total cumulative gains cannot exceed £10 million. If this is the case, any gains over this limit will be subject to the higher rates of CGT.

A qualifying business disposal includes a disposal of shares in a trading company, or the holding company of a trading group.

ER is normally available provided that, for a period of 12 months ending with the date of the sale, the individual holds at least 5% of the ordinary share capital, can exercise at least 5% of the voting rights and is an officer or employee of the company or of one or more of the companies which are members of the trading group.

Compliance with the rules should be checked carefully.

Business Investment Relief

This relief is aimed at UK resident non domiciled individuals and has been introduced to encourage inward investment. Subject to certain conditions, overseas income and gains can be remitted into the UK for investment into eligible trading companies, without triggering a tax charge on those funds being remitted to the UK. There is no limit to the investment and although there are some anti avoidance provisions, the rules appear to be relatively generous.

Advice should be taken to ensure an investment qualifies before funds are remitted.

Inheritance Tax

The charge to Inheritance Tax (IHT) is based on where the asset is situated and the domicile of the person concerned; the place of residence is irrelevant (except when determining whether an individual has become deemed domiciled in the UK).

Deemed Domicile

As discussed above, currently the concept of deemed domicile applies for IHT purposes where an individual has been resident in the UK for 17 out of 20 years. Certain Double Taxation Treaties may override these rules and should be checked carefully.

Basis of Taxation

IHT is an integrated lifetime transfer and estates tax, and is a tax on capital transfers of value by an individual on certain lifetime gifts which are taxed immediately, lifetime gifts where the donor dies within seven years from the date of the gift and the chargeable estate upon the individual's death.

Each individual is entitled to a nil rate band (NRB) which is currently £325,000 for 2017/18. Only transfers of value exceeding this band are liable to IHT. Any unused NRB can now be shared by spouses/civil partners on second death. The NRB is not an annual exemption. It is a seven year cumulative band which takes into account the previous seven years' chargeable transfers when determining whether a transfer has exceeded the NRB.

IHT is currently charged at rates of 20% on chargeable lifetime transfers and 40% on death.

There are three types of lifetime gift: exempt transfers, potentially exempt transfers and chargeable lifetime transfers.

Upon death an individual is deemed to have made a transfer of value equal to the whole of their chargeable estate, which is the total value of all their capital assets less any amounts owing at the date of death.

Examples of the most common exempt transfers are transfers between spouses and civil partners, gifts to UK registered charities, the annual exemption (the first £3,000 of gifts made each tax year) and small gifts up to £250 de minimis. There are other valuable exemptions available.

The most common chargeable lifetime transfers (CLTs) are gifts to trusts. Most gifts to trusts (except charitable trusts or trusts for the disabled) are CLTs.

Potentially exempt transfers are all lifetime gifts between individuals. During the donor's lifetime the transfers are treated as exempt from IHT and if the donor survives seven years from the date of the gift the transfer is completely exempt.

If the donor dies within seven years of the date of the gift the transfer becomes chargeable, although the amount chargeable depends on how many years have passed between the date of the gift and the date of death.

It was announced in the 2015 Summer Budget that a main residence NRB will be phased in from 2017/18. By 2020/21 this should be worth £175,000. The main residence NRB will effectively be transferable between spouses so on the death of the second spouse a family home worth £1million could be passed on to their descendants without incurring an IHT charge. This relief will be withdrawn gradually where the net value of the estate exceeds £2million. Advice will need to be taken to ensure that the appropriate amount of relief is claimed.

OTHER CONSIDERATIONS

Remuneration Packages

Any benefits provided to an employee, either in the UK or in their home country, will need to be considered when calculating the UK tax position and some of the more popular benefits are mentioned briefly below.

It is also possible to use share schemes and incentives to remunerate in a tax efficient manner and these are discussed elsewhere in the book.

Common Benefits

If accommodation is provided rent free or at a subsidised rate, the relevant benefit of that will be chargeable to both tax and NI. If the value of the property provided is in excess of £75,000, the tax benefit is particularly high and there are ways of minimising the tax liabilities.

If the employer helps with the move to the UK, there are some valuable reliefs worth up to £8,000 but it is important that advice and planning are undertaken before the move takes place.

If an employee is sent to the UK on a temporary secondment for less than 24 months it may be possible to claim tax relief in respect of the expenses in attending the 'temporary workplace' in the UK. These expenses would include, but not be restricted to, accommodation costs, utilities, ordinary commuting to the temporary workplace and subsistence. This relief may extend to cover travel between the UK and their home country.

The taxable benefit of a car is generally calculated based on its CO_2 emissions and the list price before discounts in order to encourage the use of more fuel efficient cars.

Double Taxation

It is always worthwhile to remember that there is a guiding principle that no one should suffer double taxation on the same income, gains or assets in more than one country. However, how this relief is given depends on the country of origin and any double taxation treaty which may be in force with the UK.

Taxation could be due in both countries, the country of residence only, or the country where the source is 'arising'. This changes depending on the type of income or gains and whether there is an old treaty, a new treaty or even no treaty at all.

Once again, if at all possible, the interaction between the countries should be checked before the foreign national arrives in the UK.

3.5 EMPLOYMENT LAW

Asha Kumar, Watson, Farley & Williams LLP

INTRODUCTION

Employment law in the UK has changed over the decades to reflect social and political changes, and has also been affected by the UK's historic membership of the European Union (EU).

The UK Government has made various amendments to employment law with the aim of deregulating it and making the UK more competitive and a more attractive place to do business. Any business considering the UK as a place of business needs to be aware of the employment and immigration laws that operate in the UK. Those investing in the UK will have to deal with different aspects of employment protection according to the mechanism used to invest in the UK, and it should also be noted that special protection is afforded to employees where there is a merger or acquisition of a business.

This chapter seeks to assist those unfamiliar with UK employment law by providing an overview of the rights and obligations afforded to individuals through the employment relationship.

EMPLOYMENT STATUS

In general, UK employment law distinguishes between three main types of employment status: 'employees', 'workers' and the 'self-employed'. This status is important because it determines the statutory employment rights to which a person is entitled.

Significant rights are conferred upon employees who, traditionally, have been seen as individuals with full-time jobs working under indefinite employment contracts. However, as new working arrangements emerge, the UK has seen an increase in the number of individuals whose working arrangements fall outside the traditional pattern.

There is no statutory definition of 'employee', and while case law has developed in this area, the actual finding of employment status depends upon the circumstances of each particular case. As a consequence, the growth of legislation that applies to 'workers', a term wider than 'employees', embraces certain types of self-employment. It should also be noted that there is also limited employment law protection for qualifying temporary agency workers.

Recently, a series of cases have been brought by individuals claiming worker rights against businesses which have tried to classify them as being self-employed. One of the most high profile of these cases was brought by a number of taxi drivers against Uber, a business which operates a smartphone application to enable customers to order and pay for a taxi. The tribunal found in the taxi drivers' favour and decided that they had worker status.

Given the emergence of the 'gig economy' and flexible working arrangements, the UK Government launched a study in 2016 on new models of working and the impact on the rights of workers and employer duties. The results of this are expected in the summer of 2017.

CONTRACTS OF EMPLOYMENT

A contract of employment comes into existence as soon as someone accepts an offer of employment in return for pay. It is legally binding between the employer and employee, and can be written or oral, express or implied, or a combination of these. In addition, some employment terms are imposed into contracts by statute.

While employers are obliged only to provide a written statement of the main employment particulars (see below), it is recommended that employees are given a full written contract, as it provides certainty and may help to avoid later disputes. However, even a written contract may not necessarily reflect all of the terms that apply in an employment relationship, and terms are often implied in a contract. These may be necessary to make the contract workable or may reflect custom and practice.

A contract can be for an indefinite duration, terminable on an agreed period of notice, or for a fixed term. Protection is afforded to a fixed-term worker so that he/she cannot be treated less favourably than an equivalent permanent worker, unless the treatment is objectively justified. In certain circumstances, fixed-term contracts automatically become permanent contracts.

Written particulars of employment
The Employment Rights Act 1996 obliges employers to provide employees with a written statement of employment particulars. The written statement is not necessarily a contract, but can provide evidence of the terms and conditions of employment. It must be provided to the employee within two months of the employment commencing and must contain certain basic information, including:

- the names of the employer and employee;
- the rate of remuneration and the intervals at which it is to be paid;
- the hours of work; and
- holiday entitlement.

An employee who has not been provided with the required particulars may make a complaint to the Employment Tribunal, which may award him/her between two and four weeks' pay. For these purposes, a week's pay is currently capped at £489, and this generally increases annually on 6 April each year.

Policies and procedures

Often written contracts are supplemented by the use of policies and procedures that describe the employer's more general employment practices, such as email and internet use.

MINIMUM STATUTORY PROVISIONS

In the UK, employees (and sometimes workers) are provided with minimum terms, which are aimed at providing decent minimum standards and promoting fairness at work. Many of the minimum standards were introduced in order to implement European directives, and consequently similar provisions apply throughout Europe. Minimum terms related to the following cannot be overridden:

- the national minimum wage;
- statutory sick pay;
- working hours;
- notice periods;
- employers' liability insurance; and
- health and safety.

National minimum wage

The National Minimum Wage Act applies to almost all workers and sets minimum hourly rates of pay. The national minimum wage is reviewed annually. The rates vary for different groups of workers and as of 1 April 2017 were set as follows:

National Living Wage of £7.50 an hour for workers aged 25 and over;
- £7.05 an hour for workers aged 21-24;
- £5.60 an hour for 18-20 year olds;
- £4.05 an hour for all workers aged 16-17; and
- £3.50 for apprentices.

Statutory sick pay

Eligible employees are entitled to receive statutory sick pay (SSP) for up to 28 weeks in one period, or more than one linked period, of sickness (periods with eight weeks or less between them are linked). A helpful SSP calculator can be found on the HM Revenue and Customs website[1].

The rate of SSP is reviewed annually and is currently £89.35 per week. In certain circumstances, an employer may be able to recover some or all of any SSP they have paid to their employees.

As a matter of policy, employers may choose to pay employees full pay (inclusive of SSP) for a limited period; this is referred to as 'contractual sick pay'.

Working hours

The Working Time Regulations implement a European directive aimed at protecting the health and safety of workers by ensuring that working time does not adversely affect a worker's health. In summary, the regulations provide details of:

- the 48 hour week;
- rest breaks; and
- annual leave.

The 48-hour week

An employer cannot require an employee to work more than an average of 48 hours a week, although there are a number of exceptions to this rule for senior employees and certain other categories of employment. Unlike many other European countries, Britain has negotiated an opt-out whereby this limit does not apply if an employee agrees in writing with his/her employer that it is not to be applied. It should be noted that the employer cannot compel the employee to opt-out and that the employee can reverse this opt-out by giving appropriate notice.

Rest breaks

Workers have the right to an uninterrupted rest period of at least 11 hours between working days, and to a 24-hour period clear of work each week. Additional rest breaks must be provided to workers whose pattern of work puts their health and safety at risk. The regulations also provide the right to a rest break of at least 20 minutes after six hours of consecutive work. Special provisions apply to night workers.

Annual leave

Workers currently have the right to a minimum of 5.6 weeks' paid annual leave. This right applies from the first day of employment and accrues at the rate of one-twelfth of

---

[1] http://www.hmrc.gov.uk/calcs/ssp.htm

the annual entitlement per month worked. A 'week' reflects the employee's working week. So, where an employee works a five-day week, he/she will be entitled to 28 days' annual leave, and if an employee works three days a week, he/she will be entitled to 16.8 days' annual leave. In practice, many employers offer employees the statutory minimum inclusive of bank holidays and will provide employees in senior roles with additional annual leave.

Grievance and disciplinary procedures

When resolving workplace disputes, parties should be mindful of acting in accordance with a code of practice developed by the Advisory, Conciliation and Arbitration Service (ACAS Code). The ACAS Code provides basic practical guidance to employers, employees and their representatives and sets out principles for handling disciplinary and grievance situations in the workplace. If an employee or employer is unreasonable in its failure to follow the new code of practice, employment tribunals will be able to order an increase or decrease in awards of up to 25 per cent.

Notice periods

The minimum legal notice periods to be given by an employer are:

- one week's notice if the employee has been continuously employed by the employer for at least one month but for less than two years; or
- two weeks' notice if the employee has been continuously employed by the employer for two years, plus an additional week's notice for each further complete year of continuous employment, up to a maximum of 12 weeks.

An employee's contract of employment may, however, provide for a longer notice period. An employment contract may be terminated without advance notice where the employee has committed an act of gross misconduct.

In the absence of any contrary contractual provisions, an employee who has been employed for one month or more must give their employer at least one week's notice to terminate their employment.

Employers' liability insurance

Every employer in the UK must have employers' liability insurance, which covers employers against damages and legal costs following injury or disease to its employees during their employment.

Health and safety

In the UK, employers have legal obligations to ensure a safe workplace. The health and safety obligations are extensive and if breached may give rise to criminal liabilities. Further details can be obtained from the Health and Safety Executive's website[1].

---

[1] http://www.hse.gov.uk

Work/life balance

Over the years, legislation has been brought in to enable employees to achieve a better work/life balance. It has been particularly targeted at parents to enable them to spend adequate time bringing up their children by allowing them to work around their commitments.

Maternity leave

All pregnant employees are entitled to 52 weeks' maternity leave. All employment benefits, including non-contractual benefits connected with an employee's employment that are not remuneration, continue to be provided for the full period of maternity leave.

Employees on maternity leave who are eligible are also entitled to receive up to 39 weeks' statutory maternity pay (SMP) at the rate set by statute. The first six weeks of SMP are earnings-related, and an employee is entitled to 90 per cent of her average weekly earnings with no upper limit. The remaining 33 weeks are paid at a lower rate, which is currently £140.98 (or 90 per cent of earnings if this is less).

Employees who are not eligible for SMP may be entitled to a Maternity Allowance for up to 39 weeks. This is currently £140.98 per week (or 90 per cent of earnings if this is less) and is claimed from the Department for Work and Pensions. Similar provisions to those set out above apply on the adoption of a child.

Shared Parental leave

On 5 April 2015, the Children and Families Act 2014 introduced a new system of shared parental leave (SPL) for eligible employees and agency workers. The new statutory shared parental leave scheme allows parents to share the statutory maternity leave and pay that is currently available only to mothers (and adoptive parents to share the adoption leave and pay currently only available to the primary adopter). Parents can share up to 50 weeks of SPL and 37 weeks of Shared Parental Pay. Leave does not have to be taken consecutively so both parents may be absent from work at the same time if they elect to do so.

Paternity leave

Eligible employees whose partners are expected to give birth will be entitled to time off at or around the time of the birth. They are entitled to take either one or two consecutive weeks' leave as paid paternity leave. Statutory paternity pay is either 90 per cent of an employee's weekly earnings or the prescribed amount (currently £140.98), whichever is the lesser.

Parental leave

Parents who have at least one year's continuous employment may take up to 18 weeks' unpaid parental leave for each child up to that child's 18th birthday.

Time off to care for dependants

In the UK, all employees have the right to take a reasonable amount of time off, without pay, to care for dependants. The right to time off is intended to enable employees to deal with an emergency in the short-term and/or, where necessary, to make longer-term care arrangements.

Right to request flexible working

Any employee with 26 weeks' continuous service has a right to request a flexible working arrangement, if the change relates to hours, times or place of work.

Part-time working

Protection is also afforded to those who work on a part-time basis. Regulations have introduced provisions that prevent part-time workers from being treated less favourably than equivalent full-time employees, unless this is justifiable. Part-time employees should also have access to the same rights and benefits as full-time employees, albeit on a pro-rata basis.

EQUALITY PROVISIONS

In the UK the Equality Act 2010 outlaws discrimination on the grounds of gender reassignment, marriage and civil partnership, pregnancy and maternity, sex, race, disability, sexual orientation, religion or belief and age. Generally, the law recognises the following types of discrimination:

- Direct discrimination: this is where someone is treated differently because of their sex, race, etc. It is not necessary to show an unlawful motive; it is the reason for the treatment that matters.
- Indirect discrimination: this is a less obvious form of discrimination. It occurs where certain requirements, conditions or practices imposed by an employer, although applied equally to all employees, have a disproportionately adverse impact on one group or other.
- Harassment: this is where one person subjects another to unwanted conduct related to their sex, race, etc., which has the purpose or effect of violating the other's dignity, or creating an intimidating, hostile, degrading, humiliating or offensive environment for them.
- Victimisation: this is where a person is treated less favourably because they have started proceedings, given evidence or complained about the behaviour of someone who has been harassing them or discriminating against them.

Special provisions apply to disability discrimination and age discrimination. Under the disability discrimination provisions, an employee with a particular condition may receive additional protection where this amounts to a 'disability' as defined under the legislation.

MISCELLANEOUS MATTERS

Whistleblowing

Protection is given to employees who disclose or 'blow the whistle on' wrongdoings at work. Employees are protected if they blow the whistle and, if they are dismissed or receive detrimental treatment as a result of their action, they can present a claim in an employment tribunal. Compensation for whistleblowing is uncapped. Whistleblowers are protected where they disclose in good faith something that relates to:

- the commissioning of a criminal activity;
- failure to comply with a legal obligation;
- a miscarriage of justice;
- a health and safety issue;
- damage to the environment; and/or
- the deliberate concealing of information about any of the above.

Any disclosure must be made in the public interest.

Data protection

The UK has data protection or 'privacy' laws. Data transfer to companies outside the EU is permitted only when the receiving country has data protection laws that are considered adequate by the European Commission. UK data protection laws may give individual employees access to information held on them by their employer, provided that certain conditions are satisfied.

Reporting and consultation requirements

The Information and Consultation of Employees Regulations 2004 (ICE) gives employees the right to be informed and consulted about the business they work for, including information on the employer's activities and any possible threats to their employment. ICE applies to all undertakings with at least 50 employees. The aim of ICE is to encourage people to develop their own voluntary arrangements tailored to their particular circumstances.

Termination of employment

In the UK, employees have the statutory right not to be unfairly dismissed. Generally, this right accrues after an employee has accrued two years' service. A dismissal in the UK will only be 'fair' if it falls under one of the following prescribed reasons, namely:

1   capability;
2   conduct;
3   avoidance of a legal enactment;
4   redundancy; or
5   some other substantial reason that justifies dismissal.

Even though a fair reason may be established, the employer should follow a fair procedure when dismissing an employee, and the parties should, in the majority of cases, follow the ACAS Code.

Where a dismissal is found to be unfair, an employee can recover compensation which is capped at the lower of £80,541 (reviewed annually) or one year's salary of the employee. There are, however, a number of circumstances, including in the event of whistleblowing or discrimination, where two years' service is not required and in which an employment tribunal can ignore the cap on compensation and award unlimited compensation. If the reason for dismissal is redundancy, an employee is generally entitled to a statutory redundancy payment, up to a current maximum of £14,670.

Employers should note that there are special rules concerning redundancy. An employer who proposes to make 20 or more employees redundant must consult with the relevant trade union or employee representatives beforehand. Failure to do so may result in compensation of up to 90 days' pay for each affected employee.

Breach of contract
In addition to statutory rights that apply on dismissal, if an employer does not comply with a term of the employment contract, this may be a breach of contract. An employee can bring a claim for damages or 'wrongful dismissal' if they do not receive their notice entitlement under their contract of employment. A fundamental breach of contract will also usually entitle an employee to resign and claim unfair 'constructive dismissal'. Similar principles apply where an employee breaches their employment contract.

When awarding compensation for breach of contract, UK courts will seek to place the innocent party in the position they would have been in had the contract been properly performed.

MERGERS AND ACQUISITIONS

Where a business or part of an entity is transferred to another by way of a business transfer, the employees in the transferring part are given significant legal safeguards under the Transfer of Undertakings (Protection of Employment) Regulations, 2006 (TUPE). These safeguards apply only when there is a transfer of assets and not where the employing entity is the same, as might be the case where the transfer is of shares in the company. These special provisions also apply in certain outsourcing situations.

The special protections include:

- appointment of employee representatives who must be informed (and possibly also consulted) in advance of the transfer;
- inheritance of past (undischarged) liabilities of the employer by the buyer or transferee;
- changes to an employee's terms and conditions of employment being rendered unlawful; and
- dismissals in connection with the transfer being rendered unlawful, unless they are for certain specified reasons.

CONCLUSION

It might seem at first sight that employers in the UK are subject to a considerable amount of legislative requirements. It should, however, be borne in mind that many of the provisions, particularly in the area of equal opportunities, were introduced as a result of European directives and thus apply to all EU member states.

It will be interesting to see how employment law in the UK develops in the next few years, particularly after the UK has completed the process of leaving the EU. It should be noted though that at around the same time that the UK Government served formal notice (on 29 March 2017) under Article 50 of The Treaty on the European Union to end the UK's membership of the EU, it also published a White Paper on the proposed Great Repeal Bill. According to the White Paper:

'...the Bill will convert EU law as it stands at the moment of exit into UK law before we leave the EU. This allows businesses to continue operating knowing the rules have not changed significantly overnight, and provides fairness to individuals, whose rights and obligations will not be subject to sudden change.'

Therefore, once the UK has left the EU, whilst the UK Government will be able to make changes to laws which are derived from its historic membership of the EU, it is not presently thought that we should expect sudden and drastic amendments to the detailed body of employment rights which has developed over a number of years in the UK. There are, in any event, a number of UK employment rights, such as the right not to be unfairly dismissed, which have developed independently of EU law.

3.6 PENSIONS IN THE UK

Howard Finch, Mazars LLP

This chapter gives a brief overview of the UK pensions regime for both corporations and individuals. Pensions law is subject to regular change, especially over recent years, and this section is merely a high level guide to the current position. Independent advice should be sought in all respects especially in relation to employer responsibilities or the recently introduced individual 'pension freedoms.'

SOCIAL SECURITY

The UK state pension provision has recently undergone a significant review and a fundamental change. In April 2016 a new State Pension was launched, commonly referred to as the Single Tier State Pension. The Pensions Act 2014 made provisions for this new Single Tier State Pension to replace (but still recognise) previous elements of State pension provision.

People reaching State Pension Age before April 2016 still receive the State Pension under the old rules. Males born on or after 6 April 1951 and females born on or after 6 April 1953 will be able to claim the new State Pension.

The new State Pension replaces the 'Basic State Pension' and the Additional State Pensions that provided a top up, including S2P and SERPS. The purpose of the state provision is to provide a very basic level of income at retirement based on the individual's National Insurance contribution record through their working life as paid by both the employer and employee (both compulsory for UK residents.)

The full new State Pension is £159.55 per week for 2017/2018. The actual amount is dependent on an individual's National Insurance record when they reach State Pension Age. It is usually paid every four weeks in arrears. It will increase each year by whichever is the highest between the average percentage growth in wages, the Consumer Prices Index (CPI) or 2.5%.

State Pension Age is currently undergoing radical change and transition and will be equalised at 65 for both men and women by November 2018. The retirement age is then set to continue to rise to 66, 67 and 68 for both men and women. Continued rises are expected and a mechanism has been established to review the State Pension Age every five years.

In addition to the State provision, individuals are expected and encouraged to make their own retirement provision, either through the workplace with the assistance of their employer, or via personal provision.

PRIVATE PROVISION

Until recently there was no requirement for an employer to offer any kind of employer sponsored workplace scheme. Previous attempts to encourage saving included the Stakeholder legislation, but as no employer contribution was required, these were met with little enthusiasm from workers.

The key benefits of UK private provision are the tax relief on contributions (within limits), the fact that the fund(s) can be drawn upon from age 55 even whilst still working if required and that up to 25% of the fund can be taken free of tax as a cash sum.

Since 1 October 2012 this changed with the introduction of 'Auto-Enrolment' as legislated for in the 2008 Pensions Act.

AUTO-ENROLMENT

As part of the Government's plan to encourage more people to save for retirement, they introduced auto enrolment with effect from 1 October 2012. The aim was to overcome the inertia that prevents many people from contributing to a pension scheme.

Transitioning through to 2018, auto-enrolment began with the largest companies and worked down in size (based on employee numbers). From a given date ('staging date' set by the Department of Work and Pensions (DWP)), ALL employers will be required to auto-enrol any qualifying employees into a nominated pension scheme, at least every three years. There are a broad ranging and significant set of statutory fines for non- compliance and breaches, and the Pensions Regulator has already demonstrated its ability to enforce these on employers where they deem necessary.

The staging date is determined by the number of employees on the employer's largest PAYE schedule as of 1 April 2012. This date could be amended, however, following any company acquisitions or mergers that have occurred since April 2012. Staging dates cannot be put back, although employers can postpone auto-enrolling employees by up to three months. Employees can opt-out but must be re-enrolled every three years.

Employers must nominate an appropriate scheme or category to be used for auto-enrolment as a qualifying workplace pension scheme (QWPS). This may be an existing company arrangement, providing it meets certain qualifying criteria or another scheme such as NEST (National Employment Savings Trust) which is available to employers to auto-enrol their employees. Any Scheme used for auto-enrolment, however, must meet certain standards as confirmed by the Pensions Regulator, including the following:

- All member charges are transparent and represent value for money (there are charge caps);
- Contributions must meet the required minimums (explained in the next section);
- Employees must be auto-enrolled without having to give their consent (no application form);
- There must be an appropriate Scheme default investment fund (employers responsibility to select);
- All employees must receive relevant Scheme information before being auto-enrolled.

Employee Categories

Employers are required to regularly assess their workers (usually via payroll records) to determine how they must be treated under the regulations. The automatic enrolment regulations define three different types of worker based on their total qualifying earnings as follows:

Earnings/Age	16 – 21	22 - (SPA)	SPA - 75
Under threshold (£5,876 in 2017/18)	Entitled Worker		
Between threshold and trigger (£5,876 - £10,000 in 2017/18)	Non- Eligible Jobholder		
Over trigger (£10,000 in 2017/18)	Non – Eligible	Eligible Jobholder	Non - Eligible

This categorisation then in turn determines the employer duties as follows:

Type of worker	Employer Duty
Eligible Jobholder	Must be automatically enrolled in a qualifying scheme and employer must make minimum contributions for these workers as long as they remain in the scheme.
Non-eligible jobholder	Must be offered the opportunity to opt into an automatic enrolment scheme and employer must make minimum contributions as long as they remain active.
Entitled worker	Must be offered a pension scheme for them to make contributions if they wish. There is no obligation on the Company to contribute.

Contributions

From April 2019, employers will be required to contribute at least 3% of defined employee earnings for all those to be enrolled in the pension scheme.

Employees must be assessed on their total qualifying earnings but contributions can be paid on a chosen definition of earnings, e.g. total pay, qualifying band earnings (£5,876- -£45,000) or basic / pensionable pay. Contributions can also be phased from staging date to April 2019, to help employers meet the additional costs they will face on auto-enrolment.

Communications, Records and Registration

Employers have a responsibility to provide employees with communications surrounding their entitlements and options at various stages. There is also the requirement to register the workplace scheme and complete a Declaration of Compliance within five months of the staging date. As with real-time PAYE there is the requirement to keep records such as any opt-out requests and the data sent to the pension provider.

TYPES OF OCCUPATIONAL SUPPLEMENTARY PLANS

Since the 6 April 2006 when the Finance Act 2004 came into force a single set of conditions now applies to all types of pension plan whether occupational or personal, contract or trust based. Legacy benefit limits based on length of service and/or earnings have been replaced by a lifetime allowance (LTA) which is effectively a total benefit cap and an annual allowance which is a contribution limit. Breaching these limits triggers punitive tax liabilities.

Types of scheme effectively fall under two categories: trust based and contract based.

Trust Based Plans

1. Defined Benefit – Promises to provide a retirement income as a percentage of final salary (or averaged salary over the last few years prior to retirement). Entitlement is earned by years of service providing a fraction of final salary per year of service. So, for example, 40 years' salary might equate to 40 x 1/60th i.e. 2/3rds final salary. Outside of the public sector (civil service, teachers etc.) these schemes are increasingly rare; however, many companies and scheme trustees still have liabilities and scheme management responsibilities to bear which can be increasingly costly with low interest rates and increasing life expectancy.
2. Career Average – career average is a lower cost scheme to the employer as it looks at earnings over the employee's entire service rather than just earnings prior to retirement.
3. Defined Contribution – Historically trust based, this plan largely moves risk from the employer to the employee as the employer contribution is fixed and the outcome is largely fund dependent. Again with the introduction of auto-enrolment, and due to the responsibilities on trustees, many of these schemes have now closed and converted to non-trust based defined contribution.

Contract Based Plans

1. Stakeholder – The Welfare and Pensions Reform Act 1999 required most employers (unless they already had an occupational scheme or less than five employees) to offer access to a Stakeholder scheme. No contributions were required from the employer, however. In reality, therefore, these schemes did not really take off, but they did help drive pension charges down in the market in general. Now, with the introduction of auto-enrolment, Stakeholder schemes are generally either being amended to comply with the updated regulations or replaced with a new scheme.

2. Group Personal Pensions – Each member has a personal contract under a group 'umbrella', usually to improve charges and for ease of employer administration. The pot is accrued from the combination of employee and employer contributions and the fund can be used at retirement in various ways to provide income (which may include capital sums).

There are also potentially 'SSASs' (small self-administered scheme) and 'SIPPs' (self-invested personal pension) which are contributed to through company payrolls, particularly in relation to senior management or directors, as they often allow more individual investment control and asset types. Other than to be aware of their existence, their detail is outside the scope of this chapter.

PENSIONS FREEDOMS

The recent changes (effective on pensions to which individuals become entitled on or from 6 April 2015) have been the subject of much press coverage. Initially announced in the 2014 Budget, the Taxation of Pensions Bill was introduced to Parliament in October 2014. Ultimately the aim was to allow individuals to access their money to purchase pension savings as they wished during retirement, subject to their marginal rate of tax.

Income options therefore now include one or a combination of the following:

1. **An Annuity** – several types available but generally it is an insurance contract which provides a guaranteed income in exchange for an agreed capital sum. With low interest rates and increasing longevity, income levels have dropped significantly in recent years. Along with the loss of capital on death, annuities are seeing a decline in popularity. Types of annuity include lifetime, with profits and flexi/ fixed term.
2. **Flexi Access Drawdown (FAD)** – allows the choice of income from the fund without reference to any rates or limits other than the size of the fund. Up to 25% of the fund can usually be taken as a tax free lump sum, and the remainder is subject to income tax at the individual's marginal rate.
3. **Uncrystallised Funds Pension Lump Sum (UFLPS)** – an alternative option to FAD allows flexible withdrawals directly from the pension funds . 25% of any amount taken is tax free cash and the rest is taxed income. It is important to note that once any funds are taken using the UFPLS option, a reduced money purchase annual allowance applies. This restricts any further tax relievable money purchase contributions to £4,000 per annum.

Part Four

Banking, Property and Financial Services

4.1 THE REGULATION OF FINANCIAL SERVICES

Sarah Ouarbya and Swagat Bannick, Mazars LLP

INTRODUCTION

As one of the premier global centres for financial services, the UK has always been an attractive market for overseas investors. The UK has a robust regulatory system in place and UK regulators frequently play a key role in creating and setting global regulatory standards.

The regulatory system in the UK is delegated to three bodies: the Financial Policy Committee (FPC), the Prudential Regulation Authority (PRA) and the Financial Conduct Authority (FCA). Each of these bodies play a defined role and all three work together for the supervision and management of the UK financial services industry.

Financial Policy Committee

The Financial Policy Committee (FPC) is part of the Bank of England and has the primary objective of identifying, monitoring and taking action to remove or reduce systemic risks, with a view to protecting and enhancing the resilience of the UK financial system. The FPC has a secondary objective to support the economic policy of the Government.

The Prudential Regulation Authority

The Prudential Regulation Authority (PRA) is part of the Bank of England and is responsible for the prudential regulation and supervision of banks, building societies, credit unions, insurers and major investment firms. The PRA's objectives are set out in the Financial Services and Markets Act 2000 (FSMA). The PRA's statutory objectives are:

1. A general objective to promote the safety and soundness of the firms it regulates;
2. An objective specific to insurance firms, to contribute to the securing of an appropriate degree of protection for those who are or may become insurance policyholders; and
3. A secondary objective to facilitate effective competition.

Firms regulated by the PRA for prudential purposes are also regulated by the Financial Conduct Authority (FCA) for conduct.

The Financial Conduct Authority

The Financial Conduct Authority (FCA) is responsible for the conduct regulation of all financial services firms and the prudential regulation of the remaining firms not subject to prudential regulation by the PRA.

The FCA has an overarching strategic objective to ensure that the relevant markets function well. It advances this strategic objective through the following three operational objectives:

1. Protection of consumers – to secure an appropriate degree of protection for consumers.
2. Protection of financial markets – to protect and enhance the integrity of the UK financial system.
3. Promotion of competition – to promote effective competition in the interests of consumers.

The FCA is an independent public body funded entirely by the firms it regulates; it is accountable to the HM Treasury, which is responsible for the UK's financial system, and to the UK Parliament.

SCOPE OF REGULATION

In the UK, a wide range of firms in the financial services industry are subject to regulation. Activities requiring a regulatory licence in the UK are called 'regulated activities' and these are defined in the Financial Services and Markets Act 2000 (Regulated Activities) Order 2001 (the Regulated Activities Order). The Regulated Activities Order is a piece of secondary legislation under the Financial Services and Markets Act 2000 (FSMA).

In the UK it is a criminal offence to carry out a regulated activity in relation to one or more specified investments without the appropriate permission from either the PRA and/or the FCA.

In general terms, a regulated activity is an activity specified in the Regulated Activities Order and carried on by way of business in relation to one or more of the investments specified in the Regulated Activities Order.

The following activities are specified in the Regulated Activities Order:

- Accepting deposits
- Issuing e-money
- Carrying out or helping to administer insurance contracts (as a firm's principal)
- Investments: dealing in or managing (as a principal or agent), arranging deals, safeguarding and administering, advising
- Home finance: arranging, advising on, entering into and administering
- Operating a multilateral trading facility
- Sending dematerialised instructions (electronic transfer of title in investments like securities and contractually-based investments)
- Setting up collective investment schemes
- Setting up stakeholder pensions schemes
- Providing basic advice on stakeholder products
- Lloyd's market activities
- Entering funeral plan contracts
- Agreeing to do most of the above activities

In addition to the above there are a number of consumer credit related activities that are subject to regulation by the FCA. These include:

- Credit broking where introducing customers to lenders is a main business activity
- Credit broking where the sale of goods or services takes place in the customer's home
- Debt administration and debt collection
- Debt counselling and debt adjusting on a commercial basis
- Lending which is not limited permission (such as personal loans, credit cards, overdrafts, pawnbroking, hire-purchase or conditional sale agreements)
- Providing credit information services
- Providing credit reference agency services
- Peer-to-peer lending

These are supplemented by a number of other consumer credit related regulated activities which are subject to limited regulation by the FCA.

Investments specified in the Regulated Activities Order are as follows:

- Deposits
- E-money
- Rights under an insurance contract

- Shares
- Instruments creating or acknowledging indebtedness
- Sukuk (sharia compliant debt instruments)
- Government and public securities
- Instruments giving entitlement to investments
- Certificates representing some securities
- Units in a collective investment scheme
- Rights under a stakeholder pension scheme
- Rights under a personal pension scheme
- Options
- Futures
- Contracts for differences
- Lloyd's syndicate capacity and syndicate membership
- Rights under funeral plan contracts, regulated mortgage contracts, home reversion plans, home purchase plans
- Rights to or interests in anything that is a specified investment, excluding 'rights under regulated mortgage contracts', 'rights under regulated home reversion plans' and 'rights under regulated home purchase plans'

FSMA and the Regulated Activities Order are complex. There are also a number of exclusions and exceptions that are impossible to summarise in this publication. The FCA provides guidance regarding the circumstances in which regulatory authorisation by the PRA and/or the FCA is required, or exempt person status is available, including guidance on the activities which are regulated under FSMA and the exclusions which are available. Guidance is provided in the Perimeter Guidance manual (PERG) in the FCA Handbook.

In broad terms the following types of firms are likely to perform regulated activities in respect of the Specified Investments and are therefore likely to be subject to regulation in the UK:

- Banks, building societies and credit unions
- Consumer credit firms
- Electronic money institutions
- Financial advisers
- General insurers and insurance intermediaries
- Investment managers
- Life insurers and pension providers
- Mortgage providers and intermediaries
- Mutual societies
- Payment institutions
- Investment advisers

- Wealth managers
- Peer to peer lenders and platforms

The above list is not exhaustive and should be used as a guide only as in the UK regulation is based on activities rather than types of firm.

REGULATION OF FINANCIAL PROMOTIONS

The FCA is also responsible for the regulation and supervision of any communications (or financial promotions) made by other firms in relation to one or more of the regulated activities listed above. Broadly, a financial promotion is described as an invitation or inducement to engage in investment activity.

The definition of 'invitation' and 'inducement' are not clear cut and further guidance is provided by the FCA in PERG. Broadly, PERG describes an invitation as something which directly invites a person to take a step which will result in engaging in investment activity. Examples of an invitation include: direct offer financial promotions; a prospectus with application forms and internet promotions by brokers where the response by the recipient will initiate the activity (such as 'register with us now and begin dealing online').

Guidance in PERG indicates an inducement may often be followed by an invitation or vice versa. An inducement may be described as a link in a chain where the chain is intended to lead ultimately to an agreement to engage in investment activity. PERG also makes it clear that all the links in the chain will be an inducement or that every inducement will be one to engage in investment activity. Only those that are a significant step in persuading or inciting or seeking to persuade or incite a recipient to engage in investment activity will be inducements and subject to the FCA rules.

Financial promotions can include all forms of communication such as advertising, broadcasts, websites, e-mails and all other forms of written or oral communication, whether sent to one person or many.

All financial promotions are required to be issued or approved by a regulated entity. In summary, financial promotions must be:

- fair, clear and not misleading;
- give a balanced impression of the product or service; and
- not disguise or diminish important warnings or statements.

Details of the financial promotions regime are outlined in the FSMA 2000 (Financial Promotion) Order 2005.

THRESHOLD CONDITIONS

The Financial Services and Markets Act 2000 (Threshold Conditions) Order 2013 (The Threshold Conditions Order) sets out a number of threshold conditions which are the minimum requirements a firm needs to meet to become authorised in the UK. Firms are required to meet the threshold conditions at the point of authorisation and on an ongoing basis.

The PRA's assessment focuses on its statutory objective to promote the safety and soundness of the firms it regulates, whereas the FCA threshold conditions focus on the protection of consumers, the integrity of the UK financial system and the promotion of effective competition in the interests of consumers. The threshold conditions are as follows:

PRA THRESHOLD CONDITIONS	FCA THRESHOLD CONDITIONS
Legal status – the firm must be a body corporate or partnership.	**Legal status** – the firm must be a body corporate or partnership.
Location of offices – A UK incorporated corporate body must maintain its head offices and, if one exists, its registered office in the United Kingdom.	**Location of offices** – A UK incorporated corporate body must maintain its head offices and, if one exists, its registered office in the United Kingdom.
Prudent conduct of business – The firm must conduct its business in a prudent matter, which includes having appropriate financial and non-financial resources.	**Appropriate non-financial resources** – The firm's non-financial resources must be appropriate in relation to the regulated activities it seeks to carry on, having regard to the FCA's operational objectives.
Suitability – The firm must satisfy the PRA that it is a 'fit and proper' person with regard to all circumstances to conduct a regulated activity.	**Suitability** – The firm must be a fit and proper person. The applicant firm's management must have adequate skills and experience and act with integrity (fitness and propriety). The firm has appropriate policies and procedures in place and the firm appropriately manages conflicts of interest.
Effective supervision – The firm must be capable of being effectively supervised by the PRA.	

	Business model – The firm's strategy for doing business is suitable for a person carrying on the regulated activities it undertakes or seeks to carry on and does not pose a risk to the FCA's objectives. **Effective supervision** – The firm must be capable of being effectively supervised by the FCA.

AUTHORISATION

Banks, credit unions and insurers are dual regulated by both the PRA and the FCA. Any firm falling in the scope of dual regulation is required to make a single licence application to the PRA as the PRA is the lead regulator for dual regulated firms. Once submitted the PRA will assess the application against the PRA's threshold conditions and the FCA will assess the application against the FCA's threshold conditions. The final decision on the application will be made by PRA but only once the FCA has provided consent.

All other firms are required to apply directly to the FCA for authorisation.

The authorisation process is different depending on the type of licence requested. For dual regulated firms the process will often start with a pre-application stage which will involve a number of structured formal meetings designed to help firms understand the authorisation process, understand the PRA and FCA's expectations of firms (particularly the threshold conditions) and identify any particular concerns early on.

Once the pre-application process has been completed, dual regulated firms are invited to submit a formal application to the PRA. The PRA and the FCA are required to make a decision on the application within six months of receiving a complete application and twelve months of receiving an incomplete application. The PRA determines whether the application is complete or not.

Some banks are able to enter a 'mobilisation' phase prior to full authorisation. This allows the bank to operate with limited permissions and gives them time to build IT systems, infrastructure, recruit staff or engage with third-party suppliers prior to a full launch.

The FCA application process is simpler and usually shorter and applications are made online through the FCA's Connect system. As part of the application firms are asked to complete a detailed application form and supply a comprehensive regulatory business plan. Firms are also asked to supply a range of other documents and completed forms specific to the licence application.

APPROACH TO INNOVATION

The FCA has introduced an innovation hub to provide support for new and innovative businesses looking to introduce new products and services to the financial services market. The hub provides a dedicated team and contact for innovative businesses, help and support to understand the regulatory framework and how it applies to them and assistance with the application for authorisation.

Through the innovation hub the FCA seeks to identify areas where the current regulatory framework needs to adapt to enable further innovation in the interests of consumers.

The FCA has also set up a regulatory sandbox that allows businesses to test innovative products, services, business models and delivery mechanisms in a live environment. The sandbox uses a cohort approach and currently runs two cohorts every year. Firms are invited to apply to be part of a cohort and, if selected, are allowed to test products or services in a controlled way under the supervision of the FCA.

PRA RULEBOOK

The PRA's rules are set out in the PRA Rulebook which can be found on the Bank of England website. The Rulebook contains the rules made by the PRA under powers conferred by FSMA. The Rulebook applies to all PRA-authorised persons (and in some cases, unauthorised persons and individuals) and contains the prudential requirements relevant to them.

The PRA Rulebook is divided into five different sections, each covering a different group of firms regulated by the PRA. The five sections are:

- Capital Requirement Regulation firms
- Non-Capital Requirement Regulation firms
- Solvency II firms
- Non-Solvency II firms
- Non-authorised persons

FCA HANDBOOK

The FCA Handbook contains the regulations and guidance relevant for firms regulated by the FCA. The handbook has been split into ten blocks:

- High Level Standards
- Prudential Standards
- Business Standards

- Regulatory Processes
- Redress
- Specialist Sourcebooks
- Listing, Prospectus & Disclosure Rules
- Handbook guides
- Regulatory guides (including PERG)
- Glossary

PASSPORTING AND EQUIVALENCE

As a current member of the EU, the UK is subject to a wide range of European Union treaties, some of which provide rights to firms to operate on a cross-border basis within the EEA without having to obtain local authorisation. These rights are known as 'passporting rights.' Passporting rights are provided either through exercising the right of establishment or by providing cross-border services.

Activities that are 'passportable' are set out in the relevant EU single market directives. Activities that are not covered by the directives and are not 'passportable' will mean that a firm wishing to carry on such activities may need to also be directly authorised in each relevant EEA state.

Some recent EU legislation also allows non-EEA firms to provide services into the EEA if their home country regime is considered 'equivalent'.

IMPACT OF BREXIT

On 29 March 2017 the UK Government announced its intention to exit the EU. This announcement triggered a two year negotiation period which will end on 29 March 2019. The negotiation period can only be extended if the remaining 27 European states agree, otherwise all EU treaties will cease to apply to the UK. In the absence of any other deal, this means the UK will lose its current passporting rights and firms currently providing services into the EEA by exercising the right of establishment or freedom of services will no longer be able to access those markets.

If the UK is granted an 'equivalence' status some firms may continue providing certain services to the EEA, but this is not guaranteed.

4.2 MERGER AND ACQUISITION TRANSACTION PROCESSES

Olga Diamond, Mazars LLP

This chapter will take you through the acquisition journey and will highlight the key stages in this process and what are the important issues that should not be overlooked.

The following graphic (Figure 6.3.l) provides details of the stages in an acquisition process. We go into further detail about these processes in the following sections.

FIGURE 6.3.1

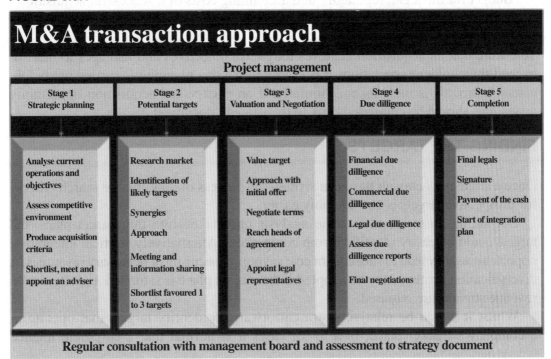

M&A transaction approach				
Project management				
Stage 1 **Strategic planning**	**Stage 2** **Potential targets**	**Stage 3** **Valuation and Negotiation**	**Stage 4** **Due dilligence**	**Stage 5** **Completion**
Analyse current operations and objectives Assess competitive environment Produce acquisition criteria Shortlist, meet and appoint an adviser	Research market Identification of likely targets Synergies Approach Meeting and information sharing Shortlist favoured 1 to 3 targets	Value target Approach with initial offer Negotiate terms Reach heads of agreement Appoint legal representatives	Financial due dilligence Commercial due dilligence Legal due dilligence Assess due dilligence reports Final negotiations	Final legals Signature Payment of the cash Start of integration plan
Regular consultation with management board and assessment to strategy document				

WHERE TO START

The essential starting point for a transaction, or indeed series of transactions, is to develop and document a strategy. This will help to drive the acquisition process towards pre-determined objectives and minimise the risks involved in acquiring companies. The strategy document should:

- Analyse your company's current operations and assess what the aims of the shareholders, management and other stakeholders are and what they are seeking to achieve;
- Consider the current and future competitive environment, the threat of new entrants and the impact acquisitions would have on this dynamic. This may be more challenging when analysing markets to which the company has no exposure, and formal market research should be considered to formulate a view;
- Thoughtfully consider the alternatives – acquisitions should be compared to a 'cold start' and the investment required under all the different options;
- Detail the desired characteristics of the target company, the funds available for transactions and the time scales involved;
- Provide consideration for the management time required for integration and the costs/cost savings that would be possible. This is particularly important in cross-border transactions;
- Budget for the legal, regulatory and accounting costs of a successful acquisition search process;

To ensure that an acquisition achieves long-term objectives and manages to meet or exceed shareholder expectations it is essential that this planning is carried out before a search process is undertaken. Similarly, if an unexpected acquisition opportunity arises, this should be compared back to the strategy document.

FINDING THE TARGETS

Once a strategy document has been written the process of defining the search criteria for prospective targets is considerably easier.

Depending on the results of the analysis undertaken into the market place, the targets could be easily identified from competitors. Alternatively, vertical integration opportunities may lead to subsequent cost savings or securing of necessary resources. A diversification strategy may be adopted if the market place is saturated and alternative revenue streams are required.

Whilst it would be relatively straightforward to identify targets that operate in a company's market place, in a lot of cases it is normal that a corporate finance agent/ broker would be engaged to undertake the search process. This enables the management of the company to continue driving the operations and organic growth strategy forward and not become distracted with another project. Similarly, when targets are being sourced from a diversified market place or vertical integration, an adviser's breadth of connections and research capability can prove invaluable. However, the support and extensive network of contacts held by a corporate finance agent/broker shouldn't be underestimated when looking for a strategic acquisition in a foreign market, especially if considering a new international market for the first time.

The criteria used for a search process are typically a mix of financial and non-financial indicators. The acquirer may be looking to achieve critical mass which would require turnover, head count, office locations or operations in key sectors. Alternatively they may be looking at adding value to their bottom line; so synergistic savings and strong profitability would be important. The strategy document would help to guide the adviser on these criteria, whilst an awareness of 'left-field' opportunities would help to supplement the target shortlist.

THE ROLE OF THE ADVISER

The adviser would be tasked with planning and executing the search and approach process within an agreed timescale and to a set of criteria which has been agreed with the company. The adviser would keep the key individuals at the company informed of progress and provide the benefit of their experience with respect to communications, negotiations and routes to targets.

There are a number of different sources which the adviser would use to identify potential targets including public companies' accounts, trade press, corporate finance websites, specialist market research providers and, increasingly, social media sites. The company would benefit by working with a UK adviser who understands the local laws, practices and forums available for corporate financiers.

The adviser would then feed his findings and thoughts back to the company, highlighting the potential targets and rating their suitability as high, medium and low for their consideration. The ranking would be dependent upon the fit with the company's acquisition criteria.

The adviser would also be able to help with preparing internal board reports that may be needed to inform the key decision makers.

EXPRESSING AN INTEREST AND OPENING DIALOGUE

Once the targets have been identified the company, usually through their adviser, would open dialogue with the target to understand their interest in a transaction. This can be done anonymously to protect the market from knowing that a particular company is acquisitive, or it can be done openly to demonstrate their strength and growth intentions. The approach is likely to differ depending on the market sector and the competitiveness of the market place.

The expression of interest is typically made through a letter or an email addressed to the main shareholder at their home/personal address. The adviser will use their experience and any connections to try to obtain a warm introduction, which has a greater chance of generating a conversation, and will always agree the target's names with their client before communicating.

The expression of interest letter may also need to include details of the acquiring company, especially if they do not have a strong brand name in the UK marketplace. Once communication commences it is important that the company is briefed by their adviser on the process that is being undertaken, just in case any direct responses are directed to the company. It is typical for all communications to go through the adviser which ensures that the acquiring company is insulated from any difficult responses and that a professional and considered approach is given to the process.

It is this professional approach that adds credibility and distinguishes genuine acquirers from those canvassing the market for competitor information.

CONFIDENTIALITY AND INITIAL INFORMATION SHARING

The area of confidentiality, especially amongst competitors, is often a major sticking point in progressing discussions.

The purchaser will often be asked, at a very early stage in the process, to sign a Non-Disclosure Agreement (NDA) before discussions progress and certainly before the sharing of information. The NDA needs to be carefully checked to ensure that the details contained within it with respect to time limits, the scope of information which is deemed confidential and the reasonable endeavours required to maintain confidentiality are not onerous.

Once an NDA has been agreed the target will then be able to provide the purchaser with any information not within the public domain which they have requested. The target may not be willing to divulge all information before a deal is agreed, especially if they are a competitor, but it is important at this stage of the transaction process that the company is able to develop a better understanding of their target. Typical initial information requested includes:

- Top 10 customers by turnover;
- A breakdown of turnover by department/service line/product line;
- Detailed profit and loss accounts for the last three years;
- Latest management accounts and forecasts for the next one to three years;
- Anonymous information on the client contracts, length, rate of churn etc.;
- Brief information on key employees and management structure;

- Diagram and details of the corporate structure and ownership percentages of any subsidiaries;
- Pension commitments;
- Any claims or law suits which are pending;
- Any unusual or one-off expenditure;
- Details of any financial implications that would be triggered by a change of
- ownership.

Whilst financial and operational questions typically form the bulk of the information requests, it is important at meetings with the target to understand their operational culture and how an acquisition would be received by key employees. The integration process should remain firmly in management's and the adviser's thoughts when they are assessing the cultures of the two companies.

VALUATION AND NEGOTIATION

Where an advisor is in place they should project manage the transaction and handle the collection of information and analysis of this information to assist with a valuation for the target (if you choose to continue the process once further information is provided).

The process of valuation is as much an art as it is a science. An understanding of the market sector which the target operates in, and knowledge of past deal multiples is essential whilst understanding possible cost savings, an interrogation of the validity of forecasts and the likelihood of customer retention will all affect the valuation. Valuing a business is only part of the requirement, with the structuring of the deal through the use of 'earn-outs' (additional consideration conditional on future results of the company) and deferred consideration (consideration that is outstanding at completion but not conditional on future events) essential tools to help mitigate the risk of the transaction.

Grasping cross-border transactions, understanding of the local market place and local valuation techniques, compared to an acquirer's own country, is vital to pricing an opportunity correctly. This valuation should then be compared to the potential time and financial cost of setting up a new operation in the UK as opposed to acquiring one.

Once the company has valued the target, the negotiation process will commence. Typically, the purchaser will provide instructions to the adviser but leave them to handle the communications. By staying removed from the process the purchaser is able to maintain a positive relationship with the target and ensure they are not viewed as the 'bad guy' through the negotiation stages.

The level of negotiation required and timescale can be affected by a number of factors, although one of the key drivers would be if the target identified is an 'on-market' (listed for sale with an adviser or in trade publications) or 'off-market' opportunity. On-market opportunities are easier to identify as they will be professionally marketed and they are more likely to conclude a transaction as the owners will be pro-actively looking to exit. However, they are likely to be subject to multiple expressions of interest which creates competition and potentially drives a higher price being paid for the target. Those which are 'off-market' opportunities should not be seen as highly unlikely to complete since companies are much more open to such approaches then they have ever been before.

HEADS OF AGREEMENT

The heads of agreement is a document which outlines the broad terms of the transaction. The main part of the document is not legally binding, but intended to cover:

- The consideration proposed for the transaction and the structure of the payments;
- The approach which the purchaser will take to due diligence;
- Restrictive covenants by which the purchaser will want any departing shareholders to abide;
- The documentation required to finalise the deal;
- A brief approach to the warranties and indemnities which will be required.

There are often a number of legally binding requirements and these are with respect to:

- Confidentiality and deal announcement protocols;
- A commitment to a deal timetable and deadline as well as an exclusivity period;
- Who pays what costs;
- Which international territories law will govern the transaction. In the UK, it is accepted practice for deals to be under English law irrespective of the jurisdiction of the acquiring company.

The heads of agreement document is normally signed by both parties before detailed due diligence is undertaken and provides the basis for legal teams to create the share and purchase agreement.

It is important to keep this document simple but as complete as possible to provide a clear starting point for the drafting of the legal documents and avoid confusion and the need for too much further negotiation as the deal progresses.

DUE DILIGENCE

The objective of due diligence is to investigate the target company, develop a level of comfort with the target's existing financial and commercial position and to validate, as much as possible, its forecast performance.

Purchasers typically select an accountancy firm to undertake the financial due diligence on their behalf. There are some standard areas which are investigated. The scope and scale of work is agreed with the purchaser before the engagement commences.

The due diligence will not only assess the financial statements but also delve deeper into the target's accounting and operational systems; for example, assessing the stock value and its saleability, supplier and customer contracts (length, terms and break clauses), fixed assets, accounting policies and contingent liabilities.

The scope of the due diligence which the accountants and the lawyers (under separate engagements) will perform needs to be wide enough to provide confidence that the target being acquired is free from material errors and risks but not so wide as to place undue financial costs on the transaction. A balance between the deal size and depth of due diligence is something which needs to be found.

Commercial due diligence is often performed in-house and will be undertaken either formally or informally when assessing the target prior to making an offer. Once the heads of agreement have been reached, and especially in instances of larger deal sizes, further commercial due diligence may be undertaken which could involve specialist market research consultants, property and environmental consultants or an in-house project team. Other areas that are also often considered include looking into the personal history of the target management team and other key employees.

REACHING COMPLETION

When purchasing a target who has maintained excellent management information, clear employment contracts, has a good stock control process and up to date property, fixed assets, environmental and data protection policies the transition between due diligence and completion can be relatively simple.

In most M&A transactions there will be issues found in either financial, commercial or legal due diligence that were not highlighted in the information memorandum or disclosed during subsequent meetings. The nature and size of these findings will have a varying impact on the transaction, from a warranty/indemnity being included through to a re-negotiation of the price or deal structure, and in the most extreme case, collapse of the deal.

It is in situations like these that the adviser really proves his or her worth, often using any findings from due diligence as leverage to achieve a more competitive price or structuring the deal or legal wording in such a way that mitigates the risk to the purchaser.

The use of a good corporate lawyer with experience of completing transactions in the UK market place but also cross-border experience is also essential to ensure that the wording of the share and purchase agreement is favourable.

POST COMPLETION

Once the company has agreed the contracts and developed the necessary level of comfort with the target's financial, commercial and legal positions, it will then be in a position to sign the share and purchase agreement and complete the transaction.

Whilst the due diligence and legal process is underway the purchaser's board or leadership team will be working on a post deal integration plan to include aspects of human resources, operations, financial, legal and other commercial requirements. This integration plan would be more detailed for an overseas acquisition as further research and consideration would need to be given to future accounting standards (for example FRSl02), the reporting currency adopted and local human resources considerations including, in the UK, minimum wage and TUPE arrangements (Transfer of Undertakings and Protection of Employment regulations 2014).

The key factor in the success of any transaction is integration; whilst on paper a target may look like the perfect bolt-on to existing operations and have numerous synergies the deal is only successful once these have been realised. Successfully managing the newly acquired company from another country will be fundamental to achieving this result. So, once the deal is complete, the real work must begin.

4.3 THE AIM MARKET OF THE LONDON STOCK EXCHANGE

Richard Metcalfe & Ben Winder, Mazars LLP

HISTORY OF AIM

Launched in 1995 as a sub-market of the London Stock Exchange (LSE), AIM was created to provide access to capital markets for smaller growing companies which, by their nature, did not qualify for a listing on the Main Market. In addition to strict eligibility criteria, such as a minimum market capitalisation and the number of shares required to be in public hands, smaller companies typically do not have the resources to commit to the ongoing reporting demands placed on a public company. The LSE addressed these issues by implementing limited entry criteria and by adopting a more balanced regulatory approach for companies listing on AIM. The ultimate goal was to create a market for entrepreneurial businesses to raise capital and to continue to focus on achieving their growth plans while at the same time maintaining the integrity of the market.

When the market was created, just ten companies were listed on AIM, with a total market capitalisation of £82 million. By the end of 2016, over 3,700 companies had used AIM to raise £100 billion in funds. By volume of companies trading on the market and their market capitalisation, AIM is the leading growth market for small and medium-sized companies in the world.

While initially intended to provide growth capital to UK businesses, over the years the market has evolved to provide access to finance to a growing number of international businesses. By the end of 2016, just under one in five of all companies listed on AIM were incorporated outside the UK. Taking account of those companies which generate the majority of their revenues outside the UK, this proportion increases to approximately one in three. AIM has developed into a global market which attracts companies from around the world due to the availability of capital, a balanced regulatory regime and the well-established infrastructure of advisory firms in London.

Companies across a broad range of sectors are represented on AIM, including financial services, manufacturing, natural resources, technology, oil & gas and consumer services.

MARKET SNAPSHOT

Below we provide a snapshot of the AIM market at the end of 2016:

At 31 December 2016 there were 982 companies listed on AIM. The majority of these companies were UK incorporated and generated the majority of their revenues from UK operations.

A sizable minority of AIM companies – 35% at the end of 2016 – either have their principal activity outside the UK or have a non-UK parent company. The countries with the largest number of AIM companies include the USA, Australia, Ireland, China, India and South Africa.

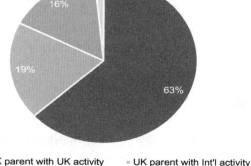

Listing profile as at December 2016

- UK parent with UK activity
- UK parent with Int'l activity
- Int'l parent with int'l activity
- Int'l parent with UK activity

The market capitalisation of companies listed on AIM ranges from less than £1 million to over £1 billion. The chart below illustrates the spread of market capitalisation, with most companies at 31 December 2016 falling in the range of £10 million to £25 million.

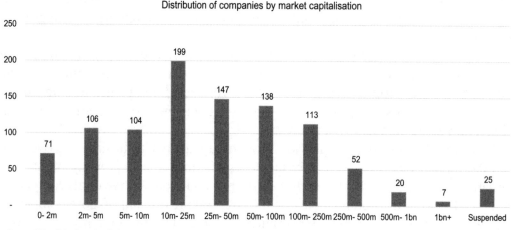

Distribution of companies by market capitalisation

Source : AIM statistics December 2016

The market is home to companies from a broad range of sectors. Using the AIM sector designations in the chart below, financial services companies, which include insurance and real estate investment vehicles, account for the largest number of companies on AIM. Companies in the consumer services sector (retailers and media companies) represent the largest market capitalisation at 31 December 2016.

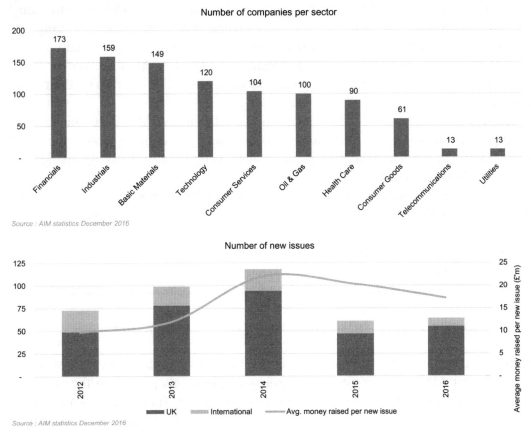

Source : AIM statistics December 2016

Source : AIM statistics December 2016

The number of listings and the value of new funds raised have fluctuated over recent years.

Over the last five years, 2014 saw a peak in the number of new listings (118) and the average new funds raised (£22 million).

Although the number of new listings decreased in 2015 and 2016 from this peak, there has been a shift towards further fund raising transactions. Total

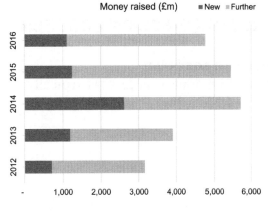

Source : AIM statistics December 2016

191

funds raised in 2015 (£5.5 billion) and 2016 (£4.8 billion) exceeded the levels achieved in 2012 and 2013.

REASONS FOR LISTING ON AIM

For many owner-managed or venture capital-backed businesses, admission to a stock exchange represents the ultimate goal. By raising funds on a stock exchange the company may be able to take the next step of investing in new products and markets or increasing the company's profile and marketability. For the shareholders, going public represents an opportunity to achieve an exit, generating a return on their initial investment.

London is one the world's truly international cities and AIM reflects this outlook, having attracted over 3,700 companies from more than 70 countries around the world. In addition, the regulatory regime in London is recognised globally for its flexible, principles-based approach.

The AIM admission criteria are less onerous than for other stock exchanges. AIM imposes few eligibility criteria, and critically for smaller growing companies there is:

- No minimum requirement for shares held in public hands;
- No minimum historical trading record required;
- No requirement for pre-vetting of the admission document by a regulatory authority;
- No minimum market capitalisation requirement for trading companies.

Although there are relatively few regulatory criteria for a company to qualify for admission to AIM, there are certain ongoing requirements placed on the company. These include the preparation and publication of regular financial information and the retention of a Nominated Adviser (Nomad), which is responsible for assisting the company with regulatory compliance.

THE AIM ADMISSION PROCESS

Standard admission
A standard admission to AIM typically comprises six distinct phases, as described below:

Strategic review	The decision to list a company's shares is one that should be taken after careful consideration of the company's goals and analysis of the potential impacts on its key stakeholders, all backed up by research.
Preparing the investment case	The investment case is the company's key selling tool and should present a compelling case to potential investors. At this stage the company will need to identify a Nomad who will help to bring the company to market.
External validation	During this phase, the company's investment case will be validated by the Nomad and a selection of potential investors.
Due diligence	With the investment case validated and a team of advisers assembled, the listing process begins in earnest. During the next five to six months, the reporting accountant, lawyers, and any specialists, will undertake due diligence on the company and prepare private reports to the company and the Nomad.
Documentation	The admission document will include details of the company, the key management team, financial performance, and how the company plans to invest the proceeds. Its content is governed by The AIM Rules for Companies. The admission document provides the basis upon which investors subscribe for shares in the company.
Marketing	Finally, the Nomad will develop a marketing strategy and issue key details of the offering to potential investors. Through a series of roadshow meetings, management will have the opportunity to bring the investment case to life and secure capital.

Raising funds

New funds raised on AIM admission transactions are typically sourced from institutional investors or a select number of individuals. Funds raised from institutional investors do not require regulatory approval prior to the listing, which makes the AIM process more attractive to smaller growing companies.

Under a public offering, which is generally defined as one made to more than 150 individuals in any member state of the European Union (EU) that is not otherwise exempted, a full prospectus under the EU Prospectus Directive (as amended) is required. As well as additional information on the company and its activities, a prospectus requires the pre-vetting and approval of the UK Listing Authority (UKLA) prior to admission.

AIM companies are not required to prepare further admission documents when they raise additional funds on the market (subject to the value of funds raised and the source). This is a significant advantage compared with other exchanges.

Fast-track admission

AIM has also introduced a streamlined secondary listing procedure – or fast-track process – which is available to companies already listed on certain designated international stock markets. Under this process, companies are not required to produce a full admission document and instead produce an expanded pre-admission announcement.

Timing and costs

Every AIM admission transaction is different. The timing and cost of an admission to AIM depend on a range of factors, including market conditions and the preparedness of the company.

As a guide, an AIM admission generally takes five to six months once the key advisers have been engaged. The planning time required in preparing and refining the company's investment plans can take up to twelve months in advance of the due diligence phase.

In terms of cost, as a guide, companies should expect the total cost of an admission on AIM to be up to 10 per cent of funds raised, with broker commissions typically representing up to five per cent of funds raised. This does, of course, depend upon the size of the fundraising and market conditions.

ADVISERS

As part of the admission process, a company will engage with a number of specialist advisers who are experts in the regulatory requirements of AIM and have experience of the process. These advisers include:

Nominated Adviser

A Nomad is the company's primary adviser, approved by the LSE, throughout the flotation process, and will help to prepare the company for its ongoing requirements and obligations post-admission.

In order for the Nomad to assess the company's potential admission on AIM, the Nomad will undertake extensive due diligence to ensure suitability of the company. In addition to assisting with the AIM admission document, the Nomad will confirm the company's suitability of admission to the Exchange and will act as the primary regulator throughout the Company's public life.

Nomads are responsible for ensuring compliance with the ongoing AIM requirements. Following admission, the Nomad advises company directors of their obligations and reviews actual trading performance against projections included in the admission document.

Brokers

Brokers are security (shares and debt) houses and members of the LSE who provide market support for trading in the company's shares and undertake fundraising activities. The broker is the key link between the company and the market; the broker provides research and sales support for the company as well as issuing information about the company to the market.

During the admission process, the broker will assess the level of investor interest in the company's securities and provide marketing and trade related advice, including the pricing of shares and investment opportunities.

All AIM companies are required to appoint and retain a broker throughout its listing on the AIM exchange. Brokers can be appointed from the same firm as the Nomad provided there are appropriate safeguards against conflicts of interest; however, some companies may prefer to appoint a broker from a separate firm.

Reporting Accountants

As one of the key advisers during the listing process, the reporting accountant is responsible for the preparation of certain documents that will be relied upon by the Nomad and potential investors. The reporting accountants are distinct from the company's own auditors.

The reporting accountant undertakes the following activities:

- An audit of the company's historical financial results covering a period of at least 36 months prior to the admission date;
- A financial due diligence review of the company and its activities, generally covering a period of 36 months prior to admission;
- A review of the company's financial reporting procedures and internal controls, including its budgeting process, to assess whether the company has appropriate

procedures in place (or will implement additional procedures post admission) to identify and report to the market any significant matters in a timely manner;

- A review of the company's working capital projections, which are prepared by management, for a period of at least 12 months following admission. The reporting accountant will "stress test" the projections by performing various sensitivities which are agreed with the Nomad.

Legal Counsel

The legal counsel works with the Nomad in regards to the preparation of the admission documents to ensure legal and regulatory compliance. The legal counsel provides advice to the company on all legal matters relating to the company's admission on AIM.

The legal counsel performs legal due diligence to address any matters regarding litigation, reorganisations, regulatory compliance, amendments to constitutional documents, directors' responsibilities and contractual arrangements. The legal due diligence seeks to ensure the company's suitability of admission and ability to meet legal and regulatory requirements.

ONGOING REQUIREMENTS

Companies listed on AIM are required to comply with the London Stock Exchange's AIM Rules for Companies (the AIM Rules) after admission. A company is expected to have established appropriate processes to help ensure compliance with the AIM Rules. AIM companies are required to have an appointed Nomad at all times during their listing on the market; a company's shares may be suspended and eventually cancelled if it does not have a Nomad.

Corporate governance relates to a company's ability to effectively govern and monitor its performance in the interest of its shareholders and is critical for public companies. The UK Corporate Governance Code is the main source of corporate governance best practice and is mandatory for fully-listed companies; however, the code is not mandatory for companies listed on AIM. In light of this, the Quoted Companies Alliance has published guidelines to enable AIM companies to establish a strong framework of corporate governance.

The AIM Rules require companies to provide certain information and ongoing disclosures to the market on a regular basis. First and foremost amongst the information to be disclosed are the annual audited accounts. The audited accounts must be published and sent to shareholders within six months of the financial year-end. These are usually prepared in accordance with International Financial Reporting Standards. The AIM Rules also require the publication of interim six monthly accounts. The interim accounts must be published within three months of the period to which they relate.

The company is expected to provide timely notifications to the market of price sensitive information as well as any changes in shareholdings and directorships. Price sensitive information ought to be published to the market as soon as is practical; this can take the form of ad hoc financial performance updates.

The company must notify the market of any substantial transactions, as defined by the AIM Rules, or related party transactions. Substantial transactions typically do not require approval by the shareholders (with reverse takeovers being the exception). If a director deals in an AIM company's shares, the transactions must be notified to the market. Prior to any director dealings, it is recommended that the company seek advice from its Nomad.

An AIM-listed company is required to maintain an up-to-date website for the disclosure of relevant information under the AIM Rules. Information to be published on the website includes an overview of the business activities, details of significant shareholders, biographical information of directors, copies of most recent announcements and copies of annual and interim accounts.

4.4 A GUIDE TO INVESTMENT IN UK COMMERCIAL PROPERTY

Gary Ritter and Charlotte Williams,
Watson, Farley & Williams LLP

The UK has historically had one of the most dynamic and transparent property markets in Europe, with a broad variety of property options, stable rents and flexible short term lease structures.

Commenting on the UK property investment market in April 2017, the London office of Cushman & Wakefield, one of the world's leading commercial property consultants, states that:

> *"As with much of the economy, the UK property market faced heightened uncertainty in 2016 as the Brexit debate and referendum rolled forward. Most notably this led to a stalling in activity as occupiers and investors paused to see what would happen. However, by the end of the year, while some occupiers remained on the sidelines or were investigating contingency plans in other markets, investment activity had sparked back into life, with quality assets in high demand, particularly from foreign investors enjoying more buying power due to the fall in the Pound.*
>
> *Total annual returns for the year dropped to 3.9% compared to 2015's 13.3%, according to the IPD UK Monthly Property Index. With a steady improvement in rental growth and sustained downward pressure on yields, the industrial sector was the strongest performer of the main commercial property sectors, with total annualised returns of 7.8%, fractionally ahead of the hotel sector, which returned 7.7%. The office market fell the most significantly from 18.3% in 2015 to 2.5% in 2016,*

with London's city core office rents experiencing a downturn, and national office rents also beginning to see slower growth as the services sector faced perhaps the most immediate uncertainty arising from Brexit. However, while year-end investment volumes into the office sector were also down on 2015, the final quarter saw an uptick in leasing activity in Central London and a pick-up in business sentiment on a national level to support demand. For the retail sector, the occupier market remained more robust through 2016, albeit with leasing activity still focussed on larger retail centres. The hotel market gained from the fall in the Pound, helping tourism and the investment market hold up well over the year, transacting just over £3.2 billion, ahead of the 10-year average.

As noted, investment activity is now being aided by the fall in sterling, with the UK's appeal to international investors increasing and Asian and Middle Eastern capital in particular coming into firstly London but also now some regional markets. Looking ahead, the long-term impact of the UK's decision to leave the EU on the real estate sector is yet to manifest. The economy has performed ahead of expectations but with higher inflation and exit talks now underway, slower rather than faster growth is generally anticipated, in the short-term at least and increased flexibility will therefore be sought by occupiers. Despite this, given the relativity of yields and, indeed, growth potential in the right assets and locations, property remains an attractive asset class for investors."

This chapter will seek to provide a legal background for overseas entities or individuals considering investing in or leasing UK commercial property (whether industrial, retail, offices or hotel/serviced apartments), either to occupy them or for investment purposes. Importantly, there are no restrictions on foreign nationals or overseas companies buying or leasing property in the UK, subject only to tax implications.

As well as acquiring the property directly, there are a number of structures through which to invest in property including:

- Property companies;
- Partnerships;
- Joint venture vehicles; or
- Real Estate Investment Trusts (REITs) A REIT is a quoted company that owns and manages income-producing property, either commercial or residential, which complies with certain conditions and may achieve certain taxation benefits.

OWNERSHIP OF LAND

The form of ownership and legal rights over a property can be very significant to an owner and/or occupier. Statute has established two forms of legal estate in land, with a relatively recent addition, namely:

- A Freehold Estate: Where the property (both land and structures) is effectively owned by the freeholder in perpetuity. An investor may prefer to own a freehold as this gives the most control, has a capital value and enables the grant of leases to secure an income stream. However, freehold ownership may nevertheless be subject to certain covenants (e.g. restricting the use of the property) and/or may be subject to the rights of others (e.g. rights of way for third parties across the property).
- A Leasehold Estate (i.e. taking a lease or renting the property): Where the leaseholder's ownership of the land is contractually limited in time to the length of the term of the lease. The lease will be granted out of a freehold or superior leasehold estate.
- Commonhold: This relatively new form of freehold tenure has existed since 2004. Commonhold is similar to the 'strata title' and 'condominium' systems that exist in Australia and the United States. Essentially, this is where each owner of a unit in a development (e.g. a flat, office or shop) owns the freehold of their unit and is also a member of a commonhold association which owns and manages the common parts of the development.

The English system enables the legal interest in the property to be split from the beneficial interest, should this be desired. The legal title holder will be the registered proprietor at the Land Registry or the legal owner of the title deeds, while the beneficial owner will be entitled to the pecuniary interest in the property and will receive the income. This would be of relevance in establishing structures for tax and accounting purposes.

As regards the beneficial interest, land can be held by more than one person in one of two ways; either as a joint tenancy or a tenancy in common. A joint tenancy is a form of ownership where, normally, should one owner die, the property will automatically vest in the surviving owner(s), regardless of the terms of the deceased's will. A tenancy in common, however, is a form of ownership where on the death of one of the joint owners, the relevant share in the property will form part of the deceased's estate and will pass to their beneficiaries by their will or, where there is no will, in accordance with the law on intestacy.

LEASEHOLD

Key elements

A lease is a contract between a landlord and tenant which creates a leasehold estate.

It is characterised by the landlord granting the tenant exclusive possession of the property for a fixed time (i.e. for a specified term or a period that is capable of being brought to an end by notice).

If these criteria are not met, a personal licence may be created instead of a leasehold estate. This is significant in terms of whether third parties will be obliged to recognise the occupier's rights and also because statute contains substantial protection for tenants, but not licensees; for example, security of tenure for certain residential and business tenancies.

Main types of lease

- The ground lease: This is a (normally residential) long lease often granted for more than 99 years, usually for a one-off sum, called a 'premium', with a nominal rent payable (sometimes called a 'peppercorn') throughout the rest of the term. A ground lease may be perceived to be closer in nature to a freehold owing to its capital value. Residential apartments/flats are normally sold or held on a long lease.
- The rack rent lease: This is the most prevalent form of commercial occupational lease, usually granted for around 5-10 years. The tenant will pay a full-market rent, normally quarterly, and, usually, no premium is payable.
- Short term residential occupational leases: These generally take the form of an Assured Shorthold Tenancy which, at the end of the lease term, entitles the landlord to possession of the premises.

COMMERCIAL LEASES

Pre-lets

Companies can take a lease of premises that are already available or may be entitled to enter into a 'pre-let' agreement with a developer to lease premises prior to the carrying out or completion of construction work, enabling the future tenant to specify the design, layout and fittings of the building.

Security of tenure

In most cases where a tenant occupies premises for business purposes, statute grants them the right to renew their lease on largely identical terms (subject to a review of rent and length of term) at the end of the term, the intention being to protect the tenant's goodwill at the premises established whilst in occupation.

Certain rights to compensation may also be available in the event that the landlord is able to rely on one or more of seven grounds to refuse to renew the lease (e.g. if

it requires occupation of the premises for its own use or wishes to redevelop the property).

Nevertheless, it is common for the parties to agree to exclude the tenant's right to security of tenure and right to compensation by 'contracting out'. A contracting out agreement will only be valid where the parties have followed a statutory process before the parties are contractually bound to enter the lease. This process requires the landlord to serve a prescribed notice on the tenant and the tenant to make a declaration that they have received the notice.

If the lease is contracted out, then the tenant must vacate the premises when the lease expires, with no right to renew and no right to compensation.

Restrictions on use

Leases usually restrict how the premises can be used. This is often linked to planning permission but sometimes, for example, with leases of commercial units in shopping centres, the use stated may be very specific so as to ensure that the landlord has a variety of businesses within the development.

Rent review

Where leases are granted for more than five years, it is standard to provide for a rent re-calculation (rent review) every fifth year. These reviews can be based on the open market rent which would be payable for a lease of the property on similar terms, may be linked to the Retail Prices Index or (less commonly) on fixed increases. Such provisions generally provide for 'upwards only' reviews.

Full repairing and insuring lease

The majority of leases of commercial premises in the UK are on a full repairing and insuring basis (FRI lease) which means that the tenant is liable for the upkeep and decoration of the property and for the costs of the landlord in insuring the building.

Service charge

Where a property is let to several different tenants, the landlord will retain responsibility in relation to the structure and the common parts of the building. The landlord will recover these costs from the tenant through charging a fee called a 'service charge'. The amount of service charge paid is generally proportionate to the size of the tenant's individual unit in relation to the lettable space in the whole building.

Break rights

Some leases include break rights giving the landlord and/or the tenant the option to end the lease before its expiry date. These provisions specify how much notice has to be given and may have financial implications.

Privity of contract

Where a lease is transferred to a new party, the original tenant will be subject to different liabilities dependent on the date of the lease.

For leases signed before 1 January 1996, the original tenant remains legally responsible for the rent and other lease commitments for the duration of the lease, regardless of whether they transfer the leasehold interest to a third party.

For leases signed after this date, subject to certain exceptions, the tenant will not remain liable after lawfully transferring the lease unless the landlord requests the tenant to sign a guarantee (known as an 'AGA'). In this situation, the tenant will remain liable during the period of ownership of the lease by the new tenant, but not beyond.

PLANNING

Prior to making certain alterations, erecting new buildings or changing the use of an existing building, businesses must contact their local authority's planning department in order to obtain planning permission. Most UK planning applications are administered by the local authority covering the area in which the particular building or site is located (contact details are available on most council websites).

The UK system is set out in statute and guidance published by the Government and by local authorities. The statutory timeframe for a planning application to a local authority to be decided is between eight and 16 weeks from the formal application, depending on whether it is treated as a major application, and whether an environmental impact assessment is required. If this timeframe is not adhered to by the local authority, the applicant may appeal. Additionally, if the application is refused, the applicant may also appeal. The appeals system in the UK also follows a statutory process.

REGISTERED LAND V UNREGISTERED LAND

Registered land

The majority of land in England and Wales is registered at the Land Registry. The register is a matter of public record and the title is guaranteed. It contains information concerning the type of estate (e.g. freehold or leasehold), the property description (through reference to a filed plan), the current owner (known as the 'registered proprietor') and details of all third party rights which have been registered against the estate or protected by notice (e.g. mortgages).

Not all information relating to the property will be displayed on the register. Certain third party rights ('overriding interests') will bind a purchaser of registered land regardless of whether they are recorded on the register, or whether a purchaser has any knowledge of them.

Unregistered land

Alternatively, where land has remained in the same hands for many years, there may not have been a trigger event requiring registration at the Land Registry and the land may still be unregistered. In the absence of a register entry, a landowner can only deduce title by proving an unbroken chain of ownership by reference to the title deeds and documents relating to the property. In practice, for a landowner to prove a good root of title, the chain of deeds must go back at least 15 years.

HOW IS LAND TRANSFERRED?

A typical sale and purchase transaction is a two-stage process involving an exchange of contracts between the buyer and the seller, followed by completion of the legal transfer. A seller's solicitor will issue a draft sale contract which will be negotiated and then exchanged with a deposit usually being paid. This is the point of no return, when both parties commit themselves to complete on a certain date. Up to this point, either party can withdraw without any liability to the other side.

Following exchange of contracts, the transfer of the property from the seller to the buyer is effected by completing the transfer deed and by complying with Land Registry registration requirements. Completion is, in effect, moving day, when the money is paid to the seller's solicitors and the keys to the property are handed over to the buyer.

Principle of 'Caveat Emptor'

In UK conveyancing, the principle of 'caveat emptor' ('let the buyer beware') is key and places the responsibility for due diligence and searches relating to a property on the buyer. It is normally the task of a lawyer to consider and negotiate the legal documentation and discover as much information as possible about the property through a variety of searches and enquiries, including, but not limited to:

- Local search – list of enquiries about property sent to the local authority which includes questions about planning, highways, drainage etc.
- Environmental search – historical information about previous uses of the land.
- Preliminary enquiries – questions about the property which are sent to the seller's or landlord's solicitors requesting information about issues such as disputes with neighbours and the use of the property.

Survey and valuation

Any property investor (whether using their own funds or funding through bank debt or sale and leaseback arrangements) should take the precaution of ensuring they have a physical survey and valuation of the property carried out by a surveyor.

Whilst not strictly property contracts, some types of real estate may be encumbered by virtue of arrangements the seller has entered into. For example, a management agreement or operating agreement may be in place which, according to the circumstances, may affect value. Any investor contemplating UK real estate investment in a specific sector will benefit from advice at an early stage to ensure that issues that may affect their investment decision are identified early in the process (e.g. any issues that go to value or may inhibit its yield, such as large scale adjoining development).

TAX IMPLICATIONS OF ACQUIRING AN INTEREST IN PROPERTY

Value Added Tax (VAT)

Commercial property transactions may be subject to VAT. Whether a commercial property transaction is subject to VAT will depend on several factors, mainly being whether it is regarded as a new property or whether the seller has opted to tax the property. VAT is currently charged at 20%.

Stamp Duty Land Tax (SDLT)

This is a mandatory tax chargeable on the purchase of property situated in England, Wales and Northern Ireland. A similar tax called 'Land and Buildings Transaction Tax' is payable in Scotland. SDLT is payable by the buyer on the purchase price, on completion or substantial performance of the contract (which generally means occupation or a payment of at least 90% of the price), whichever is earlier.

The rate of SDLT payable depends on the purchase price. For residential property, SDLT is currently chargeable at a rate of up to 15% of the purchase price. In contrast, the maximum rate of SDLT on acquisitions of UK commercial property is only 5% of the purchase price. SDLT is also payable on the grant of a lease upon both the premium (if any) and the 'net present value' of the rent payable, which is based on the value of the total rent over the life of the lease. For current rates and information on calculating SDLT please see the HMRC website[1].

There are a number of transactions which may be exempt from SDLT, such as intra-group transfers within the same group of companies.

Business rates

Business rates are a property tax that business occupiers pay towards the costs of local government services.

Details of business rates can be found at:

- England and Wales – https://www.gov.uk/guidance/valuation-office-agency-and-business-rates-non-domestic-rates

---

[1] http://www.hmrc.gov.uk/sdlt/calculate/calculators.htm

- Northern Ireland – https://www.finance-ni.gov.uk/topics/property-rating
- Scotland – http://www.gov.scot/Topics/Government/local-government/17999/11199

This chapter gives a brief summary of the legal issues relating to investment in UK commercial real estate. It is not intended to give any specific legal advice or take the place of advice from property experts.

Part Five

UK International Trade in a Wider World

5.1 WTO GROUND RULES AND UK MEMBERSHIP

The World Trade Organisation (WTO) came into effect from 1 January 1995 following signature of the Marrakesh Agreement by123 nations on 15 April 1994.

The principal features and milestones in its development are:

- The WTO replaced the General Agreement on Tariffs and Trade (GATT) which commenced in 1948. GATT followed the establishment after World War II of other new multilateral institutions to enhance international economic cooperation; in particular the International Monetary Fund (IMF) and the World Bank, two further components of the Bretton Woods system.
- Most of the features on which the WTO focuses today have their origins in previous trade negotiations from the Uruguay Round (1986-1994).
- The WTO oversees and arbitrates upon the regulation of trade between members by providing:

  * a negotiating framework for new trade agreements or amendments;
  * a dispute resolution process aimed at enforcing members' compliance to WTO agreements.

- The Doha Development Round focused on developing countries was launched in 2001; the original deadline of 1 January 2005 for its work programme of 21 subjects was missed and the round is still incomplete.
- As a result of this stalemate the launch of further new negotiations has been impossible and the number of bilateral free trade agreements between governments has proliferated.
- Under GATT a series of plurilateral agreements on non-tariff barriers aimed at improving the system were drafted, but because they were not accepted by the full GATT membership, they were informally called "codes". Several of

these codes were amended in the Uruguay Round and adopted as multilateral commitments accepted by all WTO members.

- In the Marrakesh Agreement a list of some 60 agreements, annexes, decisions and understandings were adopted. The agreements fall into six main parts:

  * Agreement establishing the WTO;
  * Multilateral Agreements on Trade in Goods;
  * General Agreement on Trade in Services;
  * Agreement on Trade-Related Aspects of Intellectual Property Rights;
  * Dispute settlement;
  * Reviews of governments' trade policies.

Principles of the trading system

The WTO's role is to establish a framework for trade policies by setting the rules rather than specifying defined outcomes. The five key principles of both the GATT pre-1994 and the WTO are:

Non-discrimination

The two components embedded in the main WTO rules on goods, services and intellectual property are:

- *The most favoured nation (MFN)* rule requiring a member to grant the most favourable conditions under which it allows trade in a certain product type to be applied to trade with all other WTO members, i.e. a special favour granted to one member must be granted to all others.
- *National treatment* requiring that imported goods should be treated no less favourably than domestically produced goods , at least post-market entry.

Exceptions to the MFN principle allow for preferential treatment among members of a regional free trade area or customs union, such as the EU or the North American Free Trade Area (NAFTA), or for developing countries.

Reciprocity

A rule reflecting both the intention to limit free-riding which might arise under the MFN rule, and the intention to obtain better access to foreign markets.

Binding and enforceable commitments

The tariff commitments made by WTO members on accession and in multilateral trade negotiations are scheduled in a list of concessions which establish "ceiling bindings."

A country can change its bindings, but only after negotiation with its trading partners. This could involve compensating partners for loss of trade. If a country does not receive satisfaction, the complainant may invoke the WTO dispute settlement procedures.

Transparency

WTO members are required to publish their trade regulations. Periodic country-specific reports through the Trade Policy Reviews Mechanism (TPRM) supplement internal transparency requirements. The WTO also tries to discourage the use of quotas and other measures used to set limits on quantities of imports.

Safety valves

Governments are able to restrict trade in specific circumstances under the WTO Agreements such as measures to protect the environment, public health, animal and plant health. The provisions fall within one or more of the following:

- articles allowing the use of trade measures to achieve non-economic objectives;
- articles safeguarding "fair competition": environmental protection measures must not be used to disguise protectionist policies;
- articles permitting intervention in trade for economic reasons.

Decision-making and Dispute Resolution

Self-described as "a rules-based, member-driven organization – all decisions are made by the member governments, and the rules are the outcome of negotiations among members", the WTO has adopted the practice of consensus as the dominant process in decision-making.

Nevertheless, the WTO Agreement foresees occasions when consensus cannot be reached and provides a dispute settlement system embodied in the Understanding on Rules and Procedures Governing the Settlement of Disputes (DSU) annexed to the Final Act signed in Marrakesh in 1994.

The DSU is regarded by the WTO as a keystone of the multilateral trading system and cited as a "unique contribution to the stability of the global economy."

How the DSU operates

The settlement process involves the appointment of case-specific panels by the WTO's Dispute Settlement Body (DSB), the Appellate Body, the Director-General and the WTO Secretariat together with arbitrators and advisory experts.

The process provides for the process to be carried out in a timely and efficient manner, normally with a panel ruling within one year and no more than 16 months if the case is appealed. Consideration should be even quicker in cases deemed urgent by the complainant.

Crucially, WTO member nations are obliged to accept the process as exclusive and compulsory.

Members

There are 164 WTO members with Liberia (2016) and Afghanistan (2016) being the two most recent. The EU, and each EU country in its own right, are members.

WTO members do not have to be fully independent states; it is sufficient that they have full autonomy in the conduct of their external commercial relations. For example, Hong Kong has been a member since 1995, predating the Republic of China which joined in 2001 after 15 years of negotiations.

As of 2007, WTO member states represented 96% of global trade and almost 97% of global GDP. In 2017, there are also 22 observer governments. Except for the Holy See, they must start accession negotiations within five years of becoming observers.

Accession

The process of becoming a WTO member takes an average of about five years, but it can last longer if the country is not fully committed or if political issues intervene. Essentially, the process for each applicant country is determined by the current trade regime and its stage of economic development. The longest on record was that of Russia, which applied to join GATT in 1993, was approved for WTO membership at the end of 2011 and acceded in August 2012. An offer of accession is only given once consensus is achieved among interested parties.

Accession process

The first step for a country wishing to accede to the WTO is to submit an application to the General Council in a memorandum with a description of its economic policies and all aspects of its trade relevant to WTO agreements. The memorandum is examined by a working party open to all interested WTO members.

The working party concentrates on issues of discrepancy between WTO rules and the applicant's international and domestic trade policies and laws after studying all necessary background information.

In the second phase of its deliberations the working party determines the terms and conditions of entry into the WTO and may consider a transitional period to allow time for the applicant nation to comply with WTO rules.

The third phase of the working party's programme involves bilateral negotiations between its members and the applicant nation regarding commitments and concessions on tariff levels for goods and services. Although the new member's commitments are negotiated bilaterally they are to apply to all WTO members under normal rules of non-discrimination.

In the final phase of the process, on conclusion of the bilateral talks, the working party sends an accession package to the general council or ministerial conference, which includes:

- a summary of all the working party meetings;
- the Protocol of Accession (draft membership treaty);
- schedules of the member-to-be's commitments.

When the terms of accession have been approved by the General Council or the Ministerial Conference, which usually meets every two years, the applicant's parliament must ratify the Protocol of Accession before it can become a member.

Some countries have undergone a rougher and longer accession process than the five years norm because of challenges by other WTO members during the period of negotiations. For example, negotiations with Vietnam took more than 11 years before it was admitted.

On accession member countries must sign all WTO agreements, of which there are currently about 60 having the status of international legal texts.

BREXIT AND BEYOND

Prior to the UK's EU referendum of 23 June 2016, Roberto Azvẽdo, WTO Director-General, warned that the UK would face complex talks with the WTO following Brexit. It has been a common assumption among many reviewing what will happen when the UK formally quits the EU in 2019 that the UK could simply operate as an ordinary WTO member. In the end this will happen but the circumstances are unprecedented and getting there might not be straightforward.

The negotiation process
Under the umbrella of EU membership and as a member in its own right, it may be that any adjustments will be of a strictly technical nature. However, negotiations will only be straightforward if the WTO membership is resolved to accommodate the UK. Recent experience of discussions during the protracted Doha Round suggests that willingness to accommodate each other's wishes is in short supply among WTO members. Therefore, a degree of careful diplomacy may be required.

These negotiations will be necessary to establish the UK's legal status in its own right within the WTO because its present membership terms are integrated into those of the EU. Both the UK and the EU will have to negotiate simultaneously with the rest of the WTO's members to extract their separate membership terms. The negotiation of free trade agreements post-Brexit with the EU itself, the US or any other WTO members on the British Government's priority list of trade partners will be separate but they will feed into discussions with the WTO. In effect, the original membership access process will have to be repeated in abbreviated form.

Agreement on the UK's membership terms will have to wait until the results of Brexit discussions are certain and it is unlikely to precede agreement on the EU's adjusted terms. Just one objection from any trading nation or group of nations which is a WTO member would be sufficient to hold up the talks.

In the event of a hard Brexit with the UK becoming more of a free trader and with low import duties across the board and minimal subsidies for farmers, the UK could achieve independent WTO membership relatively simply and quickly. However, opinion is divided on what may be the optimum scenario, and the UK government also has to balance conflicting domestic interests.

Key issues

The cause of much complexity lies in the EU's unusual situation in the WTO as 29 members: the EU itself and each of its 28 member states. The EU has agreed to keep its import duties within certain limits which apply to all its members when they import from outside the EU. The quotas agreed with the WTO allowing the EU to import maximum quantities of certain products to be imported at preferential lower-duty rates apply to the single market as a whole and not to individual countries. Likewise, limits on agricultural subsidies are also for the entire EU.

Becoming an independent WTO member will involve carving the UK's own rights and obligations out of the EU's and that will require agreement with Brussels negotiators or EU members individually.

There is a further complication. Most of the EU's current commitments to the WTO on quotas and subsidies are unknown or obscure for the reason that all the confirmed commitments pre-date 2004 when there were only 15 member states. In the intervening 13 years EU membership has expanded three times and there has been no agreement with the WTO membership on revised commitments. Shares of agricultural subsidies are likely to be particularly difficult to agree.

Other issues may be simpler, not involving a similar amount of implied work where the UK might assume existing EU commitments and no changes are required. Among these are:

- the EU's ceilings on tariffs;
- market opening pledges in services sectors;
- EU regulations on food safety, animal and plant health;
- product standards and labelling.

The bottom line

However much of the EU's commitment can be simply translated into UK undertakings, with some application of EU rules, there will still be a heavy workload to be undertaken in completing the task. Throughout the process, agreement on detailed issues as well as the complete accession package will be subject to the WTO rule of members' consensus.

5.2 THE UK EXPORT OUTLOOK POST-BREXIT

Jonathan Reuvid, Legend Business

At this early stage in negotiating the terms of the UK's departure from the EU and its future trading arrangements with the 27 remaining members it is wholly uncertain what the outlook will be for UK foreign trade within Europe from 2019.

If the UK exits the EU customs union, it will give rise to costly administrative burdens and border controls causing inconvenience to both importers and exporters, but there is no clarity on what tariffs, if any, would replace the current non-tariff basis of trade. At the extreme range of alternatives, in the event of inability to agree a trade deal or a final settlement on the UK's net liabilities, is a hard Brexit, with or without transitional arrangements, involving substitution of unilateral World Trade Organisation membership and tariff rates.

The average tariff would be about 4%, with 10% on motor cars and an upper limit of 36% on some dairy products. Plainly, the adoption of WTO tariffs would cause some market distortions and the UK government would seek bilateral trade deals with other non-EU countries to offset any diminution in exports to EU members of both goods and services.

UK trade in services with the EU, which approached US$130 billion in 2016, may be less vulnerable than trade in merchandise. The plans of some US banks to relocate staff from London to EU financial centres should not alarm unduly. The City has global strengths as the largest centre in foreign exchange trading and will remain a favoured location for securities trading and settlement thanks to its regulatory framework, the concentration of international banks and its time zone. The most significant impact will be on the clearing of euro-dominated transactions already subject to claims from Brussels negotiators and European Central Bank (ECB) attack.

Other elements of the financial services sector, such as asset management centred in Edinburgh and the big insurances companies, are unlikely to be affected by Brexit.

THE IMPLICATIONS OF A FIRM BREXIT

At this stage, we can make only preliminary assessments of the impact of Brexit on exports and how losses in value could be recovered from bilateral trade deals with other countries where a significant level of trade is already established. New trade deals will also result in some substitution of imports with a corresponding loss of exports to the UK from EU manufacturers and service providers.

The UK's overall international trade in merchandise is summarised in Figure 5.2.1 as:

Figure 5.2.1

	Exports	Imports
	US$ million	*US$ million*
Merchandise	460,446	625,806
• Agricultural products	28,405	61,498
• Non-agricultural products	423,950	558,730
Of which: EU share	43.8%	55.1%
Commercial services	345,052	207,704
• Transport	41,236	35,288
• Travel	42,869	64,148
• Other commercial services	254,271	107,212
Of which: EU share	37.2%	49.4%

Source: https://stat.wto.org/CountryProfiles - 2015
Note: Financial services (excluding insurance and pensions) account for 36.7% of other commercial services)

A worst case scenario for UK exporters collectively might involve a loss of, say, 10% of merchandise trade with the EU amounting to less than US$21 billion of annual exports.

The following is a shortlist of 11 countries with which the UK is already a trade partner and with whose governments, among others, the Department for International Trade is exploring the opportunities for bilateral trade deals post-Brexit:

- The United States of America
- Australia
- Canada
- China
- India
- Japan
- Norway
- South Korea
- Switzerland

The combined imports of these nine countries exceed US$5,700 billion and their market profiles (provided in Appendix I) yield background information to evaluate the prospects for gaining an additional U$21 billion exports from these markets over time.

The scale of the task in merchandise trade is defined in Figure 5.2.2 below, based on available 2015 trade statistics:

Figure 5.2.2 Current UK exports and total imports of export destinations

US$ billion

	UK exports		Total Merchandise imports	
	Value	*%*	*Value*	*UK share (%)*
USA	54.70	13.0	2,160.0	2.5
Australia	5.41	1.3	193.0	2.8
Canada	7.15	1.7	405.0	1.8
China	27.60	6.5	1,270.0	2.2
India	5.59	1.3	369.0	1.5
Japan	6.29	1.5	589.0	1.1
Norway	4.98	1.2	80.9	6.2
South Korea	6.47	1.5	423.0	1.5
Switzerland	32.50	7.6	262.0	12.4
Total	150.57	35.6	5,741.9	2.6

Source: https://atlas.media.mit.edu/en/profile/country

Disregarding the opportunities for growing trade with the remaining 130 WTO members that are not within the EU, the overall task of replacing a potential loss of US$21billion in exports to EU countries implies an increase of less than 14% in export sales to these nine strong markets for UK goods accounting for less than 0.4% of their total imports.

In these terms, this is a reasonable challenge given the freedom for the UK to negotiate its own trade deals and the potential to generate exponential net gains in UK exports post-Brexit.

Key product areas

Of course, the opportunities in individual export markets will vary according to the match between the products where the UK has a strong export offering and the trade partner's import demands for those products.

As an indicator of the areas where the UK will be successful, Figure 5.2.3 shows both export and import sales of the 20 product groups in which the bulk of the UK's foreign trade in goods was made in 2015.

Figure 5.2.3 – Top 20 products exported and imported by the UK in 2015

	Exports			Imports	
	£ million	Cum. %		£ million	Cum. %
Mechanical machinery	38,576	13.5	Electrical machinery	53,372	13.0
Cars	25,640	22.5	Mechanical machinery	35,865	21.7
Medical & pharma. products	24,452	31.1	Cars	31,628	29.4
Electrical machinery	24,102	39.5	Medical & pharma products	25,434	35.6
Other misc. manufactures	12,757	44.0	Other misc. manufactures	25,410	41.8
Aircraft	12,376	48.3	Other road vehicles	18,328	46.3
Scientific & photographic	11,345	52.3	Clothing	18,090	50.7
Refined oil	10,497	56.0	Refined oil	17,276	54.9
Crude oil	10,462	59.7	Crude oil	11,831	57.8

Organic chemicals	8,751	62.8	Scientific & photographic	11,505	60.6
Unspecified goods	7,857	65.6	Unspecified goods	10,428	63.1
Other road vehicles	6,444	67.9	Aircraft	10,401	65.6
Beverages	6,363	70.1	Fuels other oil	8,794	67.7
Works of art	6,083	72.2	Misc. metal manufactures	8,307	69.7
Clothing	5,788	74.2	Vegetables & fruit	7,556	71.5
Plastics	5,427	76.1	Plastics	7,459	73.3
Non-ferrous metals excl.silver	5,297	78.0	Organic chemicals	6,634	74.9
Misc. metal manufactures	5,146	79.8	Beverages	5,819	76.3
Fertilizers & other chemicals	4,916	81.5	Meat & meat preparations	5,758	77.7
Toilet & cleansing preps.	4,870	83.2	Paper & paperboard	5.642	79.1

Source: Office of National Statistics – April 2016 Trade Bulletin

From this data the following conclusions may be drawn:

1. The top 20 export product groups accounted for 83.2% of the UK's exports;
2. The top 20 import groups accounted for 79.1% of total imports;
3. The top 7 in each list accounted for 52.3 % of total exports and 50.7 % of total imports respectively;
4. Among the top 7 product groups five categories are common to both exports and imports, representing 44.2% and 41.8% respectively of total UK exports and imports:

	% exports	% imports
• Mechanical machinery	13.5	8.7
• Cars	9.0	7.7
• Medicinal& pharmaceutical prods.	8.8	6.2
• Electrical machinery	8.4	13.0
• Other miscellaneous manufactures	4.5	6.2
	44.2	41.8

The case for a firm Brexit

Taking just two of these five product groups: cars and packaged medicaments, and comparing the UK's foreign trade in these goods with that of the biggest three EU members, it is apparent that both the EU partners, as well as the UK, have much to lose potentially in the event of a hard Brexit.

In Figure 5.2.4, 2015 exports and imports of France, Germany and Italy with the UK in cars and packaged medicaments are analysed:

Figure 5.2.4 – Exports vs Imports of France, Germany & Italy with the UK

	Cars				Packaged medicaments			
	Exports		Imports		Exports		Imports	
	US$B	%	US$B	%	US$B	%	US$B	%
France	2.12	5.7	2.25	9.9	1.40	3.7	0.64	2.8
Germany	23.80	25.0	3.54	9.0	3.82	4.1	1.93	4.9
Italy	1.16	4.7	1.76	15.0	1.17	4.7	0.80	6.8

Source: https://atlas.med.edu/n/profile/country

In these two product categories, while US$2.89 billion of the UK's exports to France (representing 12.7%) are vulnerable, US$3.52 billion of France's exports to the UK (9.4%) are at risk under a hard Brexit.

More significantly, US$27.62 billion of Germany's exports to the UK (29.1%) are at risk against US$5.47 billion (13.9%) of the UK's countertrade. Italy's US$2.33 billion of exports to the UK (9.4%) are vulnerable against the UK's US$2.56 billion (21.8%). With the pound sterling's exchange rate against the EU reduced to 1.1901 (10.05.2017) and against the US$ to less than 1.28 the UK is more competitive today than in 2015 in the event of a failure to agree Brexit terms.

In light of these indicators for two major manufactured product groups, there is a clear mutual benefit to the EU and the UK in agreeing terms of trade to their joint advantage. This may not be possible for all trade, particularly agricultural products in light of the Common Agricultural Policy (CAP), but for product groups dominated by a few major multinational companies, such as the automotive and pharmaceutical sectors, an accommodation between London and Brussels would appear achievable.

Other non-trade issues, such as immigration, the Irish land border and jurisdiction, will impact the negotiation with both the EU Commission and individual national governments, but a "firm" rather than "hard" Brexit seems the more likely. Given the requirement for both the EU and UK to apply to the WTO for amended membership when the terms for UK withdrawal are certain, it also seems likely that a transitional period will be necessary after March 2019. Transitional arrangements are also probable for any complex agreements that are reached on trade.

THE CHALLENGE FOR UK EXPORTERS

The many successful UK exporters will be seeking to increase penetration in those markets beyond the EU where they are established suppliers while maintaining their market shares in EU member states. At the same time, they will be looking for opportunities to enter new markets where no initiatives have yet been made. The profiles in Appendix I of the nine priority markets for which publicly available information has been consolidated may help decision-makers to make their assessments.

Other British businesses and entrepreneurs whose experience of trading internationally is limited or who have not yet adventured beyond their home and EU markets, are being encouraged to explore export opportunities by working with the Department of International Trade, whose country specialists have established connections and can identify specific opportunities.

The 2016 FSB Report on SME exporting
The drive to engage small and medium size enterprises in proactive export initiatives was spearheaded by the Federation of Small Businesses (FSB) report, "Destination Export" which was published in July 2016 immediately following

the Brexit referendum.

The FSB report surveyed the export destinations of those small firms that are active exporters and identified that they were engaged worldwide in the following proportions:

	%
Europe (EEA plus Russia & CIS)	95
North America	61
South East Asia	56
Australia	49
Africa	35
South America	21

As to those businesses already exporting or considering engagement in export trade in comparison with those who were lapsed exporters or not considering engagement, the proportions were:

	%
Non-considerers	54
Exporters	21
Considerers	9
Lapsers	12

Within the category of non-considerers are those companies in the supply chain of currently successful exporters whose products are thereby "coat-tailing" into export markets.

In terms of business profiles, the average annual turnover of exporters was found to be £935K against £390K for the others. The majority of exports were in goods rather than services with 47% from the manufacturing industry.

Encouragingly, the ages of small firms most likely to consider exporting were less than two years (21%), two to four years (19%) and five to nine years (9%).

Survey responses identified that 37% of exporters had consulted and received advice from the Department for International Trade (DfIT). Additional sources of support were informal advice from other businesses (11%), professional associations and trade bodies (79%) and online information (7%). However, 52% of those surveyed claimed to have called for or received no support.

Making best use of desk research

Desk research is an essential first step in the decision whether or not to attempt entry into a new export market and it is also a tool to monitor market penetration for those who have already launched their products or services internationally. The appendices which follow provide extended profiles of the nine priority markets outside Europe listed in this chapter. They are a compendium of the data available from leading international institutions on which commentators and larger companies with in house economists and corporate planners rely. They offer a one-stop information shop for those embarking on their export adventures.

Each country profile will be updated twice annually according to new data filed and are available online to all accessing these chapters.

Major reference sources

UK National Statistics	https://www.gov.uk/government/statistics
The Directory of Economic Complexity	https://atlas.media.mit.edu/en/profile/country
Central Intelligence Agency	https://www.cia.gov/library
OECD	https://www.oecd-library.org/statistics
World Bank	https://www.worldbank.org
United Nations Conference on Trade and Development	https://unctad.org

5.3 BUSINESS WITHOUT BARRIERS

Glynis Whiting, Managing Partner, TIAO

What if non tariff, non-physical trade barriers were removed? British chambers of commerce in overseas markets and the UK have started using technology to facilitate international trade around the world.

Restrictions imposed by governments are not the main barriers to trade. The greatest barrier for SMEs is finding the right people to help them do business in a new market.

There is an ever growing number of online platforms which seek to use the internet to create business opportunities. Learning from Amazon and other giants, many businesses would like to find an easy and inexpensive way to extend their market and develop business. But in the online world, with scare stories every day of cyber-crime and online hackers, how do you know who you are really dealing with?

Traditional face-to-face networking, the tried and tested way to develop business with people you know, like and trust, is often very inefficient. It can be time consuming and expensive, especially for small businesses and startups with limited resources.

Chambers of commerce have traditionally provided a strong, trusted environment in which companies can build long-term lasting business relationships. Networking events, personal and business development opportunities are the mainstay of the chamber calendar. However, building your business this way can be a slow process, and chambers themselves can find recruitment and retention of their business members in a competitive environment to be challenging.

As Marc Decorte, Chair of new technology company TIAO says, "If you look at chambers from a member's perspective, after three or four years you have done the tour of all the other members. Where do you go then?"

AN ONLINE PLATFORM FOR CHAMBERS OF COMMERCE

COBCOE, the organisation representing British chambers in mainland Europe for over 40 years, has teamed up with TIAO, a new technology company based in Belgium, to put together the best of both worlds.

The challenge is how to create a global online platform which combines opportunities for every company to do business with each other in an environment in which the key ingredient is trust. Trust cannot be bought – it must be earned, and as we have seen in recent months, in an increasingly connected online world of social media, it can easily be lost.

COBCOE Connects is a matchmaking platform for businesses anywhere to find opportunities to grow their business in a trusted environment "at the click of a button".

TRUST IS THE KEY INGREDIENT

"Trust is forever fragile and attempts at control futile. Managing the message simply won't work in today's complex and interconnected world." – Robert Philips, Jericho Chambers.

Chambers of commerce know their members, often over many years. They also have unique insights into their local market place; how it works in practice, what are the key questions every business new to the area needs to ask – and all the answers.

So the COBCOE Connects platform is personally moderated at local level by chamber staff, who can also call on the expertise of their own members – an unparalleled hub of local professional knowledge and support creating a unique trusted environment for new entrants to market.

TIAO itself is predicated on this premise – TIAO stands for 'Trust is an Outcome' and this element is core to how COBCOE Connects works at every level.

WHAT DOES COBCOE CONNECTS OFFER?

The platform offers four services which together create a unique trading hub for companies:

1. The means to develop and enhance their profile, searching out the right opportunities
2. A tailored, automated 'matchmaking' service between company members within the COBCOE network
3. Facilitated transactions between members that have 'found' each other via the platform

4. A service platform for strategic partner companies – these may be at COBCOE level, like our founding partners Kompass International, or at the local network level. The offer can include visibility and branding or a more direct service offer for a limited number of selected members to assist their trading experience.

WHAT DIFFERENTIATES COBCOE CONNECTS FROM OTHER ONLINE PLATFORMS?

*   Multi-level/ multilateral – The reach and breadth of the network across Europe and beyond with companies locally and internationally, whether for export, accessing supply chain webs across the world, for joint ventures, investments in any market place – business without barriers.
*   Membership driven in-depth local knowledge in each local chamber/network, from startups to major corporates – everyone can build a profile and reputation on the platform.
*   Moderated – The unique aspect which ensures that the platform is a safe and trusted space in which to do business. Much of the matchmaking online is automated, but there will also, when needed, be personal follow-up by each chamber/network. This personal contact through known networks is a key element which builds trust for all participants.

HOW DOES IT WORK?

There are five distinctive features:

1. *Create a profile and upload opportunities*
    Each chamber becomes a network on the platform and uploads basic information about its members (company name/description/sector, etc.) Members are then individually invited to activate their membership of the platform (with acceptance of terms and conditions) and build their profile in the platform. This can include as much detail as possible about who they are, what they do, their key products and services as well as the key people running the company.

    They can also upload business opportunities – what they are looking for – to offer or state what their needs are. All key words are searchable by others, which increases the opportunity to make the right match.

2. *Intuitive search to find future business opportunity or partner*
    The COBCOE Connects search engine helps define every search using key words that match what is written in profiles and opportunities and other search criteria. Members can refine their search (location, sector, name, size of company and other keywords). Based on the information in the member profiles and the

opportunities they have posted, other members can find them.

Once they have identified a possible match, members can make direct contact with them via inline messaging directly to the primary contact of their match.

3. *No dead ends – guaranteed search results*

With COBCOE's strategic relationship with Kompass International, every member has access to the 4.8 million businesses in 68 countries around the world in the Kompass International Directory.

COBCOE and Kompass work with members to select any or all of these companies, to invite them to join the platform, and participating networks have the opportunity to offer full network membership where relevant. Each member can invite up to 100 companies (five at any one time) to join the platform and develop further contacts.

4. *Improve results by building trust*

Trust is a combination of three elements: delivery, transparency and accountability. As TIAO puts this at the heart of the platform, every member can improve their results by building trust through their TIAO score. The TIAO score rewards **delivery** by how active they are on the platform, **transparency** by the completeness level of their profile, and **accountability** by how responsive they are and how many opportunities they upload. The higher the TIAO score, the higher the company ranking in searches.

5. *Moderation – integrating digital with personal*

The role of the chamber/network moderator is a unique element in building trust in the platform.

Each chamber/network has a dedicated moderator. Although most connections in the platform are automated, the role of the moderator is a key differentiating ingredient to:

- Act as a personal point of contact for all chamber members in the platform – this works in two ways – adding value to the membership offer, plus raising the profile of the chamber with new prospects;
- Assist members in using the platform (creating profiles, doing searches and posting opportunities) and support with match-making and business development opportunities;
- Validate applications for new memberships – maintaining trust in the network and providing opportunities to recruit new members to their own network.

The moderator has real-time access via a personalised dashboard to what is happening on the site, so can make personal contact where necessary as well as monitor activity

and report back to the chamber and its members, promoting success stories.
A moderators' community has been created, which meets online fortnightly to develop ideas and share experience nationally and internationally.

IN SUMMARY

At a time of increasing global uncertainty and potential political impasse, businesses need support to weather the storms and navigate in 'choppy waters'. It is, conversely, also a good time to act and take advantage of global opportunities.

People like to do business with people they know, like and trust. Chambers and local business networks are uniquely positioned to deliver real business opportunities because of the unique combination of:

- **Local knowledge** and experience of business reality in each market or sector place, either in-house or via the breadth of existing/prospective members, who may be local SMEs or larger B2B service providers with international coverage;
- **Strong personal, often long standing relations** with members which cannot be replicated by governmental or single commercial players – ideally placed to provide personal moderation;
- **Global reach** of the COBCOE network – multi-lateral/multi-level **network of networks**;
- **Personal moderation** – COBCOE will help chambers/networks to interact and exchange **best practice**. The COBCOE accreditation process is continuously improving the effectiveness and governance of chambers and the growing 'moderators community' assists with the sharing of ideas and experience;
- **User led** – The platform is being continuously developed, facilitating more **self learning** to improve the matchmaking

---

WHO IS BEHIND COBCOE CONNECTS?

Launched as a pilot earlier this year, COBCOE Connects is now fully operational with seven partner networks already online, plus COBCOE to moderate companies from further afield and two additional networks joining every month. As of June 2017 participating chambers were Thames Valley Chamber Group and Hertfordshire Chamber of Commerce in the UK, with British Chambers of Commerce in Belgium, Italy, Lithuania, Slovenia and Bulgaria in mainland Europe.

It is early days in the development of the platform, but feedback from companies is already positive. As one of the UK's largest electronics distributors said at the Hertfordshire Chamber launch in June 2017: "COBCOE Connects is an opportunity to both procure products throughout Europe and possibly sell as well. We do appreciate that it is early days for this platform, but this makes for exciting times."

The TIAO team, which has developed the software as a service for COBCOE Connects, has in-depth understanding of both technology and, more importantly, how chambers and their members work.

The Chairman of TIAO is Marc Decorte, President and CEO of Shell in Belgium and Luxembourg with considerable experience in chambers of commerce and technology startups. Explaining what attracted him to TIAO, he said: "I only look at startups that have a disruptive element in their business model. They must create a new opportunity that did not exist before. One of the criteria for success is that TIAO starts from the customer, and that's what I liked. They didn't start with the technology. They knew that business was missing an element and that it was an opportunity for the chambers, and from that they generated the idea.

"TIAO has a very clear understanding of what chambers do, what chambers need, what the opportunities are, and what members are looking for. And they can position themselves as partners, rather than suppliers to chambers. That's essential."

He believes that the platform offers a unique win-win opportunity, adding, "Being active in chambers of commerce, I see two key elements:

1. The number one hope that members have on joining a chamber is that they will grow their business
2. Growing business very quickly equates to going international, for exporting, finding distributors and partners they can trust

"For chambers, to go on a platform is a unique opportunity that nobody else can offer. It's like virtual networking. It creates the possibility to do commercial business in a digital way. If I was a chamber, this would be the tool to give my members a concrete offer about what the value-add is of joining and staying a member."

ABOUT THE TEAMS

COBCOE
COBCOE is the Council of British Chambers of Commerce in Europe. Established 45 years ago, it is the not-for-profit membership body for British chambers of commerce located in continental Europe. Since 2017, UK chambers can also join.

The member chambers of COBCOE are currently based in 36 countries. Their combined membership stands at around 12,000 companies.

COBOE acts as an umbrella organization and works with its members and supporting partners, such as Jaguar Land Rover, to promote international trade and business. It also seeks to protect and promote the interests of members and their business members through united representation and initiatives on current topics such as Brexit.

A further 40 organisations are affiliate partners of COBCOE. These include UK chambers of commerce, British chambers of commerce around the world and other related membership organisations. This global network provides access to local market expertise and assists in building the local relationships and stakeholder engagement that helps businesses to succeed.

TIAO

TIAO is one of the fastest growing business development platforms in Europe. The founders and team members bring together a unique set of relevant experiences and expertise: experienced serial entrepreneurs, management and board experience in chambers of commerce and governmental agencies, multinational global sales, marketing and strategy expertise, plus in-house tech entrepreneurs with a solid track record of building platform startups and online services.

Marc Decorte, Chairman of TIAO has 35 years' experience in technology, business development, marketing and in driving the bottom line of B2C and B2B businesses at global level. In the last six years, he has built up extensive expertise in digital transformation through his current position as CEO of Belgian Shell and former position as Global VP Connected Digital Technologies at Shell.

5.4 STARTING OUT IN EXPORTING

Marcus Dolman, Co Chairman BExA, and Susan Ross, MBE, Vice President, BExA British Exporters Association

Department for International Trade (DIT) research suggests around a third of exporters begin exporting in response to customer demand, many working through social or family ties. Exporting involves several layers of complexity that sit above domestic trade, and therefore needs to be managed proactively and accurately. In any case, even if a business begins exporting by chance, it must be with the intention that exporting will become a profit contributor, and to achieve this, it is helpful to develop an export strategy. This strategy should identify where it is easiest to do business, culturally and linguistically, and which markets offer the best sales opportunities.

The key question is, how do you get started? What kind of selling mode should you use? Which are the best countries to start in? How do you get your goods there? What information do you need to make the sale? Who is going to do each task?

Text book marketing theory talks about entry modes. In simple terms, that means the method of selling goods or services, and how the business should be organised to do it. The choice revolves around three issues:

1. Business risk taken by exporter
2. Exporter's management control and visibility of the destination market
3. Flexibility

The good news is that you can be an arm's length exporter – by selling through a trader, manufacturer or consolidator that has experience and existing trading patterns with the destination. However, by involving an intermediary, you are giving away margin, but then you are also insulating yourself from the inevitable extra risks of getting the goods to their destination, physical loss or damage, export and import customs duties, currency, overseas regulation, law and jurisdiction, and export payment risk.

Direct exporters who want to have a regular flow of sales tend to have representation in the destination country. This ranges from having an overseas agent working on your behalf, or appointing a distributor or dealer that resells your product under your brand, through to establishing an office or joint venture partner abroad.

Each route has its place but the resources available to exploit the market and the level of risk the seller is prepared to take will determine which is most appropriate in the circumstances. For example, the sheer size and strategic potential of China may suggest a direct investment, whereas Zambia would suggest a distributor method. A very small market like Ascension may best be served by exporting directly from head office.

A good place to start for help and information is with DIT. This government-funded agency supports UK exporters and helps companies realise their international business potential through knowledge transfer and ongoing support. The DIT and Exporting is GREAT websites contain country information and details of the services on offer. 'Open to Export' has useful resources and pointers and you can submit questions to a panel of experts.

START WITH A PROFITABLE PRODUCT LINE

It is very difficult to start your first business with exporting. However, if you have a successful product in your home market, exporting can help you to grow and diversify. So, if you have a product that sells well here and is successful and profitable, you can understand its ins and outs and what works and doesn't work in the UK before going overseas. If your UK domestic business doesn't enjoy good margins, do not assume that, by adding export markets, you can improve your company's finances. It is only worth venturing overseas if the product is already profitable: exporting is going to take a lot of your time and is likely to cut into your margins. The cost of every aspect of business is higher, and your overseas representative will also want a percentage of sales.

BEGIN CLOSE TO HOME

With exporting, you need to take one step at a time: don't try to launch in every market. The nearest market to the UK is Ireland: they speak the same language, use the euro, and have strong ties with the UK.

If your product works in Ireland, look to countries with a similar customer profile, needs and wants. This may be to larger English speaking countries such as the USA or Canada, or closer to home into Europe. Benelux countries are physically close, speak English, and their population of 29m (under half that of the UK[1]) belies their trading skills. The Netherlands has its own industrial and agricultural exports and also acts as

---

[1] CIA World Fact Book

a distribution centre for continental Europe and is the world's eighth largest exporter, exporting four times as much per head of population as the UK.

> Notwithstanding this, one exporter writes, "Export strategies for new exporters often suggest concentrate on easy, near markets. Sensible strategy, but in practice a good order from Japan is worth two promises from Ireland".

Once your target list of destinations is established, start with the ones that you can get to easily on low cost direct flights: your time is precious.

DEVELOPING YOUR PRODUCT FOR EXPORT

Look at what adaptations your product will need for your chosen export market. Is your product right? Get to know the competition. Look at the customer requirements. Try to imagine the position of the customer, the wholesaler and the retailer. What do they want? You are going to make a big investment in exporting, you need to protect your brand and provide good quality and service to encourage your customers to choose your product instead of their familiar locally produced product. You cannot afford to get it wrong.

> To enter the Japanese market, a consumer engineering company needed to design a tiny machine that could be put away in a cupboard in a typical Japanese home. Subsequently, the company discovered that customers in Europe also wanted a tiny machine.

Consider your Intellectual Property Rights, and be careful about which entities you licence to distribute your products, for which sectors or geography, and if exclusive or not. You do not want to have a licensee that has acted as a 'brand collector' and is not working hard enough for you. The BExA Guide to Export Compliance[1] has a useful checklist on this subject.

---

[1] http://www.bexa.co.uk/bexa-guide-to-export-compliance-2/

RESEARCH

Make sure you have time to spend to research the market properly. Understand the culture and demographics of the country. Find out what sells locally, what price it is and what its shortcomings are. Understand what will be the best way to promote/market/advertise your product. Who are the key players? What can you learn from them? Taking a key UK customer out to your golf club might be a pleasant way to spend an afternoon and initiate some useful discussion, but it won't necessarily suit a French customer where golf is less popular, and instead an activity that demonstrates your appreciation of France's fine food could result in a stronger relationship.

Perfecting the image

A young electronics company had developed a calibration system to enable installers of digital TV to achieve the best reception. Exports were mainly to the USA and comprised 10% of turnover. An approach was made to DIT for advice about growing exports. The recommended strategy included being more proactive in seeking out new opportunities, using on-the-ground market information from overseas embassies, who also supplied useful leads, and understanding the technology and consumer needs of each market before visits were made. New European markets were established and exports grew to 70-80% of turnover.

There is a lot of information on the internet, but the key is its interpretation. Ensure the data obtained is pertinent to the question. For example, some countries' economic and demographic information may be controlled by their governments. It may have been produced to toe the party line, may be misleading, inaccurate or even blatantly untrue.

If you are selling consumer products, information such as GNP and GDP are useful for identifying the bigger markets, but consider also the disposable income of the people: China, for example, has the world's largest economy, but 1.4 billion people spreads that wealth out dramatically. Per Capita Income is an important measure if the product is a mass market product, but if you are selling luxury goods, the real measure is the disposable income of the richest segment of the population, the A, B, C1 demographic strata.

Checklist: Awareness of local customs and practices
- Check local, national and religious holidays, and summer factory/office shutdowns. The working week may not be 9am-5pm Monday to Friday.
- What is the normal dress code?
- Be sensitive to your customer's religion:
  - * Foods or food combinations to avoid
  - * Fasting times
  - * Prayer times
- Understand the politics and other newsworthy events in the territory, including when elections and major sporting events are being held.
- Understand the business etiquette on greetings and meetings. If in doubt, always shake hands with your right hand, address as Mr/Mrs, and receive a business card with both hands, taking care to read it. Practice these things at home so that you do not feel shy doing them when you arrive.
- Smiles can go a long way, but don't try British or self-deprecating humour too early in your relationship, and certainly not by email where it can be read very differently. Taking the blame and playing the eccentric Brit can have benefits, so long as you don't repeat this too often.

MAKE IT A BUSINESS

Don't try to take on overseas markets until you have the resources (in terms of people and money) to do things properly. Too often people go into exporting via an export agent, assuming this will be a useful add-on for the domestic business, but it isn't wise to treat export as an add-on. Take it very seriously. And think: you need to have a success early on or the team will become disillusioned.

This is where working with third parties can help. Much expertise is available from sales agents and export houses, from freight forwarders for the logistics, and the bank and factoring houses who can help with payment and credit collections. You don't have to do it all yourself to be successful!

Choose your customers wisely. Seasoned exporters make the availability of credit insurance on a customer a part of the decision about whether to bid. The value of the credit insurance is that if the customer does not pay in good time, the credit insurer can help with debt collection and if that is also unsuccessful, pay a claim.

FINANCE

When you start exporting, you will have an extra cash requirement. Suppliers may demand payment at 30 days, but because the goods take longer to get to their destination, you have to give longer credit on your sales. You may need to compete with local suppliers in your destination market where the usual credit terms may be longer. For example, Germany and Netherlands tend to pay strictly 30 days after invoice date; whereas in France and Belgium, 60-90 days is the norm and Portugal, Spain, Greece and Italy ask for long credit terms and take longer to pay! How will you fund this? You may be able to negotiate longer terms from suppliers because you are winning more business for them. Export factoring can be used to close the gap. However, factoring only works once the sale has been made. Prior to that, you may need to look at procurement finance or sources of additional working capital, not forgetting 'non-bank finance' such as peer-to-peer lending. The Government has an Export Working Capital Scheme to help address the working capital needs of exporters[1]. See also BExA's Guide to Financing Exports[2].

> Terms of payment must relate to something under your control; the despatch date or invoice date are usual. Avoid "30 days from date of arrival at customer's site": What if the goods are delayed? How do you prove they have arrived? What if your goods arrive at the beginning of a public holiday and have to be stored?

ROUTE TO MARKET

Work out how you are going to get the goods there, including delivery (Incoterms®) and management/organisation. Use the four Ps:

---

[1] Details of Government Export Finance schemes can be found on the UK Export Finance website: https://www.gov.uk/government/organisations/uk-export-finance

[2] http://www.bexa.co.uk/bexa-guide-to-financing-exports-2/

Product – what are you selling; how is it packaged, what are the warranty obligations? What substitute product is available? Will you have issues with Intellectual Property?

Place – destination; how you will transport the goods there, how you will get them in front of your customer. What is your method of distribution/logistics? Who will provide after sales services?

Price – check what else sells in the market and at what price. What are the usual payment terms, and what will you have to offer to be competitive?

Promotion – how do you get the customer to buy? How do you get the message out – advertising, trade shows, brochures, sales force, distributors? Will you sell directly or engage a local representative? How does the local market normally sell goods?

> Sometimes it is better not to follow the crowd. One British exporter had a choice of two trade shows: Moscow supported by DIT or Prague with no support. The exporter writes: "We went to Prague and were the only foreign company. We established business with four different Czech importers."

WHERE TO START

Identify your new market from research with the help of DIT. British embassies and consulates, through their commercial staff, provide invaluable help to new exporters in a number of different ways, including helping identify potential agents and local organisations and give you an understanding of local commercial practices. There is no substitute for visiting the market. Consider taking part in a trade mission organised by a UK Chamber of Commerce or Trade Association. And get networking: experienced exporters are usually happy to share their experiences of overseas markets.

Appendix I

Priority Trade Markets
beyond the EU

PRIORITY MARKETS FOR UK TRADE:

UNITED STATES OF AMERICA

THE ECONOMY

In perspective

The United States of America (USA) remains the largest global economy. World Bank estimates of 2015 nominal GDP with comparatives for the next five leading economies with GDP in excess of US$2 trillion and the EU total in descending order are:

	US$ million	GDP real growth (%)
USA	18,036,648	1.6
China	11,064,665	6.6
Japan	4,383,076	0.5
Germany	3,363,447	1.7
United Kingdom	2,861,091	1.8
India	2,088,841	7.7
EU	16,314,942	2.2

In terms of purchasing power parity (PPP), while US GDP trebled between 1990 and 2015, China's GDP multiplied 17.6 times. Since then, US GDP has continued to be outshone by China and more recently India. As a result, the Chinese economy has overtaken the US with a 2016 GDP of US$21.270 trillion at PPP compared to US18,560 trillion for the USA and US$19,180 for the European Union including the UK.

With a more positive outlook for the world economy and the US in 2017 and 2018 in both IMF and OECD forecasts and with America as the UK's second trade partner after the EU, the US is a prime target for increased exports.

The US economy today
The headline statistics for 2015 relating to GDP of US$18 trillion and the estimated population of 323 million highlight the USA's foreign trade performance as:

	% GDP	$ per capita
GDP		54,307
Foreign trade	14.5	11,817
Current account balance	(2.4)	

Source: WTO statistics

Composition of GDP

	By end use %		By sector of origin %
Household consumption	68.6	Agriculture	1.1
Government consumption	17.7	Industry	19.4
Investment in fixed capital	15.9	Services	79.5
Investment in inventories	0.5		

Source: CIA World Fact Book

In respect of household consumption, household debt is recorded as 79.75% of disposable income for the first quarter of 2016 and had risen to US$12.58 trillion by the year-end.

The industrial production growth rate is estimated at 2.1% for 2016.

International Trade

In world trade the US ranked 3rd in merchandise exports after the EU and China and 2nd in imports before China but again after the EU; the same world ranking as for both exports and imports of services. US merchandise exports and imports each declined by 3% in 2016 but a modest recovery is expected in 2017 and 2018 in line with world trade trends. Conversely, US exports and imports of services in 2016 increased by 0.3% and 3.2% respectively.

The USA urrently has 14 free trade agreements in force , of which all but the North American Free Trade Agreement (NAFTA) with Canada and Mexico are bilateral. It has been in protracted negotiations with the EU, currently halted by the new US administration since 2013, on the proposed Transatlantic Trade and Investment Partnership (TTIP) and is engaged in discussions on 14 other bilateral and regional agreements.

Ease of entry

US market entry is not easy for foreign exporters in spite of the open business environment. UK exporters without previous engagement in America need to identify carefully the geographical locations where there are specific opportunities for their products and that the local market is receptive to imports. Direct representation rather than the use of export agents is more likely to be successful.

Merchandise Trade

US merchandise exports at US$1,505 billion (f.o.b.) in 2015 accounted for 9.13% of the global total, while its merchandise imports (c.i.f) at US$2,307 billion represented 13.8% of the global total. The current account deficit of US$802 billion is echoed in imbalances with China and the EU, notably Germany.

By contrast, the US ran a surplus in its trade in commercial services of US$221 billion with exports of US$690 billion (14.5% of world exports) against imports of US$469 billion (10.2%).

The composition of merchandise trade is summarised as:

By main commodity group	Exports %	Imports %
Agricultural products	10.7	6.8
Fuels and mining products	9.4	10.7
Manufactures	74.8	78.4
Other	5.1	4.2
By destination & origin		
Canada	18.6	13.0
China	7.7	21.8
EU	18.2	18.9
Mexico	15.7	12.9
Other	39.7	33.4.1

Source: WTO statistics

Agricultural products

The top imported agricultural products, together amounting to US$27,852 million in 2015, are alcoholic liquor, coffee and bakery products. Together they accounted for 22% of the total.

The top five exported agricultural products are soya beans, maize, fresh or dried nuts, wheat and meslin and other food preparations which amounted to US$46,320 million in 2015, representing 33% of exports. There was a trade surplus of US$15,714 million in overall agricultural products.

Non-agricultural products

America's top imported and manufactured products are passenger cars, crude petroleum oils, automatic data processing machines, automotive parts and medicaments in measured dosages. Together amounting to US$524.2 billion in 2015 they accounted for 25% of total manufactures and fuels imports at US$2,101 billion.

Non-agricultural exports totalled US1,201 billion, resulting in a 2015 trade deficit of US$900 billion. The top five product categories in descending order are refined petroleum oils, passenger automobiles, auto parts, electronic integrated circuits and automatic data processing machines. Together they accounted for US$235.5 billion, representing 20% of the total.

Trade in commercial services

Compared to trade in non-agricultural merchandise, the imports and exports of commercial services, at US$469 billion and US$690 billion respectively, are relatively low. The pattern of this trade is:

	Exports	Imports
By main service	%	%
Transport	12.2	20.7
Travel	25.8	25.7
Other commercial services	58.5	51.7
Goods-related services	3.5	2.0
By main destination & origin		
EU	31.6	35.2
Canada	8.8	6.6
Japan	6.7	6.2
Other*	52.9	52.0

*Other export destinations include China (6.1%) and other origins include Bermuda (5.5%)

Source: WTO statistics

CURRENT UK TRADE WITH THE UNITED STATES

Total merchandise exports to the US in 2015 were US$54.7 billion against imports of US$44.8 billion. The top eight export and import product groups in which the UK traded with the US in 2015 were:

	Exports			Imports	
	US$ billion	%		US$ billion	%
Cars	6.9	13.0	Planes, helicopters	5.7	13.0
Packaged medicines	4.7	8.5	Aircraft parts	2.0	4.4
Nucleic acids	4.3	7.9	Refined Petroleum	1.5	3.4
Gas turbines	2.8	5.2	Human or animal blood	1.1	2.4
Hard liquor	1.8	3.3	Gas turbines	0.7	1.5
Aircraft parts	1.4	2.6	Valves	0.6	1.4
Paintings	1.4	2.6	Telephones	0.6	1.4
Share of UK/US trade	13.7	37.2		24.7	27.5

Source: https://atlas.media.edu/en/profile/country

OPPORTUNITIES FOR UK EXPORTERS

UK products are likely to be more competitive in the US against exports from its EU partners than from the US's NAFTA partners or imports from Asia. The 2015 exports of the top eight product groups for Germany, Italy and France, the other three major EU suppliers, are:

	Germany	Italy	France
	US$ billion	US$ billion	US$ billion
Cars	27.3	4.1	5.4
Vehicle parts	5.8	0.6	-
Planes, helicopters etc.	4.2	-	4.9
Medical instruments	2.4	-	-
Gas turbines	2.3	-	-
Hard liquor	-	-	1.9
Engine/vehicle parts	1.3	1.4	-
X-ray equipment	1.2	-	-
Centrifuges	1.0	-	-
Wine	-	1.7	1.6
Leather footwear	-	1.1	-
Aircraft parts	-	1.0	1.2
Passenger & cargo ships	-	0.9	-
Beauty products	-	-	0.8
Trunks & cases	-	0.7	0.6

Source; https://atlas.media.edu/en/profile/country

Detailed information and advice on entry strategy to US markets is provided by Britain is Great from its Intralink source.

PRIORITY MARKETS FOR UK TRADE:

AUSTRALIA

THE ECONOMY

In perspective

Having enjoyed two decades of continuous growth with contained inflation, low unemployment and public debt and a solid financial system, by the last quarter of 2015 Australia faced a range of challenges to future growth. Contributory factors were the fall in global prices of key export commodities coupled with reduced demand for mineral resources and energy from Asia, notably for mineral resources from China. Although Australia's strong banking system and its control of inflation had mitigated the after effects of the global financial crisis, its record of continuous growth over 103 successive quarters came to an end in the first quarter of 2017.

The World Bank estimates of Australia's 2016 nominal GDP with comparatives for 10 other leading economies with GDP in excess of US$1.3 trillion and the EU total in descending order are:

	US$ million	GDP real growth (%)
USA	18,036,648	1.6
China	11,064,665	6.6
Japan	4,383,076	0.5

Germany	3,363,447	1.7
United Kingdom	2,861,091	1.8
India	2,088,841	7.7
Italy	1,821,497	0.8
Canada	1,552,808	0.9
S. Korea	1,377,873	2.7
Russian Federation	1,365,865	(0.8)
Australia	1,339,141	2.9
EU	16,314,942	2.2

In terms of purchasing power parity (PPP), Australia's GDP ranked 20th in 2016 compared to the UK in 10th and Canada in 17th place.

Comparative real growth rates in 2016, detailed in the last column of the table, confirm that the developing Asian economies continued to outpace those of the USA, Canada and Western Europe while Japan's economy continued to languish and that of Russia was negative.

With a more positive outlook for the world economy in 2017 and 2018 in both IMF and OECD forecasts, Australia may hope to avoid recession but a further slowdown of the Chinese economy could override the global trend. Nevertheless, given Australia's standing as a leading fellow member within the British Commonwealth, it is clear that it should be a prime target for increasing investment and exports when the UK gains freedom to form its own trade agreements outside the EU.

Australia's economy today
The headline statistics for 2015 relating to GDP of more than US$1.34 trillion relative to its estimated population of 23 million highlight Australia's rather weaker foreign trade performance compared to that of Canada on a per capita or proportion of GDP basis. However, the Australian trade deficit of US$19,974 was less significant.

	% GDP	$ per capita
GDP		61,339
Foreign trade	19.7	12,215
Current account balance	(1.5)	

Source: WTO statistics

Composition of GDP

	By end use		By sector of origin
	%		%
Household consumption	58.5	Agriculture	3.6
Government consumption	18.7	Industry	28.2
Investment in fixed capital	24.3	Services	68.2
Investment in inventories	-		

Source: CIA World Fact Book

The industrial production growth rate for 2016 is estimated as 2.2%.

Australian household debt as a percentage of GDP has been rising continuously for several decades and reached 123% in December 2016, the third highest ratio among the 36 OECD countries

Australia's principal industries are mining, industrial and transportation equipment, food processing, chemicals and steel.

Employment

The labour force was estimated at 12.63 million in 2016 with an unemployment rate of 5.8%. Employment by sector was reported in 2010 as 3.6% in agriculture, 21.1% in industry and 75.3% in services.

Australia does not have an official poverty line but the lowest 10% in income was last estimated to account for 2% of consumption and the highest 10% for 25.4%. Recent data is unavailable.

International Trade

In world trade Australia ranked 23rd in merchandise exports in 2016 after Poland as 22nd and compared with the UK in 10th and Canada in 12th place. In imports Australia ranked 22nd after Switzerland, the UAE and Turkey with the UK in 4th and Canada in 9th place. In services Australia ranked 12th in exports and 14th in imports.

Australia's merchandise exports and imports declined by 22% and 2% respectively in 2015. Exports recovered by 1% in 2016 while imports declined by a further 6%. A modest recovery is expected in 2017 and 2018 in line with world trade trends. Australian exports and imports of services in 2015 decreased by 9% and 14% respectively but exports recovered strongly in 2016 by 8.6% while imports declined further by 1.5%.

Australia is a member of the East Asia Summit which consists of the original Association of South East Asia Nations (ASEAN) Free Trade Area plus Three (China, Japan and South Korea) together with India, New Zealand, Russia and the US as well as itself. It currently has bilateral agreements in force with CARICOM, Chile, China, Japan, Malaysia, New Zealand, Singapore and South Korea.

Merchandise Trade

Australian merchandise exports at US$188.4 billion (f.o.b.) in 2015 accounted for 1.14% of the global total, while its merchandise imports (c.i.f) at US$208.4 billion represented 1.25% of the global total. The current account deficit of US$20 billion is echoed in imbalances with China and the United States of a similar order. Imports from the EU are unmatched. Australia also ran a deficit in its trade in commerce of US$5.3 billion with exports of US$48.4 billion similar to Canada against imports of US53.7 billion.

The composition of merchandise trade, with commodity groups, is summarised as:-

By main commodity group	Exports %	Imports %
Agricultural products	10.0	7.3
Fuels and mining products	57.3	12.5
Manufactures	13.7	75.7
Other	10.0	4.6
By destination & origin		
United States	5.3	11.3
China	32.5	23.1
Japan	15.9	7.4
South Korea	7.1	-
Other (including the EU)	39.2	40.09

Source: WTO statistics

Agricultural products

Imported agricultural products in 2015, together amounting to US$3.4 billion, included wine of fresh grapes, bread, pastry and other bakery products, other food preparations, cigars, cheroots and cigarillos, and alcohol of less than 80% proof. Together these top imports accounted for 27% of the total.

Australia's top five exported agricultural products are frozen meat of bovine animals, wheat and meslin, chilled fresh bovine meat, uncarded or uncombed wool and fresh meat of sheep or goats, which together represented 34% of total exports of US$33.9 billion in 2015. There was a trade surplus of US$21.5 billion in overall agricultural products.

Non-agricultural products

Australia's top imported and manufactured products are passenger cars, petroleum oils other than crude, automatic data-processing machines, crude petroleum oil and medicaments in measured doses. Together amounting to US$48.9 billion in 2015 they accounted for 27% of total manufactures imported at US$182.3 billion.

Non-agricultural merchandise exports totalled US$146,783 billion, resulting in the 2015 trade deficit of US$35.5 billion. The top five export categories in descending order are iron ores, coal briquettes and ovoids, petroleum gases, gold and artificial corundum. Together they accounted for US$93.4 billion representing 64% of the total.

Trade in commercial services
Compared to trade in non-agricultural merchandise, the imports and exports of Australian commercial services at US$53.7 billion and US$48.4 billion respectively are low. The pattern of this trade is:

	Exports	*Imports*
	%	%
By main service		
Transport	10.5	24.5
Travel	61.4	40.8
Other commercial services	28.0	34.0
Goods-related services	0.2	0.7
By main destination & origin		
China	13.8	23.0
US	10.7	18.8
New Zealand	6.8	4.9
Singapore	5.8	7.8
Other (including Japan)	62.9	64.6

Source: WTO statistics

Among other commercial services, financial services have a share of 21.8% greater than the share of 14.9% for ICT. Other business services account for the majority share at 48.4%.

Intellectual property

The number of applications for registration in 2014 by residents and non-residents was:

	Resident	Non-resident	Total
Patent	1,988	23,968	25,956
Trademark	41,677	22,825	64,502
Industrial design	2,630	3,967	6,597

Foreign Direct Investment (FDI)

UNCTAD recorded Australia's FDI stocks abroad at 2016 year end as US$402 billion and at home as US$576 billion.

During 2016, Australia's FDI inflows were US$48,190 million and outflows a modest US$6,012 million.

BUSINESS ENVIRONMENT

Living standards

The OECD Better Life Index, based on 11 factors, ranks Australia 2nd among 38 OECD countries after Norway, three places ahead of Canada, seven places ahead of the US and against the UK at 16th. By contrast, in a global context the Quality-of- life index places Australia 9th out of 67 entries, after the US in 7th place and before the UK in 13th. The Human Development Index also ranks Australia 2nd only to Norway.

TAXATION

Corporate tax

The basic rate of corporate tax for 2017/18 is 30% for companies with turnover over a threshold of $25 million with the lower rate of 27.5% for smaller companies. For the 2018/19 to 2023/24 financial years the higher rate threshold is raised to $50 million.

CURRENT UK TRADE WITH AUSTRALIA

Total merchandise exports to Australia in 2015 were US$5.41 billion against imports of US$2.81 billion. The top eight export and import product groups in which the UK traded with Australia in 2015 were:

	Exports			*Imports*	
	US$ million	*%*		*US$ million*	*%*
Cars	979	18.0	Raw lead	418	15.0
Packaged medicaments	343	6.3	Wine	329	12.0
Hard liquor	170	3.1	Gold	310	11.0
Machinery	147	2.7	Orthopaedic appliances	219	7.8
Brochures	111	2.0	Coal briquettes	110	3.9
Hormones	95	1.8	Sheep and goat meat	86	3.1
Gold	86	1.6	Bovine meat	67	2.4
Newspapers	90	1.7	Human/animal blood	44	1.6

Source: https://atlas.media.edu/en/profile/country

The top eight export categories account for 37.2% of total UK exports to Australia representing 1.3% of all UK exports worldwide. Australia's exports to the UK are rather less diverse with the top eight categories representing 56.8% of total imports from Australia and the UK sourcing less than 0.5% of its imported merchandise from Australia.

Similar data for other export fields in which the UK is less established can be derived from the same source.

NEW OPPORTUNITIES FOR UK EXPORTERS

Given the low share (2.8%) at present enjoyed by the UK of Australia's imports, the dominance of its imports from China (12%), the US (12%) and other Asian economies, opportunities for UK exporters to improve their weak penetration of Australian markets must focus on the categories of merchandise currently imported from the US and the EU (in particular from Germany with a 4.8% share). At the same time, the UK government will be focusing on constructing a bilateral trade deal post-Brexit with Australia.

PRIORITY MARKETS FOR UK TRADE:

CANADA

THE ECONOMY

In perspective

Canada has a high-tech industrial economy, with a pattern of production, high living standards and market-orientation similar to the USA. There has been impressive growth in the mining, manufacturing and services sectors since World War II, transforming a largely rural economy into a largely industrial and urban society. More recently, the petroleum sector has expanded rapidly since Canada's proven oil reserves were greatly boosted by finds in Alberta and now rank third in the world after Venezuela and Saudi Arabia. Canada has become the world's fifth largest oil producer.

Solid economic growth from 1993 to 2007 was interrupted by the global financial crisis and the economy dropped into recession in the final quarter of 2008 with the first fiscal deficit for 12 years posted in 2009. Thanks to the Bank of Canada's early action and conservative lending policies, coupled with strong capitalisation, the major banks emerged from the crisis as among the strongest.

The World Bank estimates of Canada's 2015 nominal GDP with comparatives for 10 other leading economies with GDP in excess of US$1.3 trillion and the EU total in descending order are:

	US$ million	GDP real growth (%)
USA	18,036,648	1.6
China	11,064,665	6.6
Japan	4,383,076	0.5
Germany	3,363,447	1.7
United Kingdom	2,861,091	1.8
India	2,088,841	7.7
Italy	1,821,497	0.8
Canada	1,552,808	0.9
S. Korea	1,377,873	2.7
Russian Federation	1,365,865	(0.8)
Australia	1,339,141	2.2
EU	16,314,942	2.2

In terms of purchasing power parity (PPP), while the US GDP more than trebled between 1990 and 2015, ahead of Canada and the UK (2.8 times), Germany (2.5 times) and Japan (2.2 times), their growth was dwarfed by the performance of leading Asian economies: China (17.6 times), India (8.9 times) and South Korea (4.8 times). The Chinese economy has now overtaken the USA with a 2016 GDP of US$21,270 trillion at PPP compared to US$18,560 trillion for the USA, US$19,180 for the European Union (including the UK) and US$1,586,725 for Canada.

Comparative real growth rates in 2016, detailed in the last column of the table, confirm that the developing Asian economies continued to outpace those of the USA, Canada and Western Europe while Japan's economy continued to languish and that of Russia was negative.

With a more positive outlook for the world economy, Canada and the USA in 2017 and 2018, in both IMF and OECD forecasts and given Canada's status as a leading fellow member within the British Commonwealth, it is clear that Canada should be a prime target for increasing investment and exports when the UK gains freedom to form its own trade agreements outside the EU.

Canada's economy today
The headline statistics for 2015 relating to GDP of more than US$1.5 trillion relative to its estimated population of 35.3 million highlight Canada's strong foreign trade performance compared to the neighbouring USA on a per capita basis as:

	% GDP	*$ per capita*
GDP		48,538
Foreign trade	31.8	15,456
Current account balance	(2.9)	

Source: WTO statistics

Composition of GDP

By end use	*%*	By sector of origin	*%*
Household consumption	57.9	Agriculture	1.6
Government consumption	21.3	Industry	27.7
Investment in fixed capital	22.2	Services	70.7
Investment in inventories	0.3		

Source: CIA World Fact Book

In respect of household consumption, household debt, recorded as 167% of consumption in February 2017, exceeded GDP for the first time in the second quarter of 2016 and is the highest among G7 countries.

The principal industrial products manufactured or processed domestically and exported include motor vehicles and parts, industrial machinery, aircraft, telecommunications equipment, chemicals, plastics, fertilizers, wood pulp, timber, crude petroleum, natural gas, electricity and aluminium. Imports also include machinery and equipment, motor vehicles, crude oil, chemicals, electricity and more general consumer durables. The industrial production growth rate was estimated at 5.1% in March 2017 against 2.8% a year earlier.

Employment

The labour force, estimated at 19.4 million in 2016 with an unemployment rate of 7.1%, is employed as to 2% in agriculture, 13% in manufacturing, 6% in construction, 76% in services and 3% in other occupations.

Canada does not have an official poverty line but 94% of the population is estimated to be living below the Low Income Cut-Off. The lowest 10% in income was last estimated to account for 2.6% of consumption and the highest 10% for 24.8%. Data more recent than 2000 is unavailable.

International Trade

In world trade Canada ranked 12th in 2016 in merchandise exports with the EU, China and the USA in the top places and the UK as 11th. In imports Canada ranked 9th with the UK in 6th place, and immediately after Hong Kong but before South Korea. In services Canada ranked 18th in exports and 14th in imports. Canada's merchandise exports and imports declined by 14% and 9% respectively in 2015 and by a further 2.5% and 4% in 2016. A modest recovery is expected in 2017 and 2018 in line with world trade trends. Canadian exports and imports of services in 2015 decreased by 10% and 11% respectively.

Canada currently has five free trade agreement in force , of which two, the North American Free Trade Agreement (NAFTA) with the USA and Mexico and the Agreement with EFTA (Iceland, Liechtenstein, Norway, Switzerland) are multilateral. It has a negotiated agreement with the EU, which was signed in 2016 but is not yet in force. Negotiations are in hand for three further free trade agreements

The NAFTA, signed in 1992, is the most significant current agreement. It removed taxes on products traded and protects copyrights, patents and trademarks between the three countries. Under the agreement trade with the USA, Canada's principal partner with whom it has a significant surplus, has flourished. Canada is the USA's largest foreign supplier of energy, including oil, gas and electric power and a major source of US uranium imports.

Merchandise Trade

Canadian merchandise exports at US$408.5 billion (f.o.b.) in 2015 accounted for 2.48% of the global total, while its merchandise imports (c.i.f) at US$436,4 billion represented 2.61% of the global total. The current account deficit of US$27,897 million is echoed in imbalances with China and the EU, notably Germany.

By contrast, Canada ran a surplus in its trade in commerce of US$1.7 billion with exports of US$46.9 billion against imports of US$45.1 billion. The composition of merchandise trade, with commodity groups similar to that of the US, is summarised as:-

	Exports	Imports
By main commodity group	%	%
Agricultural products	15.6	9.1
Fuels and mining products	25.6	9.9
Manufactures	51.1	77.2
Other	7.8	3.8
By destination & origin		
United States	76.7	53.3
China	3.9	12.3
EU	7.2	11.5
Other (including Japan and Mexico)	12.3	23.0

Source: WTO statistics

Agricultural products

Imported agricultural products, together amounting to US$34.3 billion in 2015, include wine of fresh grapes, bread, pastry and other bakery products, other food preparations, coffee and chocolate or cocoa food. Together these top imports accounted for 20% of the total.

Conversely, Canada's top five exported agricultural products are soya beans, maize, fresh or dried nuts, wheat and meslin and other food preparations, which represented

38% of total exports of US$44.3 billion in 2015. There was a trade surplus of US$10.1 billion in overall agricultural products.

Non-agricultural products
Canada's top imported and manufactured products are passenger cars, automotive parts, crude petroleum oils, other petroleum oil and motor vehicles for goods transport. Together amounting to US$83 billion in 2015 they accounted for 22% of total manufactures imported at US$376.6 billion.

Non-agricultural merchandise exports totalled US$345.9 billion, resulting in the 2015 trade deficit of US$30.7 billion. The top five export categories in descending order are crude petroleum oils, passenger automobiles, gold, other petroleum oils and auto parts. Together they accounted for US$129.8 billion, representing 38% of the total.

Trade in commercial services
Compared to trade in non-agricultural merchandise, the imports and exports of commercial services at US$95.4 billion and US$76.3 billion respectively are relatively low. The pattern of this trade is:

	Exports	Imports
	%	%
By main service		
Transport	15.5	23.0
Travel	20.9	30.8
Other commercial services	61.4	47.3
Goods-related services	2.1	0.9
By main destination & origin		
USA	55.5	56.6
EU	31.6	35.2
Other	52.9	52.0

Source: WTO statistics

Among other commercial services, financial services have a share of 16.5% similar to 15.2% for ICT. Other business services account for the majority at 51.1%.

Intellectual property

The number of applications for registration in 2014 by residents and non-residents was:

	Resident	Non-resident	Total
Patent	4,198	31,283	35,481
Trademark	21,348	29,680	51,028
Industrial design	859	4,908	5,767

Foreign Direct Investment (FDI)

UNCTAD recorded Canada's FDI inflows in 2016 at US$33,721 million and outflows at US$66,403 million.

At 2016 year-end, Canada's FDI stocks were US$1,220 billion abroad and US$956 billion at home.

BUSINESS ENVIRONMENT

Living standards

The OECD Better Life Index, based on 11 factors, ranks Canada 5th among 34 OECD countries, four places ahead of the US and against the UK at 16th. By contrast, in a global context the Quality-of- life index places Canada 17th out of 67 entries after the USA in 7th place and the UK in 13th. The Human Development Index ranks Canada in 10th place, alongside the US, out of 188.

TAXATION

Corporate tax – Federal

The basic rate of federal tax is 38% less federal tax abatement – i.e. 28%. After the general rate reduction for manufacturing and processing deduction at its current rate, the net tax rate is 15% after the first CAD500,000 of active business income. There is also a small business deduction for Canadian controlled private corporations with active business incomes in Canada of less than CAD500,000 that reduces the net federal tax rate to 10.5%.

Provincial or territorial rates

Provinces and territories other than Manitoba have a lower rate and a higher rate of income tax. The lower rate applies to the income eligible for the federal small business deduction. The higher rate applies to all other income.

Rates very between provinces and territories. The lower rate varies from nil (Manitoba) to 4.5% (Ontario and Prince Edward Island) and the higher rate from 11% (British Columbia) to 16% (Nova Scotia and Prince Edward Island).

CURRENT UK TRADE WITH CANADA

Total merchandise exports to Canada in 2015 were US$7.15 billion against imports of US$8.23 billion. The top eight export and import product groups in which the UK traded with Canada in 2015 were:

Exports			*Imports*		
	US$ billion	*%*		*US$ billion*	*%*
Gold	1.13	16.0	Gold	1.79	22.0
Aircraft parts	0.68	9.5	Nickel mattes	1.50	18.0
Cars	0.61	8.6	Planes, helicopters	0.40	4.9
Gas turbines	0.45	6.3	Precious metal scraps	0.38	4.6
Packaged medicaments	0.32	4.4	Diamonds	0.37	4.5
Refined petroleum	0.24	3.3	Radioactive chemicals	0.30	3.6
Hard liquor	0.17	2.4	Gas turbines	0.24	2.9
Human & animal blood	0.13	1.8	Crude petroleum	0.23	2.7

Source: https://atlas.media.edu/en/profile/country

The top eight export categories account for 52.3% of total UK exports to Canada, representing 1.7% of total UK exports worldwide. Canada's exports to the UK are rather less diverse with the top eight categories representing 63.2% of UK imports from Canada and the UK sourcing 1.4% of its imported merchandise from Canada.

Similar data for other export fields in which the UK is less established can be derived from the same source.

NEW OPPORTUNITIES FOR UK EXPORTERS

Given the dominance of US trade with Canada, opportunities for UK exporters to improve their weak penetration of Canadian markets must focus on the 11.5% of merchandise currently imported from the EU in the expectation of a similar trade deal post-Brexit and seeking advantage from the longstanding Commonwealth relationship.

PRIORITY MARKETS FOR UK TRADE:

CHINA

THE ECONOMY

In perspective

China is the largest economy in S.E Asia. World Bank estimates of 2016 nominal GDP with US and EU comparatives indicate:

	US$ million
China	11,064.665
Japan	4,383,076
India	2,088,841
S. Korea	1,377,873
USA	18,036,648
Germany	3,363,447
United Kingdom	2,861,091
EU	16,314,942

In 2014 China overtook the USA to become the world's largest economy in terms of purchasing power parity (PPP). For 2016 China's GDP at PPP of US$21,270 compares with the US at US$18,560 trillion. Its GDP nearly quadrupled between 1980 and 1990, two and a half times ahead of India and in line with South Korea. Since then, it has continued to grow strongly each year but has been outshone more recently by growth in India. For the last three years comparative real growth rates, greatly exceeding those of the EU and US, have been:

	China	India	S. Korea
	%	%	%
2014	9.2	9.2	5.2
2015	8.0	8.7	3.7
2016 (est)	6.6	7.7	2.7

China's spectacular economic progress began with the introduction of its "open door" policy from the late 1970's. Since then, China has moved from a centrally controlled command economy to a more market oriented one. The Government, under the control of the Chinese Communist Party (CCP), has phased out agricultural collectives, gradually liberated prices, increased autonomy for state enterprises and, above all, encouraged and stimulated growth of the private sector by adopting international standards and business practices including the development of stock markets and a modern banking system. An exchange rate system that references a basket of currencies has been introduced, moving towards full convertibility of the renminbi since it was accepted as part of the IMF's special drawing rights basket. State enterprises in sectors considered as important to "economic security" are still government supported. As a result of the complete economic restructuring and efficiency gains, China's real GDP has increased more than ten times since 1978. Higher paid job opportunities in urban areas, particularly the coastal cities, have generated an aspiring middle class with more than 274 million rural workers and their families migrating from the countryside. The growth of the last 20 years up to the millennium was bootstrapped by exports and foreign direct investment in Chinese enterprises but rising domestic consumption is now a prime stimulus.

As an exporter, the UK's penetration of Chinese markets has been weak, but most proactive British companies now regard China as a major opportunity for investment and export and as a target for a free trade agreement when the UK gains freedom from its EU membership.

The Chinese economy today

The headline statistics for 2016 relating to GDP of US$11.06 trillion and the estimated population of 1,373 million highlight foreign trade performance as:

	% GDP	$ per capita
GDP		7,503
Foreign trade	22.3	1,677
Current account balance	2.1	2.5

Source: WTO statistics

Composition of GDP

	By end use		*By sector of origin*
	%		*%*
Household consumption	38.7	Agriculture	8.6
Government consumption	14.2	Industry	40.7
Investment in fixed capital	42.3	Services	50.7
Investment in inventories	1.6		

Source: CIA World Fact Book

Chinese household debt reached 44.4% of GDP in the fourth quarter of 2016, having climbed steadily from 34.5% from the beginning of 2014 as the propensity to save by a more prosperous urban population declines.

Principal components of industrial output in which China is the world leader in gross value include mining and ore processing, iron, steel, aluminium and other metals; coal; machine building; armaments; textiles and apparel; petroleum; cement; chemicals; fertilizers; and consumer products (including footwear). The industrial production growth rate for 2016 was estimated as 6.1%.

Employment

The labour force, estimated at 805.9 million in 2016 with an unemployment rate of 4.2%, is employed as to 33.6% in agriculture, 30.3% in industry and 36.1% in services. Only 6% now of the population is estimated to be living below the poverty line set at approximately US$400 in 2011. At the last count the lowest 10% of the urban population accounted for 1.7% of consumption and the highest 10% for 30.0%.

International Trade

Having become the world's largest merchandise exporter in 2010, by 2016 China remained in 3rd place as an importer after the EU and the US. In commercial services China is ranked 3rd in both exports and imports after the EU (excluding intra-EU trade) and the US. In merchandise trade China's exports declined by 8% and imports by 5% in 2016 in line with world trade trends but a modest recovery is expected in 2017 and 2018. In services, Chinese exports fell 4.3% while imports continued to grow by 3.7%.

Through its membership of the China Free Trade Area (ACFRA) China has had a bilateral agreement with the ASEAN bloc since 2010 and with the Caribbean Community (CARICOM) subsequently. It also has bilateral agreements with its two special administrative regions (Hong Kong and Macau) and with 12 other countries: Australia, New Zealand, Pakistan, Singapore, South Korea, Taiwan, Thailand, Chile, Costa Rica, Peru, Switzerland and Georgia.

Merchandise Trade

China's share in world total merchandise exports at US$2,278 billion (f.o.b.) in 2015 accounted for 13.8% of world total exports, while its share in merchandise imports (c.i.f) at US$1,682 billion represented 10.1% of the global total.

The composition of merchandise trade is summarised as:-

By main commodity group	Exports %	Imports %
Agricultural products	3.2	9.5
Fuels and mining products	2.4	21.3
Manufactures	94.3	64.4
Other	0.1	4.8
By destination & origin		
United States	18.0	9.0
EU	15.6	12.4
Hong Kong	14.6	-
South Korea	-	10.4
Japan	6.0	-
Taiwan	-	8.6
Other	45.8	59.6

Source: WTO statistics

Agricultural products

The top imported agricultural products, together amounting to US$47,326 million in 2015, are soy beans, palm oil and its fractions, grain sorghum, malt extract and barley. Together they accounted for 44% of the total.

Conversely, the top five exported agricultural products are dried vegetables, preserved plants' parts, non-frozen vegetables and anim preparations, which amounted to US$11,246 million in 2015, representing 22% of all exports from this sector.

Non-agricultural products

China's top imported commodities and manufactured products include electronic integrated circuits, crude petroleum oils, iron ores and concentrates, optical appliances and line telephony electrical apparatus. Together they amounted to US$415.9 billion, accounting for 28% of non-agricultural imports totalling US$1,492 billion in 2015.

Non-agricultural exports totalled US$2,229 billion of which the top five product categories in descending order are electronic integrated circuits, refined petroleum oils, automobiles, auto parts and other optical appliances. Together amounting to US$486 billion, they accounted for 22% of the total.

Trade in commercial services

Compared to trade in non-agricultural merchandise, the imports and exports of commercial services at US$466,330 million and US$285,476 million respectively are relatively low. The pattern of this trade is:

	Exports	*Imports*
	%	%
By main service		
Transport	13.5	16.2
Travel	40.0	62.7
Other commercial services	38.1	20.8
Goods-related services	8.4	0.3

Source: WTO statistics

Other commercial services other than transport and travel have a minor role, accounting for 21% of imports and 35% of exports:

By contrast, intellectual property (IP) registrations are significant. The number of applications registered in 2014 by residents and non-residents was:

	Resident	Non-resident	Total
Patent	801,135	127,042	928,177
Trademark	1,997,014	107,520	2,104,534
Industrial design	548,428	16,127	564,555

The focus on trademark registration reflects the concerns of leading internationals already doing business in China and seeking to protect their brands.

Foreign Direct Investment (FDI)
China's FDI is advancing rapidly. UNCTAD statistics for 2016 record inflows at US$133,700 million and outflows on investment abroad at US$183,100 million compared with UK inflows of US$253,826 million. Inward FDI stocks stand at US$1,354 billion and FDI stocks of US$1,281 billion abroad, both approaching UK levels. China is now deploying its US$3 trillion foreign exchange reserves on infrastructure and high tech business investment in developed economies. The UK is a major beneficiary.

BUSINESS ENVIRONMENT

Taxation
Corporate taxes are set and administered by the State under laws enacted by the National People's Congress or by its Standing Committee. There are 26 types of tax including Excise Tax, many related to real estate but the principal taxes levied on business are:

	Current rate %
- Corporate Tax, levied on net income	25
- Sales Tax, based on sales or turnover (applied to taxpayers in the manufacturing, circulation or service sectors)	17

CURRENT UK TRADE WITH CHINA

Total UK merchandise exports to China in 2015 were US$27.6 billion against imports of US$62.8 billion. The top eight export and import product groups in which the UK traded with China in 2015 were:

	Exports			*Imports*	
	US$ billion	*%*		*US$ billion*	*%*
Gold	10.20	37.0	Computers	5.27	8.4
Cars	5.03	18.0	Broadcasting equipment	3.12	5.0
Packaged medicaments	1.15	4.2	Telephones	2.03	3.2
Crude Petroleum	0.94	3.4	Models/stuffed animals	1.87	3.0
Recovered paper	0.53	1.9	Other furniture	1.53	2.4
Scrap copper	0.44	1.6	Light fixtures	1.31	2.1
Vehicle parts	0.42	1.6	Trunks & cases	1.25	2.0
Gas turbines	0.38	1.4	Knitwear	1.14	1.8

Source: https://atlas.media.edu/en/profile/country

Similar data for other export fields in which the UK is less established can be derived from the same source.

OPPORTUNITIES FOR UK EXPORTERS

British companies that do best are those which have set out to establish a long-term relationship, often through contractual or equity joint ventures. These have taken the form of establishing processing plants or parallel manufacturing operations but as China has become less cost competitive there is now a growing reverse trend to establish Chinese operations in the UK, which are planned to export technical development and know-how back to China as well as product on world markets.

The first step is to identify which Province, Municipality or major city in China is the most suitable for a UK company's initiative and the China Britain Business Council (CBBC), with its 13 offices in strategic locations in China and 10 offices in the UK is a long established and valuable resource.

PRIORITY MARKETS FOR UK TRADE:

INDIA

THE ECONOMY

In perspective

India has the second largest economy in S.E Asia among those in transition and the third including Japan. World Bank estimates of 2016 nominal GDP with US and EU comparatives indicate:

	US$ million
China	11,064.665
Japan	4,383,076
India	2,088,841
S. Korea	1,377,873
USA	18,036,648
Germany	3,363,447
United Kingdom	2,861,091

In terms of PPP, India's 2016 GDP is estimated at US$8.7 trillion. For many years the real growth of the Indian economy lagged behind that of China but more recently has powered ahead. For the last three years comparative real growth rates of the three largest Asian developing countries, greatly exceeding those of the EU and US, have been:

	China	India	S. Korea
	%	%	%
2014	9.2	9.2	5.2
2015	8.0	8.7	3.7
2016 (est)	6.6	7.7	2.7

On this evidence alone and having regard to fellow membership of the British Commonwealth, India is a market on which British companies should focus seriously as an opportunity for investment and exports, whether or not the UK gains freedom to form its own trade agreements outside the EU. In 2015 India imported only 1.5% of its requirements from the UK which hardly reflects the longstanding relationship between the two countries.

The Indian economy today
A period of growth from 1997 to 2011 when GDP averaged less than 7% followed extensive liberalisation of the economy from the early 1990s, which included industrial deregulation, privatisation of state-owned industries and reduced controls on foreign trade and investment. However, growth began to falter in 2011 as a consequence of slow world growth, investor pessimism about the Government's commitment to further economic reforms, rising macroeconomic imbalances and a decline in investment under conditions of high inflation and interest rates. The sharp depreciation of the rupee following a shift of capital from India by Western investors was a contributory factor.

However, the economy rebounded in 2014 with growth returning to more than 7%. In the past three years a reduction of the current account deficit and the improved perception of investors of forthcoming economic reform under the new Government has resulted in inbound capital investment and stabilisation of the rupee.

The headline statistics for 2015 relating to real GDP of US$2.08 trillion and the estimated population of 1.27 billion highlight foreign trade performance as:

	% GDP	$ per capita
GDP		1,539
Foreign trade	24.8	382
Current account balance	6.6	2,080

Source: WTO statistics

Composition of GDP

By end use	%		By sector of origin	%
Household consumption	60.8	Agriculture	16.5
Government consumption	11.4	Industry	29.8
Investment in fixed capital	27.6	Services	45.4
Investment in inventories	3.0		

Source: CIA World Fact Book

In respect of household consumption, household debt rose above 10% GDP for the first time in March 2013. India ranks 15th among countries having the highest household debt.

Principal industrial products manufactured domestically include textiles, chemicals, food processing, steel, transportation equipment, cement, petroleum, machinery, software and pharmaceuticals. The industrial production growth rate for 2016 was estimated as 7.4%.

Employment

The labour force, estimated at 513.7 million in 2016 with an unemployment rate of 8.4%, is employed as to 49% in agriculture, 20% in industry and 31% in services.

In 2010, 29.8% of the population was estimated to be living below the poverty line. The lowest 10% accounted for 3.6% of consumption and the highest 10% for 31.1%. Two years later, the proportion living below the poverty line had fallen to less than 22%.

International Trade

In world trade India ranks 18th in merchandise exports and 11th in imports (13th and 9th excluding intra-EU trade). Its higher rankings in commercial services are 5th and 6th respectively. Total merchandise exports in 2016 are reported as US$271,600 billion and imports at US$402,400 billion.

India's merchandise exports declined by 1% and imports by 9% in 2016 in line with world trade trends but a modest recovery is expected in 2017 and 2018. Trade in the export of commercial services increased by 3.5% while imports rose by 8.4%.

India has had a Free Trade Area agreement with the ASEAN Group since 2010 and bilateral agreements with Sri Lanka, Singapore, Thailand and Malaysia. The last two are separate from the FTA agreement with ASEAN. Negotiations with the EU and European Free Trade Association (EFFTA) have stalled.

Merchandise Trade

India's share in world total merchandise exports at US$267,147 million (f.o.b.) in 2015 accounted for 1.6% of world total exports, while its share in merchandise imports (c.i.f) at US$391,977 million represented 2.3% of the global total.

The composition of merchandise trade is summarised as:-

	Exports	*Imports*
By main commodity group	%	%
Agricultural products	13.2	7.1
Fuels and mining products	15.7	33.1
Manufactures	68.4	47.8
Other	2.7	12.0

By destination & origin

China/Hong Kong	4.6	15.8
United States	15.2	-
EU	16.9	11.2
Saudi Arabia	-	5.5
Switzerland	-	5.4
Other	51.9	62.1

Source: WTO statistics

(Exports to Saudi Arabia and Switzerland and imports from the US are low and are included as "other")

Agricultural products

The top five imported agricultural products, together amounting to US$14,900 million in 2015, are: palm oil and its fractions, dried leguminous vegetables, soya-bean oil and its fractions, Brazil and cashew nuts, coconuts and sunflower seed or cotton oil. Together they accounted for 66% of the total.

Conversely, the top five exported agricultural products are: rice, frozen meat of bovine animals, raw cotton, cane or beet sugar and vegetable saps and extracts which amounted to US$14,453 million in 2014, representing 49% of all exports from this sector.

Non-agricultural products

India's top imported and manufactured products are crude petroleum oils, gold, diamonds, coal as briquettes and ovoids and petroleum gases. Together they totalled US$149,710, accounting for 41.9% of manufacture and fuels imports, which amounted to US$357,476 million in 2015.

Non-agricultural exports totalled US$232,472 million, of which the top five product categories in descending order are: refined petroleum oils, diamonds, medicaments in measured doses, jewellery and automobiles for people transport. Together totalling US$78,949, they accounted for 34.0% of the total.

Trade in commercial services

Compared to trade in non-agricultural merchandise, the imports and exports of commercial services at US$122,225 million and US$155,225 million respectively are relatively high. The pattern of this trade in 2015 was:

	Exports	*Imports*
	%	*%*
By main service		
Transport	9.2	42.8
Travel	11.5	12.2
Other commercial services	77.0	44.8
Goods-related services	0.2	0.2

Source: WTO statistics

Among other commercial services, financial services have a minor role, accounting for only 4.5% of exports.

By contrast, intellectual property (IP) registrations are more significant, particularly for trademarks. The number of applications registered in 2014 by residents and non-residents were:

	Resident	*Non-resident*	*Total*
Patent	12,040	30,814	42,854
Trademark	200,137	22,098	222,235
Industrial design	6,168	3,141	9,309

Foreign Direct Investment (FDI)

UNCTAD statistics for 2016 record India's FDI inflows at US$44,486 million and outflows on investment abroad at US$5,120 million compared with UK inflows of

US$253,826 million for the same year. As an economy in transition, inward FDI stock is reported at a relatively modest level of US$319 billion with investment abroad at US$144 billion.

Annual inward investment has grown by 58% since 2013, reflecting the relaxation of investment controls, including restrictions on equity participation in Indian companies.

BUSINESS ENVIRONMENT

Living standards

The standard of living in India varies from state to state, reflecting the degree of industrialisation, with 75% of the poor living in rural areas. Estimates of middle-class households are forecast to double from 2015/16 levels to 113.8 million by 2030 and average real wages to quadruple between 2013 and 2030, when another estimate projects the middle class population to number 475 million people. Nevertheless, a rural middle class is emerging in India, with some rural areas enjoying increasing prosperity. The southern state of Kerala ranks top in most indices. In the Numbeo quality of life index India now ranks 51st ahead of Pakistan in 55th place.

Taxation

Corporate income taxation

India maintains a differential between the corporate income tax (CIT) applicable to an Indian company and a foreign company. The basic rates for the year 2017/18 are 25% on an Indian company's net income up to 500 million INR and 30% above and on the net income of all foreign companies at 40%. Effective rates include surcharge, education cess and secondary and higher education cess which vary according to income level and are applied as follows:

Income	Domestic company (%)	Foreign company (%)
Less than 10 million rupees (INR)	25.75	41.20
More than 10 million INR but less than 100 million INR	27.55	42.04
More than 100 million INR	28.84	43.26
More than 500 million INR	34.61	43.26

CURRENT UK TRADE WITH INDIA

Total merchandise exports to India in 2015 were US$5.59 billion and against imports of US$9.24 billion. The top eight export and import product groups in which the UK traded with India in 2015 were:

	Exports			*Imports*	
	US$ million	*%*		*US$ million*	*%*
Silver	1,380	25.0	Packaged medicaments	463	5.0
Scrap iron	338	6.0	Leather footwear	449	4.9
Gas turbines	314	5.6	Jewellery	355	3.8
Gold	179	3.2	Non-knit women's suits	322	3.5
Hard liquors	171	3.1	Refined Petroleum	308	3.3
Aircraft parts	153	2.7	Trunks and cases	235	2.5
Scrap aluminium	148	2.7	Non-knit women's shirts	218	2.4
Scrap copper	84	1.5	Knit T-shirts	214	2.3

Source: https://atlas.media.edu/en/profile/country

Similar data for other export fields in which the UK is less established can be derived from the same source.

OPPORTUNITIES FOR UK EXPORTERS

The top eight export categories account for just over 50% of the UK's export trade with India, of which only 11% are in manufactured product. This is a weak basis for gaining serious market penetration in manufactured goods. However, Germany managed to export US$10.7 billion and America exported $20 billion into India in the same period and their performance sets the benchmark for a focused UK export drive.

Detailed information and advice on entry strategy to the Indian consumer market is provided by Britain is Great from its Intralink source.

PRIORITY MARKETS FOR UK TRADE:

JAPAN

THE ECONOMY

In perspective
Japan is a mature, developed economy and ranks second only to China in size among the SE Asia countries. World Bank estimates of 2016 nominal GDP with US and EU comparatives indicate:

	US$ million	GDP real growth (%)
China	11,064.665	6.6
Japan	4,383,076	0.5
India	2,088,841	7.7
S. Korea	1,377,873	2.7
USA	18,036,648	1.6
Germany	3,363,447	1.7
United Kingdom	2,861,091	1.8
EU	16,314,942	2.2

In terms of PPP, Japan's 2016 GDP is estimated at US$4.8 trillion, in 5th place after China, the EU, the US and India. For many years the real growth of the Japanese economy has lagged behind those of other leading developed economies and of the three other Asian economies targeted as priority export markets for the UK.

After World War II Japan developed its advanced economy with close interlocking structures of suppliers, manufacturers and distributors built on a strong work ethic, a concentration on high technology and with guaranteed lifetime employment for much of the urban workforce. These successful elements of Japanese industry were then subject to erosion in the face of global competition and domestic demographic change. The days of impressive annual growth rates averaging 10% in the 1960s, 5% in the 1970s and 4% in the 1980s have long since passed. The after effects of inefficient investment and an asset price bubble reduced growth to an average 1.7% in the 1990s and heralded a long period of near stagnation with the economy falling into recession four times since 2008.

The Japanese economy today

Government stimulus spending aided a recovery from late 2009 through to 2011 when Japan was hit by a massive earthquake and tsunami which disrupted most economic activity. The Three Arrows economic revitalisation policies introduced from 2013 and revised in 2015 have stimulated the real economy to start growing again.

Japan has always been dependent on imported fossil fuels and the shutdown of Japan's nuclear reactors after the tsunami increased that dependency. The re-start of two nuclear reactors at the Sendai Nuclear Power Plant have restored a welcome base-load electricity source. However, an ongoing weakness of the economy is reliance on a high proportion of imported food in spite of self-sufficiency in rice production and high crop yields from a subsidized agricultural sector. More generally, six years after the tsunami the Japanese economy has largely recovered, although output in the affected areas is still below the national average.

The headline statistics for 2015 relating to real GDP of US$4.12 trillion and the estimated population of 127 million highlight foreign trade performance as:

	% GDP	$ per capita
GDP		1,539
Foreign trade	18.9	6,766
Current account balance	0.8	1,386

Source: WTO statistics

Composition of GDP

	By end use		By sector of origin
	%		%
Household consumption	58.3	Agriculture	1.2
Government consumption	20.4	Industry	27.7
Investment in fixed capital	21.7	Services	71.1
Investment in inventories	(0.0)		

Source: CIA World Fact Book

Household consumption reached 60.7% of GDP in 2014 and household debt rose to 140% GDP in 2015, ranking Japan 12th highest among countries for which debt ratios are recorded. Public debt for 2016 is estimated at 235% GDP.

Renowned as one of the world's largest and most technologically advanced producer of motor vehicles, electronic equipment and machine tools, Japan also processes or manufactures steel and nonferrous metals, ships, chemicals, textiles and processed food. However, the industrial production growth rate for 2016 was estimated at 0.5%.

Employment

The labour force, estimated at 65.3 million in 2016 with an unemployment rate of 3.2%, is employed as to 3% in agriculture, 26% in industry and 71% in services.

In 2013, 16.1% of the population was estimated to be living below the poverty line. In 2008 the lowest 10% accounted for 2.7% of consumption and the highest 10% for 24.8%. More recent data is not available.

International Trade

In world trade Japan ranks 5th in both merchandise exports and imports (4th and 9th excluding intra-EU trade). Its higher rankings in commercial services are 5th and 6th respectively. Total merchandise exports in 2016 are reported as US$641,400 billion and imports at US$629,800 billion.

Japan's merchandise exports grew by 3% while imports declined by 6% in 2016 but, in line with world trade trends, a modest recovery is expected in 2017 and 2018. Trade in the export of commercial services increased by 6.5% while imports rose by 8.4%.

Japan has had a Free Trade Area agreement with the ASEAN Group since 2008 and has bilateral agreements with Australia, Brunei, Chile, India, Indonesia, Malaysia, Mexico, Mongolia, Peru, Philippines, Singapore, Switzerland, Thailand and Vietnam. The first of these was signed with Singapore in 2002 and the last with India in 2011. Japan has conducted early stages of negotiation with the Gulf Cooperation Council, India, Australia and New Zealand

Merchandise Trade

Japan's share in world total merchandise exports at US$624,939 million (f.o.b.) in 2015 accounted for 3.8% of world total exports, while its share in merchandise imports (c.i.f) at US$648,494 million represented 3.9% of the global total.

The composition of merchandise trade is summarised as:-

	Exports	*Imports*
By main commodity group	%	%
Agricultural products	1.6	11.3
Fuels and mining products	4.3	29.4
Manufactures	87.2	57.1
Other	6.9	2.2
By destination & origin		
United States	20.2	10.9
China	17.5	26.7

EU	10.6	11.4
South Korea	7.0	-
Australia	-	5.6
Other	44.7	46.5

Source: WTO statistics

(Exports to Australia and imports from South Korea are low and are included as "other")

Agricultural products

The top five imported agricultural products, together amounting to US$14,161 million in 2015 are: fresh chilled and frozen swine meat, maize, cigars, cheroots and cigarillos, other prepared or preserved meat and soya beans. Together they accounted for 26% of total imports.

Conversely, the top five exported agricultural products are: food preparations, sauces and their ingredients, bread, pastry and other bakery products, cigars, cheroots and cigarillos and waters containing added sugar which together amounted to US$1,350 million in 2015, representing 36% of all exports from this sector.

Non-agricultural products

Japan's top imported and manufactured products are: petroleum gases, crude petroleum oils, medicaments in measured doses, electronic integrated circuits, coal briquettes and ovoids. Together they totalled US$149,652, accounting for 26% of manufactures and fuels imports, which amounted to US$561,150 million in 2015.

Non-agricultural exports totalled US$159,866 million, of which the top five product categories in descending order are: motor cars, vehicle parts, electronic integrated circuits, vessels for transport and special purpose machines. Together totalling US$159,866, they accounted for 27% of the total.

Trade in commercial services

The imports and exports of commercial services at US$173,689 million and US$157,863 million respectively represent less than a third of trade in non-agricultural merchandise. The pattern of this trade in 2015 was:

	Exports %	Imports %
By main service		
Transport	22.5	23.6
Travel	16.1	9.2
Other commercial services	60.8	62.7
Goods-related services	0.6	4.6
By destination and origin		
United States	20.2	10.9
China	17.5	25.7
South Korea	7.0	-
Australia	-	5.6
Other	44.7	46.5

Source: WTO statistics
(Exports to Australia and imports from South Korea are low and are included as other)

Among other commercial services, intellectual property (IP) has a leading role, accounting for 37.6% of trade. Patent registrations are more the most significant, confirming Japan's continuing focus on technological innovation The number of IP applications registered in 2014 by residents and non-residents was:

	Resident	Non-resident	Total
Patent	265,959	60,030	325,989
Trademark	100,036	24,566	124,602
Industrial design	24,868	4,870	29,738

Foreign Direct Investment (FDI)
UNCTAD statistics for 2016 record Japan's FDI inflows at US$11,388 million and outflows on investment abroad at US$145,242 million compared with UK inflows of US$253,826 million for the same year. As a mature economy inward FDI stock is reported at a modest level of US$187 billion with investment abroad at US$1,401 billion comparable to China's outward FDI stock of US$1,281 billion.

BUSINESS ENVIRONMENT

Living standards
The population of Japan is highly urbanised with 93.5% living in major towns and cities. In terms of life expectancy, Japan ranks 3rd globally with an average expectancy of 85 years. By the early 1990s, 90% of Japanese people considered themselves middle class and were relatively content. However, inequality has grown over the past two decades following the end of Japan's economic boom and the international financial crisis of 2008/9. Nevertheless, the Numbeo quality of life index today ranks Japan 17th, one place behind the UK.

Taxation

Corporate income taxation

Corporation tax
Domestic Japanese corporations are taxed on their worldwide income, including foreign branch income, while 95% of dividends received from a foreign company may be excluded, provided that the Japanese holding, established for more than 6 months, holds at least 25% of the outstanding shares.

A foreign company is taxed only on its Japan-source income at the rates from fiscal years beginning on or after 1 April 2016 and 1 April 2018 as follows:

Company size and income (Japanese yen JPY)	Corporate tax rate (%)	
	1 April 2016	1 April 2018
Paid-in capital of more JPY 100 million	23.4	23.2

Paid-in capital of JPY 100 million or less except for a company wholly owned by a company with paid-in capital of JPY 500 million or more:

	1 April 2016	1 April 2018
First JPY 8 million p.a.	15.0	15.0
Over JPY 8 million p.a.	23.4	23.2

National corporate tax
As of 1 April 2017, corporate taxpayers are required to file and pay the national local corporate tax at a fixed rate of 10.3% of their corporate tax liabilities.

Standard enterprise tax and local corporate special tax
Enterprise tax is levied on a corporate's income allocated to each prefecture according to the number of employees and number of offices in each location. The standard rates of enterprise tax including local corporate special tax are:

Taxation base	Enterprise tax (%)
First JPY 4 million p.a.	3.4
Next JPY 4 million p.a.	5.1
Over JPY 8 million p.a.	6.7

A lower standard rate of enterprise tax at 0.9% is charged for utilities and insurance companies.

CURRENT UK TRADE WITH JAPAN

Total merchandise exports to Japan in 2015 were US$6.29 billion against imports from Japan of US$10.50 billion. The top eight export and import product groups in which the UK traded with Japan in 2015 were:

	Exports			*Imports*	
	US$ million	*%*		*US$ million*	*%*
Packaged medicaments	806	13.0	Cars	2,060	20.0
Cars	714	11.0	Gold	832	7.9
Gas turbines	500	8.0	Vehicle parts	662	6.3
Hard liquors	195	3.1	Gas turbines	428	4.1
Nitrogen Heterocyclic compounds	173	2.8	Construction vehicles	291	2.8
Platinum	148	2.4	Photographic chemicals	254	2.4
Combustion engines	123	2.0	Engine parts	216	2.1
Radioactive chemicals	119	1.9	Electrical ignitions	164	1.6

Source: https://atlas.media.edu/en/profile/country

Similar data for other export fields in which the UK is less established can be derived from the same source.

OPPORTUNITIES FOR UK EXPORTERS

The top eight export categories account for just 44.2% of the UK's export trade with Japan, of which all are manufactured or processed products. This 1.1% share of Japanese imports is a foothold for gaining serious market penetration in manufactured goods. However, Germany managed to export US$19.3 billion (3.3%) and America exported $63.5 billion (11%) into Japan in the same period and their performance sets the benchmark for a more intensive UK export drive.

More detailed information and advice on entry strategy to the Japanese consumer market is provided by Britain is Great from its Intralink source.

PRIORITY MARKETS FOR UK TRADE:

SOUTH KOREA

THE ECONOMY

In perspective

The Republic of South Korea has the third largest economy in S.E Asia among those in transition and the fourth including Japan. World Bank estimates of 2016 nominal GDP with US and EU comparatives indicate:

	US$ million
China	11,064.665
Japan	4,383,076
India	2,088,841
S. Korea	1,377,873
USA	18,036,648
Germany	3,363,447
United Kingdom	2,861,091
EU	16,314,942

South Korea's GDP in terms of purchasing power parity (PPP) nearly quadrupled between 1980 and 1990 in line with China and two and a half times ahead of India. Since then, it has continued to grow strongly each year but has been outshone by growth in China and more recently in India. For the last three years comparative real growth rates, greatly exceeding those of the EU and US, have been:

	China	India	S. Korea
	%	%	%
2014	9.2	9.2	5.2
2015	8.0	8.7	3.7
2016 (est)	6.6	7.7	2.7

The IMF forecasts that by 2021 South Korea's GDP at PPP will have grown a further 23 per cent. On this evidence alone South Korea is a market on which British companies should focus seriously as an opportunity for investment and exports when the UK gains freedom to form its own trade agreements outside the EU.

The South Korean economy today
The headline statistics for 2016 relating to GDP of US$1.38 trillion and the estimated population of 50.9 million highlight foreign trade performance as:

	% GDP	$ per capita
GDP		27,071
Foreign trade	47.8	12,940
Current account balance	6.6	2,080

Source: WTO statistics

Composition of GDP

	By end use		By sector of origin
	%		%
Household consumption	49.0	Agriculture	2.3
Government consumption	15.4	Industry	37.8
Investment in fixed capital	29.3	Services	60.2
Investment in inventories	0.1		

Source: CIA World Fact Book

In respect of household consumption, household debt is recorded as 69.9% of disposable income.

Principal industrial products manufactured domestically include electronics, telecommunications equipment, automobiles, chemicals, shipbuilding and steel. The industrial production growth rate for 2016 was estimated as 1.8%.

Employment

The labour force, estimated at 27.25 million in 2016 with an unemployment rate of 4.0%, is employed as to 5.7% in agriculture, 24.2% in industry and 70.2% in services. In 2013, 14.6% of the population was estimated to be living below the poverty line. In 2014 the lowest 10% accounted for 6.8% of consumption and the highest 10% for 37.8%.

International Trade

In world trade the Republic of South Korea ranks 6th in merchandise exports and 9th in imports (5th and 8th excluding intra-EU trade). Its lower rankings in commercial services are 16th and 11th respectively (9th and 7th excluding intra-EU trade). Total exports in 2016 are reported as US$509,800 billion and imports at US$405,100 billion.

South Korea's exports declined by 6% and imports by 7% in 2016 in line with world trade trends but a modest recovery is expected in 2017 and 2018.

South Korea is the only country that has free trade agreements with the EU, US and China. The EU FTA allows the tax-free import of products with a value of less than £104 per shipment. Some 97% of tariff barriers between South Korea and the EU were abolished progressively by the end of 2014.The EU holds a 9% share of South Korea's global trade in which the UK is the second largest partner.

The South Korean government encourages direct purchases from overseas suppliers as an alternative to the high consumer prices charged by those import and sales channels which are dominated by local conglomerates which have the benefit of exclusive distribution agreements.

Merchandise Trade

South Korea's share in world total merchandise exports at US$526,755 million (f.o.b.) in 2015 accounted for 3.2% of world total exports, while its share in merchandise imports (c.i.f) at US$436,499 million represented 2.6% of the global total.

The composition of merchandise trade is summarised as:-

	Exports	*Imports*
By main commodity group	%	%
Agricultural products	2.1	7.6
Fuels and mining products	8.3	30.6
Manufactures	89.4	61.6
Other	0.3	0.4
By destination and origin		
China	25.4	17.1
United States	12.3	8.7
EU	9.1	11.9
Japan	5.6	10.2
Other	47.6	52.1

Source: WTO statistics

Agricultural products

The top imported agricultural products, together amounting to US$7,264 million in 2014, are maize, frozen bovine meat, wheat and meslin, fresh, chilled and frozen pork and solid residues from soya bean oil. Together they accounted for 28% of the total.

Conversely, the top five exported agricultural products are cigars, cheroots etc., other food preparations, liquids containing added sugar, pasta, bread and other bakery products which amounted to US$2,233 million in 2014, representing 40% of all exports from this sector.

Non-agricultural products

South Korea's top imported and manufactured products are crude and refined petroleum oils, petroleum gases, electronic integrated circuits, coal as briquettes and ovoids. Together they account for 40.7% of manufacture and fuels imports, which amounted to US$499,763 million in 2014.

Non-agricultural exports totalled US$567,495 million, of which the top five product categories in descending order are electronic integrated circuits, refined petroleum oils, automobiles, auto parts and other optical appliances. Together they accounted for 34.3% of the total.

Trade in commercial services

Compared to trade in non-agricultural merchandise, the imports and exports of commercial services at US$112,345 million and US$96,844 million respectively are relatively low. The pattern of this trade is:

	Exports	*Imports*
	%	%
By main service		
Transport	33.7	26.4
Travel	15.8	22.2
Other commercial services	47.2	43.6
Goods-related services	3.3	7.8

By main destination and origin

China	20.0	12.5
United States	15.4	24.8
EU	10.3	18.5
Japan	9.1	7.6
Other	45.3	36.5

Source: WTO statistics

Among other commercial services, finance and insurance have a minor role, accounting for less than 4% of both imports and exports:

	Imports	Exports
	US$ million	*US$ million*
Finance	1,692	1,410
Insurance	812	684
	2,504	2,094

By contrast, intellectual property (IP) registrations are at a significant level. The number of applications registered in 2014 by residents and non-residents was:

	Resident	*Non-resident*	*Total*
Patent	164,073	46,219	210,292
Trademark	138,040	22,604	160,644
Industrial design	60,797	3,777	64,574

Indeed, South Korea is focused on innovation and technology with some 4.9% of GDP spending on Research andDevelopment.

Foreign Direct Investment (FDI)

UNCTAD statistics for 2016 record South Korea's FDI inflows at US$10,827 million and outflows on investment abroad at US$27,274 million, compared with UK inflows of US$253,826 million for the same year. As an economy in transition, inward FDI stock is reported at a relatively modest level of US$185 billion with investment abroad at US$306billion.

Incentives in the form of cash grants, site location support and tax support are offered mainly in the eight South Korean Free Economic Zones.

BUSINESS ENVIRONMENT

Living standards

Average wages per annum are US$33,130, with 70% of the 26.9 million workforce employed in services, 24% in industry and less than 6% in agriculture. Hours worked exceed 2,000 per annum compared with less than 1,700 by UK workers.

Disposable income averages £2,225 per month of which £1,756 is spent on living expenses:

While taxes average £322 per month, the balance is saved or invested. The target market for UK exporters is assessed as 32.4% of total monthly living expenses, approximately £426.

Taxation

Value Added Tax (VAT)

The basic rate of VAT is set at 10% with books, newspapers, magazines and some other cultural items exempt. Zero rate tax status is awarded to the export of goods and services, the supply of international transportation services outside South Korea and certain goods and services paid for in foreign exchange.

Corporate taxation

As at June 2015, the tax bands were:

- on the first KRW 200 million	10%
- from KRW 200 million to KRW 20 billion	20%
- in excess of KRW 20 billion	30%

Income tax

South Korea levies income tax for non-residents on their Korean earned income only. Taxpayers have the option of 17.5% flat rate or a progressive scale reflecting income.

Entry controls

Valid passports and visas are required for foreign visitors. UK nationals can stay for up to 90 days without a visa. After 90 days anyone staying longer in South Korea must apply for an alien registration card via the embassy.

Foreign investors need to apply for a Foreign Investment Visa (Form D-8) from their local South Korean embassy.

CURRENT UK TRADE WITH SOUTH KOREA

Total merchandise exports to South Korea in 2015 were US$6.47 billion against imports of US$9.14 billion. The top eight export and import product groups in which the UK traded with South Korea in 2015 were:

	Exports			Imports	
	US$ million	*%*		*US$ million*	*%*
Crude petroleum	1,520	23.0	Special purpose ships	3,000	33.0
Cars	783	12.0	Machinery	1,638	17.5
Gas turbines	188	2.9	Cars	1,500	16.0
Hard liquors	183	2.8	Refined Petroleum	551	6.0
Packaged medicaments	159	2.5	Passenger & cargo ships	500	5.5
Machinery	147	2.3	Other floating structures	250	2.7
Liquid preparations	105	1.6	Electrical products	235	2.6
Gold	82	1.3	Office machinery	223	2.4

Source: https://atlas.media.edu/en/profile/country

Similar data for other export fields in which the UK is less established can be derived from the same source.

NEW OPPORTUNITIES FOR UK EXPORTERS

With an urbanised population representing 82.5% of the total 51 million population, a 0.53% population growth rate and an urbanisation rate of 0.66%, the consumer market, particularly in FMCG and online retail, is concentrated in the following six major urban areas:

	Population (million)
Seoul (the capital)	9,774
Busan	3,216
Incheon	2,685
Daegu	2,244
Daejon	1,564
Gwangju	1,536

The net migration rate is 2.6 migrants per 1,000 head of population. Some 60% of the urban population live in high-rise apartment buildings.

Korea is a sophisticated market with 72% under the age of 54, of which 26% are under 25.

e-commerce
98.5% of South Korean households have internet access and wireless, mobile and broadband subscriptions run at 106.5 per 100 inhabitants. Consequently, South Korea enjoys the world's seventh largest e-commerce market, trailing only China and Japan among APAC countries. The value of e-commerce in 2015 was £25 billion, amounting to 9.8% of retail sales and forecast to reach 12.8% by 2017. With 13% y.o.y growth, e-commerce sales are forecast to top £32 billion by 2018.

M-commerce has been a national priority for internet investment since the 1990s and South Korea occupies a leading position in broadband with download speeds of 205 mbs compared to Japan (154 mbs) and the UK (13 mbs). Some 80% of the population use smartphones and there is a correspondingly high usage for e-commerce.

In South Korea 45% of e-commerce transactions are by smartphone compared to 41% in Japan and 18% in the UK. Other significant features of this retail market are that 74% of payments are made by credit card compared to the global average of 53% and that the conversion rate on mobile transactions is twice that of the UK.

International online retailers have found South Korea a difficult market to enter; both e-Bay and Groupon were rebuffed at the first attempt. Among open-market retailers the heavyweights offering services similar to Amazon are Coupang (enjoying a 55.2% share of social commerce at £2 billion sales), Ticket Monster (£967 million) and We Make Price (sales £1.4 billion).

Leading online shopping malls are provided by:

- Ellotte Group (sales £38 billion);
- Shinsae Group (sales £3.3 billion), SouthKorea's oldest department store and largest hypermarket chain, formerly a subsidiary of Samsung;
- Hmall - Hyundai Department Store group (sales £6 billion)
- Gmarket (sales £482 million) and Auction (£482 million),subsidiaries
- of e-Bay

Cross-border e-commerce through these outlets was £1 billion in 2015 and is forecast to reach £6 billion in 2018. To date, the UK share of this rapidly growing market via the EU FTA is limited to just 1.4% compared to Germany's 5.4%. Cross-border sales are dominated by US suppliers (74%) with Chinese sites holding 11%. Globally, by contrast, the UK accounts for 11% of internet sales.

The opportunities for British manufacturers are significant but require detailed planning, careful selection of channels to market and administration both locally and at distance. Particular attention should be paid to providing high levels of customer service and support to the very demanding South Korean consumer.

Detailed information and advice on entry strategy to the South Korean consumer market is provided by Britain is Great from its Intralink source.

PRIORITY MARKETS FOR UK TRADE:

NORWAY

THE ECONOMY

In perspective

World Bank estimates of 2015 nominal GDP for Norway, with comparatives for 11 leading economies with GDP in excess of US$1.3 trillion, the EU and Switzerland are tabled as:

	US$ million	GDP real growth (%)
USA	18,036,648	1.6
EU	16,324,942	2.2
China	11,064,665	6.6
Japan	4,383,076	0.5
United Kingdom	2,861,091	1.8
India	2,088,841	7.7
Canada	1,552,808	0.9
S. Korea	1,377,873	2.7

Australia	1,339,141	2.2
Germany	3,363,447	1.7
France	2,418,838	1.3
Italy	1,821,497	0.8
Switzerland	670,790	0.8
Norway	386,578	0.8

Norway's GDP at PPP has differed little from real GDP. At an estimated US$364,700 billion Norway ranked 49th in 2016 when its real GDP growth rate slackened to 0.8% from 1.6% in 2015. However, some improvement is expected in 2017 and 2018 in line with IMF and OECD forecasts.

Natural resources are the bedrock of Norway's economy. In addition to oil and gas, they include hydropower, fish, forests and minerals. The country's petroleum resources are carefully regulated by the Government. Oil production peaked in 2000 but Norway remains a leading global exporter, having reduced production by 50% up to 2015. Conversely, annual gas production more than doubled over the same time period. As a hedge against the eventual decline of both oil and gas production, the Government saves state revenue from the sector in the world's largest sovereign wealth fund, valued at US$800 billion in 2016. Up to 4% of the fund's value, the expected annual rate of return, is deployed by the Government towards balancing the federal budget each year.

After solid growth in the 2004-2007 period, the Norwegian economy slowed in 2008 and went into reverse in 2009; it returned to modest growth from 2010 to 2015 when lower oil prices caused slower growth, increased unemployment and weakened the currency. If necessary, the government is prepared to use the sovereign wealth fund to subsidise public spending and help to avoid a recession.

The Norwegian economy today

The headline statistics for 2015 relating to GDP of US$386.6 billion and the estimated population of 5.3 million highlight Norway's foreign trade performance as:

	% GDP	$ per capita
GDP		91,585
Foreign trade	33.9	31,031
Current account balance	10.4	5,516

Source: WTO statistics

Composition of GDP

By end use	%	By sector of origin	%
Household consumption	44.0	Agriculture	1.8
Government consumption	24.3	Industry	34.7
Investment in fixed capital	23.3	Services	63.5
Investment in inventories	5.4		

Source: CIA World Fact Book

In respect of household consumption, household debt is recorded as 222% of disposable income, the 3rd highest among developed countries on the OECD scale after Denmark and the Netherlands.

The principal industrial manufactures produced or processed domestically include petroleum and gas, shipping, fishing, aquaculture, food processing, ship building, pulp and paper products, metals, chemicals, timber, mining and textiles. The industrial production growth rate is estimated at (0.5) % for 2016, ranking Norway 177th globally.

Employment

The labour force, estimated at 2.794 million in 2016 with an unemployment rate of 4.8%, was employed in 2015 as to 2.7% in agriculture, 18.3% in industry and 79% in services. The petroleum sector provides about 9% of jobs and 15% of GDP.

Norwegian incomes are broadly distributed. In 2014 the lowest 10% in household income accounted for 3.8% and the highest 10% for 21.2%. More recent data is unavailable although any recent change is unlikely to be significant.

International Trade

In world trade Norway ranked 36 in merchandise exports (23 excluding intra-EU trade) and 38 in imports (24 excluding intra-EU trade.) In services, Norway holds the same world ranking of 17 (excluding intra-EU trade) for both exports and imports. Merchandise exports declined by 7% in 2015 and imports by 1% but some recovery is expected in 2017 and 2018 in line with world trade trends. Norway's exports and imports of services fell in 2015 by 11%and 1% respectively.

Through its EFTA membership Norway is party to the 23 bilateral free trade agreements currently in force and to further bilateral agreements, planned or under negotiation, with the MERCOSUR bloc, Algeria and Albania.

Merchandise Trade

Norway's merchandise exports at US$105,372 million (f.o.b.) in 2015 accounted for 0.64% of the global total, while its merchandise imports (c.i.f) at US$75,228 million represented 0.46% of total world imports. The current account surplus of US$29 billion is mainly attributable to sales of petroleum products.

By contrast, in commercial services Norway ran a trade deficit of US$5.5 billion with exports of US$40.3 billion (0.8% of world exports) against imports of US$45.8 billion (1.0%).

The composition of merchandise trade is summarised as:-

	Exports	Imports
By main commodity group	%	%
Agricultural products	10.2	10.9
Fuels and mining products	64.6	9.7
Manufactures	74.8	78.4
Other	5.1	4.2
By destination and origin		
EU	79.4	60.9
United States	4.4	6.3
China	2.8	10.4
South Korea	1.9	4.2
Other	11.5	18.2

Source: WTO statistics

The top five imported agricultural products, together amounting to US$1,901 million in 2015, are: food preparations, wine, bread, pastry and other bakery products, rape, colza or mustard oil and flours, meals and pellets. Together they accounted for 28% of total imports.

The top five exported agricultural products are: food preparations, flours, meals and pellets, solid residues from soya-bean oil, anim preparations and cheese and curd which together amounted to US$503 million in 2015, representing 55% of exports. There was a trade deficit of US$5,831 million in overall agricultural products.

Non-agricultural products
Norway's top imported and manufactured product groups are passenger cars, vehicles not mainly for navigability, refined petroleum oils, automatic data processing machines and nickel mattes and oxide sinters. Together, amounting to US$12.5 billion in 2015, they accounted for 18% of manufactures and fuels imports at US$69.3 billion.

Non-agricultural exports totalled US$101 billion, resulting in a 2015 trade deficit of US$31.8 billion. The top five product categories in descending order are petroleum gases, crude petroleum oil, fish chilled and fresh, refined petroleum oils and unwrought aluminium. Together they accounted for US$68.9 billion, representing 68% of the total.

Trade in commercial services
Compared to trade in non-agricultural merchandise, the imports and exports of commercial services at US$45.8 billion and US$40.3 billion respectively are significant. The pattern of this trade is:

	Exports	*Imports*
	%	%
By main service		
Transport	44.3	22.4
Travel	12.3	34.6
Other commercial services	41.1	41.0
Goods-related services	2.3	2.1

Source: WTO statistics

Among other commercial services, financial services and ICTs play minor roles of 12% each. Intellectual property applications in 2014 were also at modest levels:

	Resident	*Non-resident*	*Total*
Patent	1,106	457	1,563
Trademark	4,022	11,453	15,475
Industrial design	335	881	1,216

Foreign Direct Investment (FDI)

UNCTAD reported minimal FDI inflows and outflows in 2016 with a negative adjustment for inflows and Norwegian outward investment at US$14.9 billion, representing 16.7% of GDP

At 2016 year-end, FDI stocks at home were estimated to be US$136 billion and abroad at US$188 billion. Much of the latter represents outward investment by the Norwegian sovereign wealth fund.

BUSINESS ENVIRONMENT

Living standards

The average household net-adjusted disposable income per capita in Norway is US$33,393 a year, above the OECD average of US$29,016 a year. However, there is a considerable gap between the poorest and richest with 20% of the population earning almost four times more than the bottom 20%.

The OECD Better Life Index, based on 11 factors, and the Human Development Index rank Norway 1st among 34 OECD countries. Strongest factors are life satisfaction, the environment, safety, work-life balance and health. In a global context, the Quality-of-life Index ranks Norway 20th out of 111, well behind the other Scandinavian states, Switzerland and the UK. By comparison, consumer prices in the UK excluding rent are 47.3% lower than in Norway (27.8% including rent) but the local purchasing power in Norway is almost the same.

TAXATION

Corporate tax

Norway's corporate income tax rate is 24%, having declined from 28% since 2012. Resident companies are charged CIT on worldwide income and non-resident companies are liable for CIT in Norway when engaged in business in Norway or managed from Norway.

In addition there are a number of special tax regimes:

- Petroleum tax: All upstream petroleum activity on the Norwegian Continental Shelf (NCS) is charged at the special rate of 54% on top of CIT (a marginal tax rate of 78% on net income). There are various investment-based 'supplementary depreciation' allowances granted on investments in installations for exploitation and production as well as pipelines;
- Hydro power tax: Income from the production, sales, transfer or distribution of hydro power is subject to a 34.3% resource rent tax in addition to CIT (a marginal tax rate of 58.3%). The resource rent is generally calculated per hydro power plant on spot market price per hour multiplied by production;

- Shipping tonnage tax regime: The rules in Norway are in line with those of other EU/EEA countries and imply that shipping income will be exempt on a permanent basis so that only CIT is levied.

Sales tax

The standard rate of VAT is 25% with lower rates of 15% applied to foodstuffs and 8% on transport, hotel rooms and holiday homes, and tickets to cultural and entertainment events.

CURRENT UK TRADE WITH NORWAY

Total merchandise exports to Norway in 2015 were US$4.98 billion against imports of US$18.8 billion. The top eight export and import product groups in which the UK traded with Norway in 2015 were:

	Exports			*Imports*	
	US$ million	*%*		*US$ million*	*%*
Cars	398	8.0	Crude petroleum	9,380	50.0
Machinery (specific)	269	5.4	Petroleum gas	6,350	35.0
Excavation machinery	246	5.0	Refined Petroleum	356	1.9
Valves	205	4.1	Raw Zinc	160	0.9
Surveying equipment	196	3.9	Hydrocarbons	146	0.8
Iron pipes	123	2.6	Insulated wire	108	0.6
Gas turbines	121	2.4	Newsprint	98	0.5
Planes, helicopters etc	110	2.2	Valves	83	0.4

Source: https://atlas.media.edu/en/profile/country

The top eight export categories account for 33.6% of UK exports to Norway, representing less than 1.2% of total UK exports worldwide. Norwegian exports to the UK are concentrated heavily on petroleum and products, with the top eight categories representing 90.1% of UK imports from Norway and 3.1% of the UK's total imported merchandise.

Similar data for other export fields in which the UK is less established can be derived from the same source.

NEW OPPORTUNITIES FOR UK EXPORTERS

Norway is of particular interest to the UK as a major supplier of oil and gas through the North Sea pipeline and as a member of the European Economic Area (EEA), which it joined at the end of 1994 when it opted out of the EU following a referendum. As an EEA member Norway continues to make a substantial contribution to the EU budget, and is subject to most of the EU single market rules imposed by Brussels without being able to influence them. However, as a non-member of the customs union Norway does have the ability to make trade deals and EEA membership does not include conformity to the EU directives on agriculture and fisheries. For these reasons the 'Norway option' is under consideration as an exemplar for the UK in seeking transitional arrangements to cover its exit process before a more permanent divorce from the EU.

PRIORITY MARKETS FOR UK TRADE:

SWITZERLAND

THE ECONOMY

In perspective

World Bank estimates of 2015 nominal GDP for Switzerland, with comparatives for 11 leading economies with GDP in excess of US$1.3 trillion, the EU and Norway are tabled as:

	US$ million	GDP real growth (%)
USA	18,036,648	1.6
EU	16,324,942	2.2
China	11,064,665	6.6
Japan	4,383,076	0.5
United Kingdom	2,861,091	1.8
India	2,088,841	7.7
Canada	1,552,808	0.9
S. Korea	1,377,873	2.7
Australia	1,339,141	2.2

Germany	3,363,447	1.7
France	2,418,838	1.3
Italy	1,821,497	0.8
Switzerland	670,790	0.8
Norway	386,578	0.8

Switzerland's GDP at PPP is somewhat less than real GDP. At an estimated US$494,300 billion Switzerland ranked 40th in 2016 when its real GDP growth rate advanced to 1% from 0.8% in 2015, having fallen below 2% from 2011. Further improvement is expected in 2017 and 2018 in line with IMF and OECD forecasts.

Switzerland occupies a unique position at the heart of Western Europe with an advanced and prosperous economy, retaining strong links with the EU but without formal membership. Having maintained neutrality for centuries including the period of two World Wars in the 20th century, Switzerland is famed for its financial services within its vibrant and sophisticated services sector. Its manufacturing industry is based on high-technology, knowledge-based production and a highly skilled labour force. Coupled with exceptional infrastructure and a transparent legal system, Switzerland's efficient capital markets, low corporate tax rates and political stability have combined to make it one of the most competitive global economies.

Together with Norway, Iceland and Liechtenstein Switzerland is a member of the European Free Trade Area (EFTA) having joined in 1960 but unlike others rejected EEA membership in 1992 and EU membership in a series of referenda. It shares a common VAT area and customs territory with Liechtenstein, enjoys the benefits of the EU single market without being a member of its customs union but has retained protection for its agricultural sector. Nevertheless, its economy is closely linked to those of its Eurozone neighbours who purchase the lion's share of Switzerland's exports. Inevitably, this dependence drove the Swiss economy into recession in 2008 during the global financial crisis but the Swiss National Bank (SNB)'s zero interest rate policy helped recovery to set in in 2010.

The tendency of international investors to drive up demand for the Swiss franc as a safe currency caused the SNB to abandon its peg to the euro from January 2015. A strengthening currency remains a permanent threat to competitiveness and active SNB intervention has become a necessary feature of Swiss monetary policy. As a result of international pressure from its trading partners Switzerland now conforms to OECD regulations in tax matters and is considering the possibility of imposing taxes on bank deposits held by foreigners.

The Swiss economy today

The headline statistics for 2015 relating to GDP of US$664.7 billion and the estimated population of 8.2 million highlight Switzerland's foreign trade performance as:

	% GDP	$ per capita
GDP		83,480
Foreign trade	60.1	50,185
Current account balance	10.4	9,246

Source: WTO statistics

Composition of GDP

By end use	%	By sector of origin	%
Household consumption	54.0	Agriculture	0.7
Government consumption	11.2	Industry	25.9
Investment in fixed capital	23.8	Services	73.4
Investment in inventories	(0.9)		

Source: CIA World Fact Book

In respect of household consumption, household debt is recorded as 211% of disposable income, the 5th highest among developed countries on the OECD scale.

The principal manufacturing service activities in which Switzerland is engaged domestically include machinery, chemicals, watches, textiles, precision instruments, tourism, banking and insurance. The industrial production growth rate is estimated at 2.1% for 2016, ranking Switzerland 100th globally.

Employment

The labour force, estimated at 5.173 million in 2016 with an unemployment rate of 4.4%, was employed in 2015 as to 3.4% in agriculture, 23.4% in industry and 73.2% in services.

Swiss incomes are broadly distributed. At the last count the lowest 10% in household income accounted for 7.5% and the highest 10% for 19%. In 2011, when last reported, 7.6% of the population were estimated to be below the poverty line.

International Trade

In world trade Switzerland ranked 15 in merchandise exports, (17 excluding intra-EU trade) and 17 in imports (20 excluding intra-EU trade.) In services, Switzerland ranks 17th globally in exports and 9th in imports. Merchandise exports declined by 7% in 2015 and imports by 9% but some recovery is expected in 2017 and 2018 in line with world trade trends. Switzerland's exports and imports of commercial services fell in 2015 by 7% and 6% respectively.

Through its EFTA membership, Switzerland is party to the 24 bilateral free trade agreements currently in force, as well as its customs union with Liechtenstein, and to eight further bilateral agreements, planned or under negotiation since 2010, including those with Hong Kong, India and the USA.

Merchandise Trade

Switzerland's merchandise exports at US$289,874 million (f.o.b.) in 2015 accounted for 1.76% of the global total, while its merchandise imports (c.i.f) at US$251,873 million represented 1.51% of total world imports. The current account surplus of US$38 billion is rather more than Norway. In commercial services Switzerland ran a trade surplus of US$15.6 billion with exports of US$108 billion (2.3% of world exports) against imports of US$92.4 billion (2.0%).

The composition of merchandise trade is summarised as:-

	Exports	Imports
By main commodity group	%	%
Agricultural products	3.2	5.0
Fuels and mining products	2.6	5.4
Manufactures	68.5	61.6
Other	25.7	28.1
By destination and origin		
EU	43.4	64.5
United States	10.6	8.0
China/Hong Kong	8.7	5.1
India (Turkey imports)	7.4	2.4
Other	30.0	19.92

Source: WTO statistics

The top five imported agricultural products, together amounting to US$3,037 million in 2015 are: wine, coffee, bread, pastry and other bakery products, other food preparations and cheese and curd. Together they accounted for 26% of total imports.

The top five exported agricultural products are: coffee, waters containing added sugar, chocolate and other cocoa food, other food preparations and cheese and curd which together amounted to US$6,028 million in 2015, representing 66% of exports. There was a trade deficit of US$2,449 million in overall agricultural products.

Non-agricultural products
Switzerland's top imported and manufactured product groups are: gold, medicaments in measured doses, passenger cars, articles and parts of jewellery and human and animal blood. Together amounting to US$112.4 billion in 2015, they accounted for 47% of non-agricultural merchandise imports at US$241.3 billion.

Non-agricultural exports totalled US$279.2 billion, resulting in a 2015 trade surplus of US$37.9 billion. The top five product categories in descending order are: gold, medicaments in measured doses, human and animal blood, wristwatches and other articles and parts of jewellery. Together they accounted for US$156.2 billion, representing 56% of the total.

Trade in commercial services
Trade in commercial services with exports at US$108 billion and imports at US$92.4 billion respectively is substantial and generates a surplus of US$15.6 billion. The pattern of this trade is:

	Exports	Imports
	%	%
By main service		
Transport	10.1	9.5
Travel	15.0	17.3
Other commercial services	70.2	70.7
Goods-related services	4.7	2.5

Source: WTO statistics

Among other commercial and goods-related services and amounting to US$5.1 billion in exports against US$2.3 billion of imports, financial services are dominant, accounting for 27% with intellectual property accounting for 19%. In 2014 intellectual property applications recorded were relatively modest:

	Resident	Non-resident	Total
Patent	1,480	568	2,048
Trademark	11,588	17,332	28,920
Industrial design	1.112	1,613	2,725

Foreign Direct Investment (FDI)

UNCTAD reported FDI inflows and outflows in 2016 with a negative adjustment for inflows of US$26.3 billion and Swiss outward investment at US$30.6 billion, representing 16.7% of GDP.

At 2016 year-end, Switzerland's FDI stocks at home were estimated to be US$793 billion and abroad at a massive US$1.1 trillion of which US$145 billion was in services.

BUSINESS ENVIRONMENT

Living standards

The average household net-adjusted disposable income per capita in Switzerland is US$35,952 a year, above the OECD average of US$29,016 a year but lagging behind the US average of US$41,071.

The OECD Human Development Index ranks Switzerland 3rd and the Better Life Index, based on 11 factors, ranks Switzerland 4th among 34 OECD countries. Strongest factors are life satisfaction, safety, work-life balance and jobs. In a global context, the Quality-of-life Index ranks Switzerland 12th out of 111, after the Netherlands in 11th place and before the UK in 13th place. By comparison, consumer prices in the UK excluding rent are 81.7% lower than in Switzerland (68.4% including rent) with Switzerland ranking 2nd after Bermuda in the Numbeo cost-of-living index against the US in 18th and the UK in 29th place respectively.

TAXATION

Legal framework

As a federation the authority to levy taxes is vested in the individual states (cantons) of Switzerland, which delegate common powers of taxation to the federal government and individual powers to the municipalities within each of the 26 cantons.

Corporate income tax (CIT)

Resident companies are charged CIT on their taxable profits generated in Switzerland at federal, cantonal and communal level. Foreign-source income attributable to foreign permanent establishments or real estate property is excluded from the Swiss tax base. However, they are taken into account by cantons that levy progressive tax rates.

Non-resident companies are liable for tax on their income generated in Switzerland only if they are partners of a Swiss business, own real estate there, have a PE in Switzerland or deal with or have receivables secured by mortgage on Swiss real estate property.

Federal level

Federal CIT is levied at a flat rate of 8.5% on profit after tax (i.e. approximately 7.83% on profit before tax). No corporate capital tax is levied.

Cantonal/communal level

Each canton has its own tax laws and levies cantonal and communal income tax and capital taxes at different rates, in some cases at progressive rates.

Overall tax rates

The overall approximate range of the maximum CIT rate on profit before tax for federal, cantonal and communal taxes varies between 11.5% and 24.2%, depending on the location of corporate residence in Switzerland.

CURRENT UK TRADE WITH SWITZERLAND

Total merchandise exports to Switzerland in 2015 were US$32.5 billion against imports of US$11.2 billion. The top eight export and import product groups in which the UK traded with Switzerland in 2015 were:

	Exports			Imports	
	US$ million	%		US$ million	%
Gold	25,000	77.0	Packaged medicaments	3,530	31.0
Jewellery	1,270	3.9	Gold	912	8.1
Nitrogen Heterocyclic compounds	1,030	3.2	Paintings	493	4.4
Cars	755	2.3	Precious metal watches	489	4.4
Planes, helicopters etc.	276	0.9	Human or animal blood	476	4.3
Packaged medicaments	258	0.8	Base metal watches	409	3.7
Paintings	232	0.7	Diamonds	370	3.3
Gas turbines	160	0.5	Platinum	288	2.6

Source: https://atlas.media.edu/en/profile/country

The top eight export categories account for 89.3% of UK exports to Switzerland, heavily concentrating on gold and representing 7.6% of total UK exports worldwide. Switzerland exports to the UK are more diverse with packaged medicaments (pharmaceuticals) dominant and the top eight categories representing 61.8% of UK imports from Switzerland and 1.8% of the UK's total imported merchandise. The UK provides just under 3% of Switzerland's imports (excluding gold) and is the market for 4 % of Switzerland's exports.

Similar data for other export fields in which the UK is less established can be derived from the same source.

NEW OPPORTUNITIES FOR UK EXPORTERS

Switzerland is of similar interest to Norway for the UK in considering transitional arrangements to cover its exit process before a more permanent divorce from the EU. However, Switzerland has a separate series of bilateral agreements with the EU rather than EFTA membership and it is less likely that the UK would be accepted on these terms.

APPENDIX II

CONTRIBUTORS' CONTACTS

British Exporters Association (BExA)
5th Floor
88 Victoria Street
Westminster
London SW1H 0HW
Tel: +44 (0) 207 222 5419
Contact: Michelle Treasure
e-mail: michelle.treasure@bexa.co.uk

Carter Jonas LLP
One Station Square
Cambridge CB1 2GA
Tel: +44 (0) 1223 348 607
Contact: Nick Hood
e-mail: Nick.Hood@carterjonas.co.uk

Council of British Chambers of Commerce in Europe (COBCOE)
Registered address:
Worth Corner
Turners Hill
Crawley
West Sussex RH10 7SL
Tel: +44 (0) 203 290 1468
Contact: Anne-Marie Martin
e-mail: anne-marie.martin@cobcoe.eu

Legend Business Books Ltd
107-111 Fleet Street
London EC4AB 2AB
Tel: +44 (0) 207 93 9941/8
Contact: Tom Chalmers
Direct line: +44 (0) 207 9948
e-mail: tomchalmers@legend-paperbooks.co.uk
Jonathan Reuvid
Direct line: +44 (0) 1295 738 070
e-mail: jreuvidembooks@aol.com

Mazars LLP
Tower Bridge House
St Katharine's Way
London E1W 1DD
Tel: +44 (0) 20 7063 4000

and

Times House
Throwley Way
Sutton SM1 4JQ
Tel: +44 (0) 208 661 1826
Contact: Toby Stanbrook
Tel: + 44 (0) 20 8661 4195
e-mail: toby.stanbrook@mazars.co.uk

PNO Consultants Limited
Dunham House
Brooke Court
Lower Meadow Road
Wilmslow
Cheshire SK9 3ND
Tel: +44 (0) 161 488 3488
Contact: Olaf Swanzy
e-mail: olaf.swanzy@pnoconsultants.com

UK Intellectual Property Office
1sr Floor
Abbey Orchard Street
London SW1P 2HT
Contact: Nic Fearon-Low
Tel: +44 (0) 207 034 2841
e-mail: nic.fearon-low@ipo.gov.uk

Watson Farley & Williams LLP
15 Appold Street
London EC2A 2HB
Tel: +44 (0) 20 7814 8000
Contact: Asha Kumar
Direct line: +44 (0) 20 7814 8182
e-mail: AKumar@wfw.com